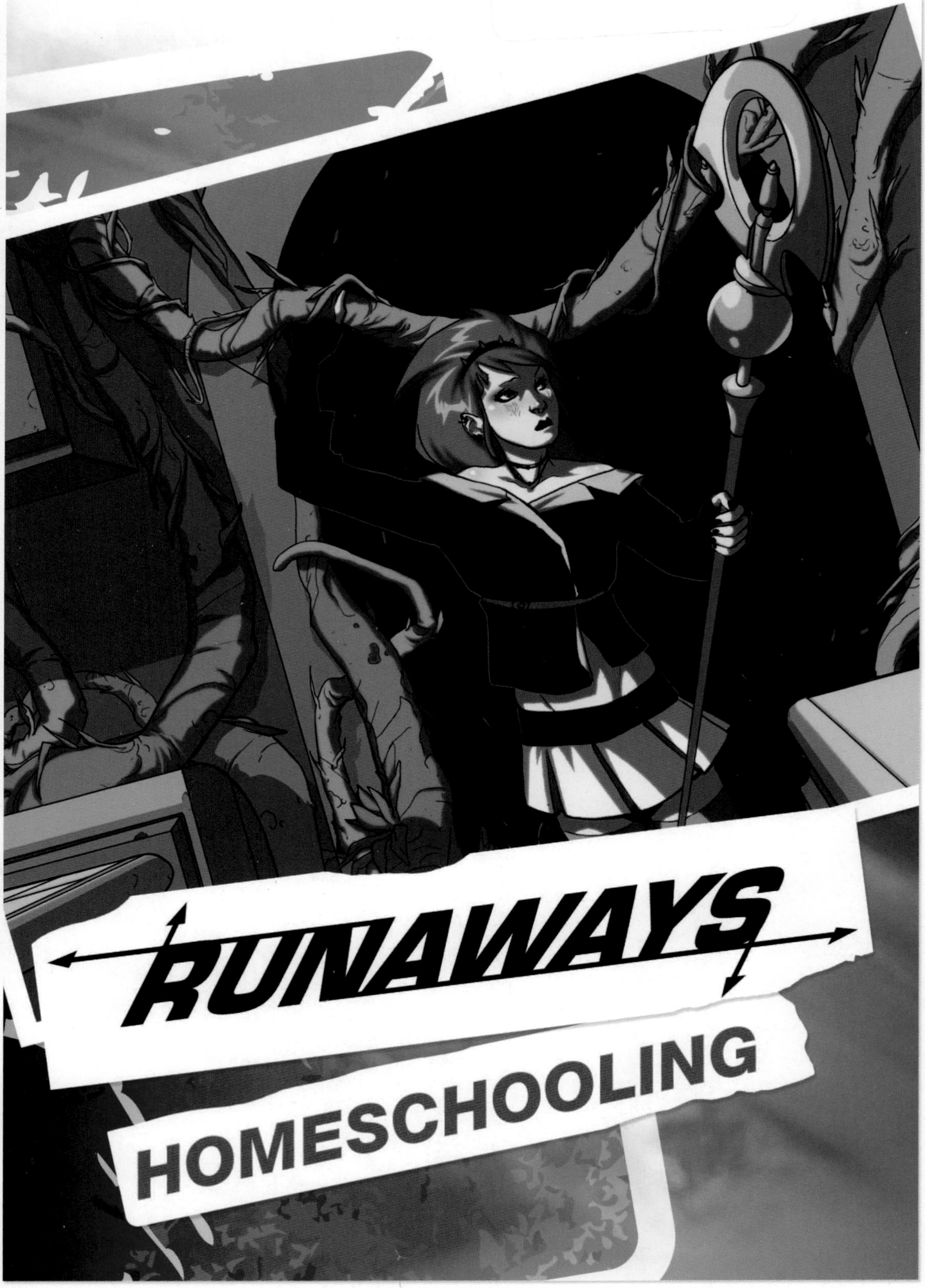
RUNAWAYS
HOMESCHOOLING

RUNAWAYS
HOMESCHOOLING

WRITER: **KATHRYN IMMONEN**
ARTIST: **SARA PICHELLI**
COLORIST: **CHRISTINA STRAIN**
LETTERERS: **VC'S AUDRA ELIOPOULOS, JOE SABINO** & **JOE CARAMAGNA**
COVER ART: **DAVID LAFUENTE** & **CHRISTINA STRAIN**
ASSOCIATE EDITOR: **DANIEL KETCHUM**
EDITOR: **NICK LOWE**

"WHAT IF THE RUNAWAYS BECAME THE YOUNG AVENGERS?"
WRITER: **C.B. CEBULSKI**
PENCILER: **PATRICK SPAZIANTE**
INKER: **VICTOR OLAZABA**
COLORISTS: **JOHN RAUCH** WITH **CHRISTINA STRAIN** & **PATRICK SPAZIANTE**
LETTERER: **JEFF POWELL**
ASSISTANT EDITOR: **JORDAN D. WHITE**
ASSOCIATE EDITOR: **CHRIS ALLO**
CONSULTING EDITOR: **MARK PANICCIA**
EDITOR: **JUSTIN GABRIE**

RUNAWAYS CREATED BY **BRIAN K. VAUGHAN** & **ADRIAN ALPHONA**

COLLECTION EDITOR: **JENNIFER GRÜNWALD**
ASSISTANT EDITORS: **ALEX STARBUCK** & **JOHN DENNING**
EDITOR, SPECIAL PROJECTS: **MARK D. BEAZLEY**
SENIOR EDITOR, SPECIAL PROJECTS: **JEFF YOUNGQUIST**
SENIOR VICE PRESIDENT OF SALES: **DAVID GABRIEL**

EDITOR IN CHIEF: **JOE QUESADA**
PUBLISHER: **DAN BUCKLEY**
EXECUTIVE PRODUCER: **ALAN FINE**

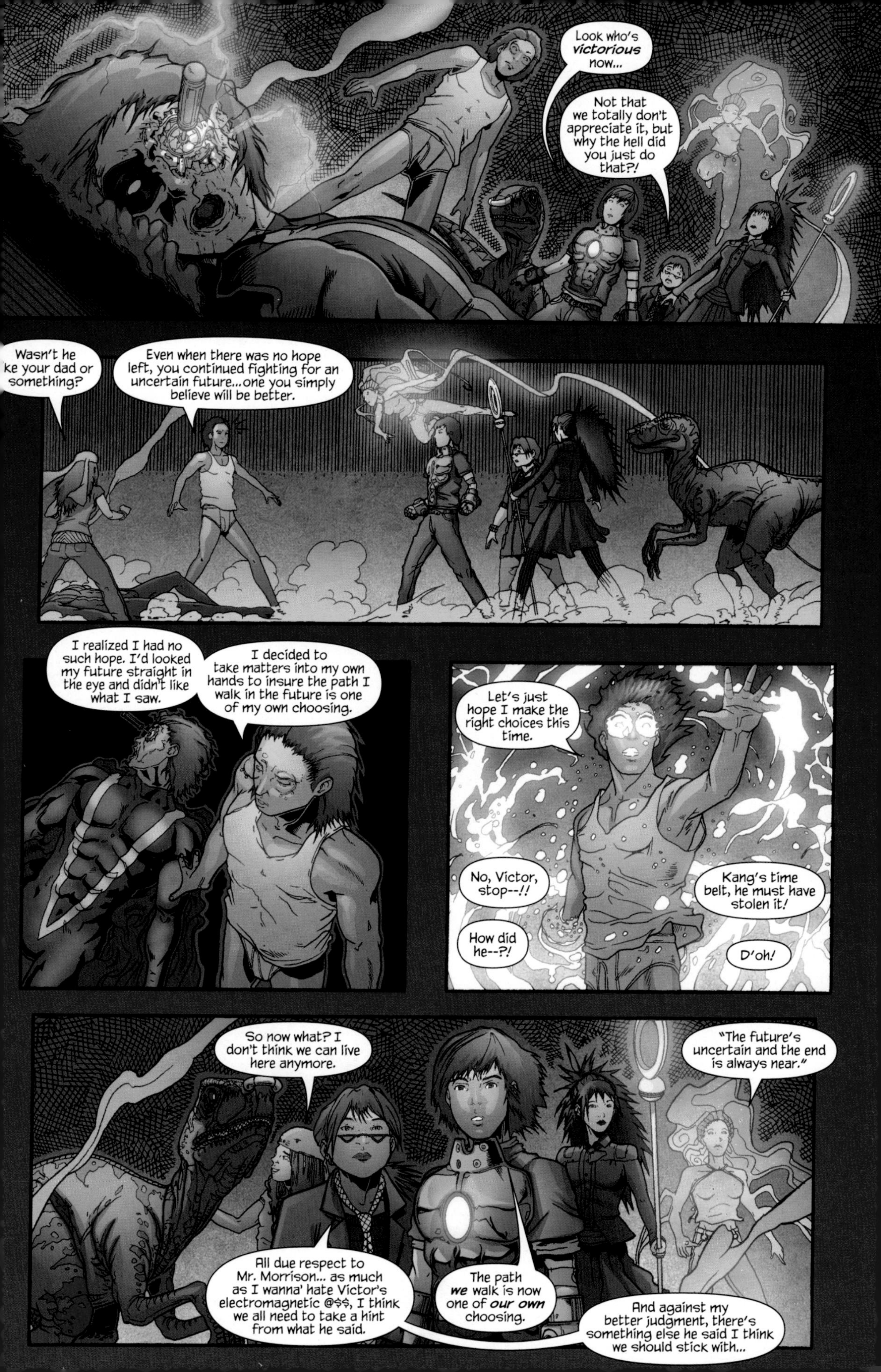

Look who's *victorious* now...
Not that we totally don't appreciate it, but why the hell did you just do that?!
Wasn't he ke your dad or something?
Even when there was no hope left, you continued fighting for an uncertain future...one you simply believe will be better.
I realized I had no such hope. I'd looked my future straight in the eye and didn't like what I saw.
I decided to take matters into my own hands to insure the path I walk in the future is one of my own choosing.
Let's just hope I make the right choices this time.
No, Victor, stop--!!
How did he--?!
Kang's time belt, he must have stolen it!
D'oh!
So now what? I don't think we can live here anymore.
"The future's uncertain and the end is always near."
All due respect to Mr. Morrison... as much as I wanna' hate Victor's electromagnetic @$$, I think we all need to take a hint from what he said.
The path *we* walk is now one of *our own* choosing.
And against my better judgment, there's something else he said I think we should stick with...

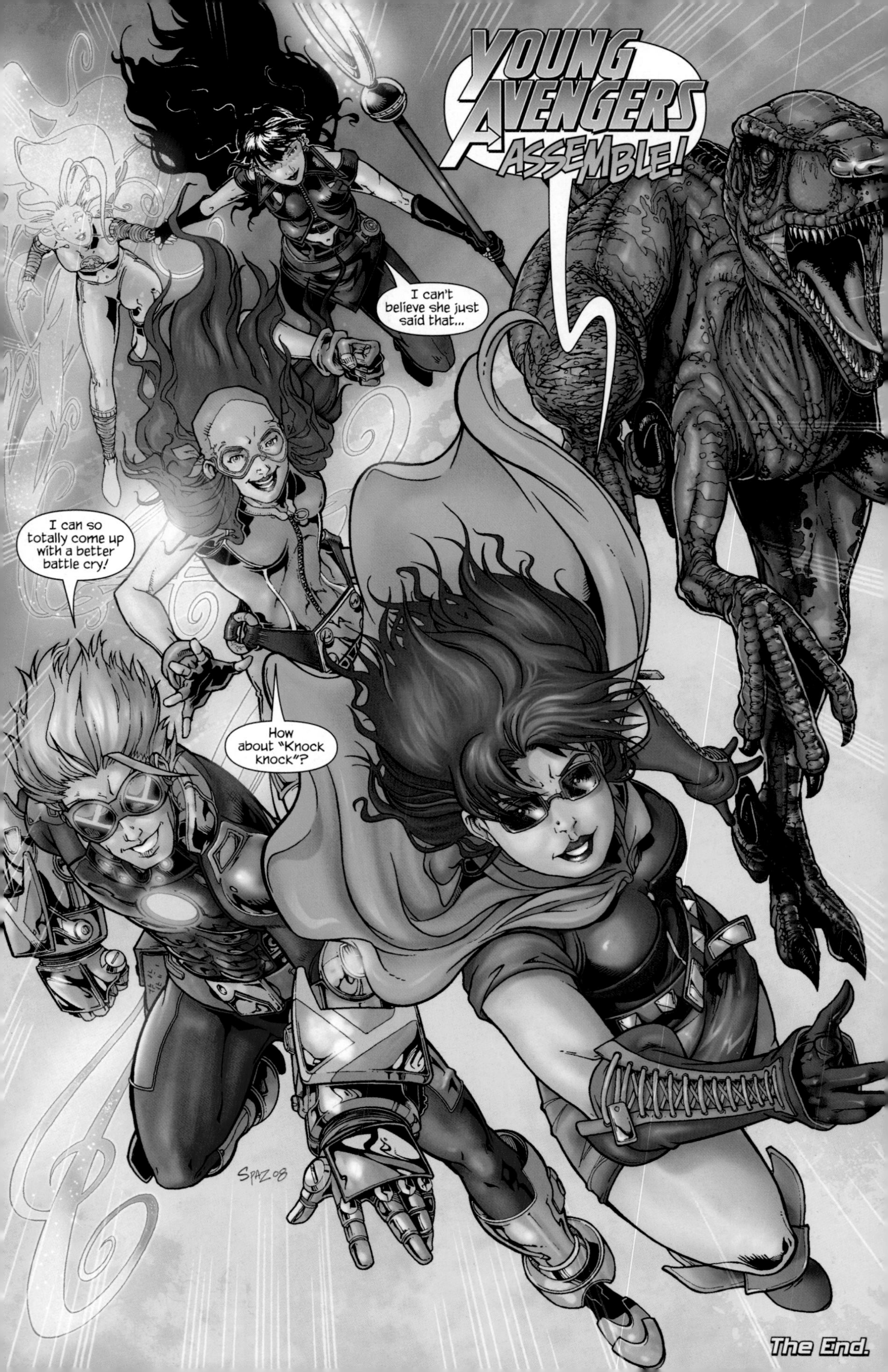
YOUNG AVENGERS ASSEMBLE!
I can't believe she just said that...
I can so totally come up with a better battle cry!
How about "Knock knock"?
SPAZ '08
The End.

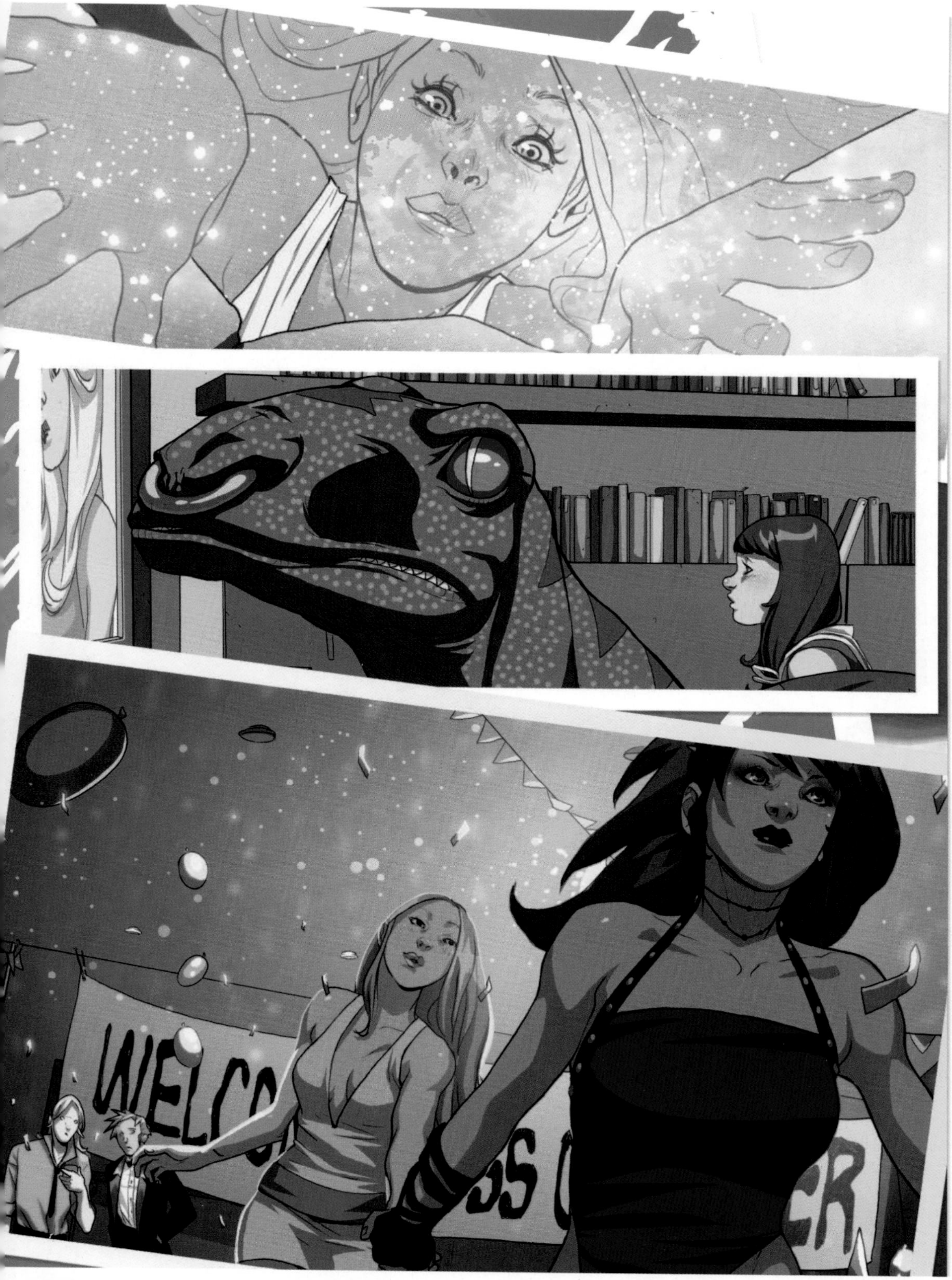
WELCO

RUNAWAYS: HOMESCHOOLING. Contains material originally published in magazine form as RUNAWAYS #11-14; and WHAT IF? SECRET WARS, CAPTAIN AMERICA: FALLEN SON, HOUSE OF M, SPIDER-MAN: BACK IN BLACK and NEWER FF. First printing 2009. Hardcover ISBN# 978-0-7851-4037-5. Softcover ISBN# 978-0-7851-4039-9. Published by MARVEL PUBLISHING, INC., a subsidiary of MARVEL ENTERTAINMENT, INC. OFFICE OF PUBLICATION: 417 5th Avenue, New York, NY 10016. Hardcover: $19.99 per copy in the U.S. (GST #R127032852). Softcover: $14.99 per copy in the U.S. (GST #R127032852). Canadian Agreement #40668537. **Printed in the U.S.A.** ALAN FINE, EVP - Office Of The Chief Executive Marvel Entertainment, Inc. & CMO Marvel Characters B.V.; DAN BUCKLEY, Chief Executive Officer and Publisher - Print, Animation & Digital Media; JIM SOKOLOWSKI, Chief Operating Officer; DAVID GABRIEL, SVP of Publishing Sales & Circulation; DAVID BOGART, SVP of Business Affairs & Talent Management; MICHAEL PASCIULLO, VP Merchandising & Communications; JIM O'KEEFE, VP of Operations & Logistics; DAN CARR, Executive Director of Publishing Technology; JUSTIN F. GABRIE, Director of Publishing & Editorial Operations; SUSAN CRESPI, Editorial Operations Manager; ALEX MORALES, Publishing Operations Manager; STAN LEE, Chairman Emeritus. For information regarding advertising in Marvel Comics or on Marvel.com, please contact Mitch Dane, Advertising Director, at mdane@marvel.com. For Marvel subscription inquiries, please call 800-217-9158. **Manufactured between 10/5/09 and 11/4/09 (hardcover), and 10/5/09 and 3/10/10 (softcover), by R.R. DONNELLEY, INC., SALEM, VA, USA.**

10 9 8 7 6 5 4 3 2 1

11

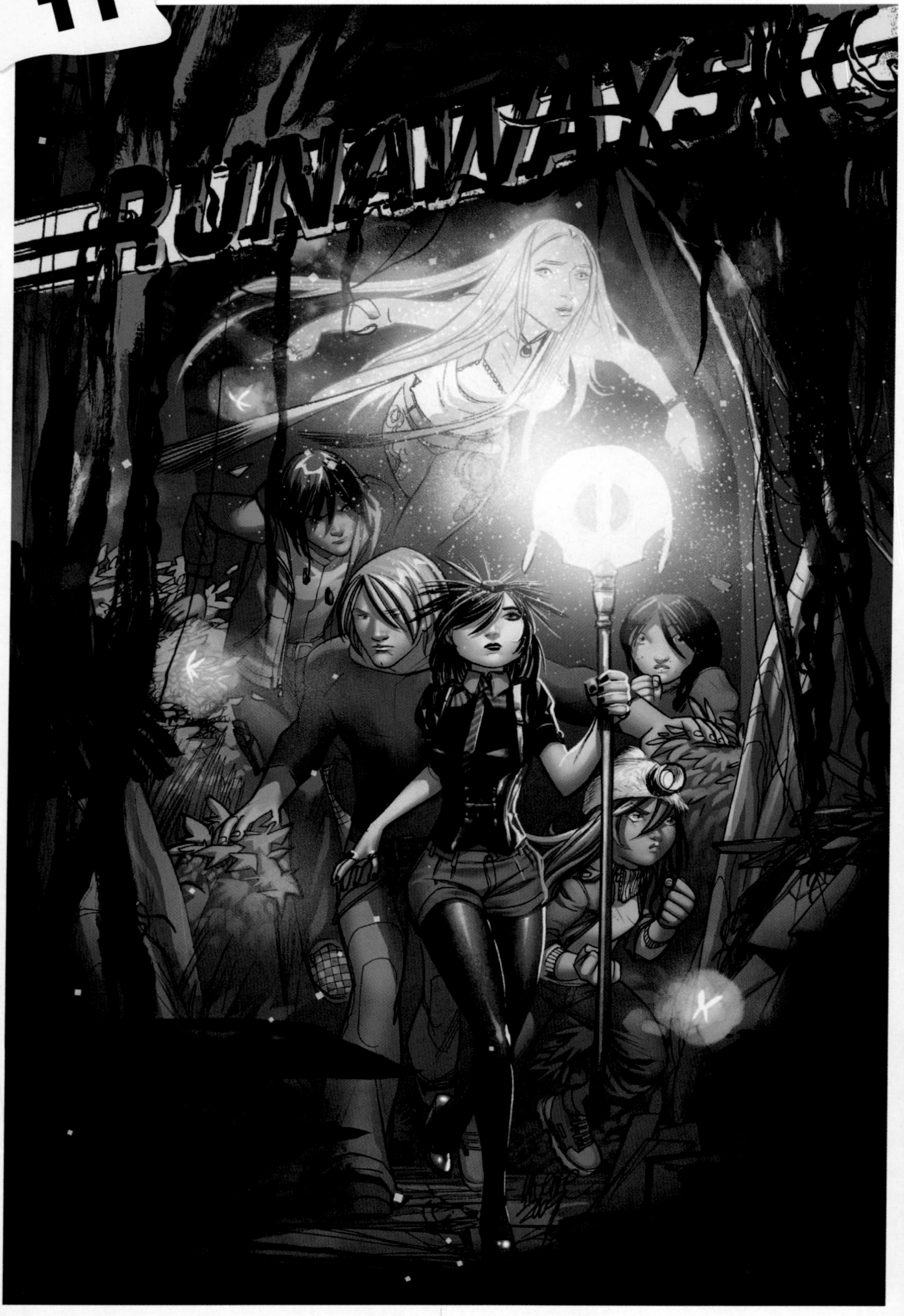
RUNAWAYS

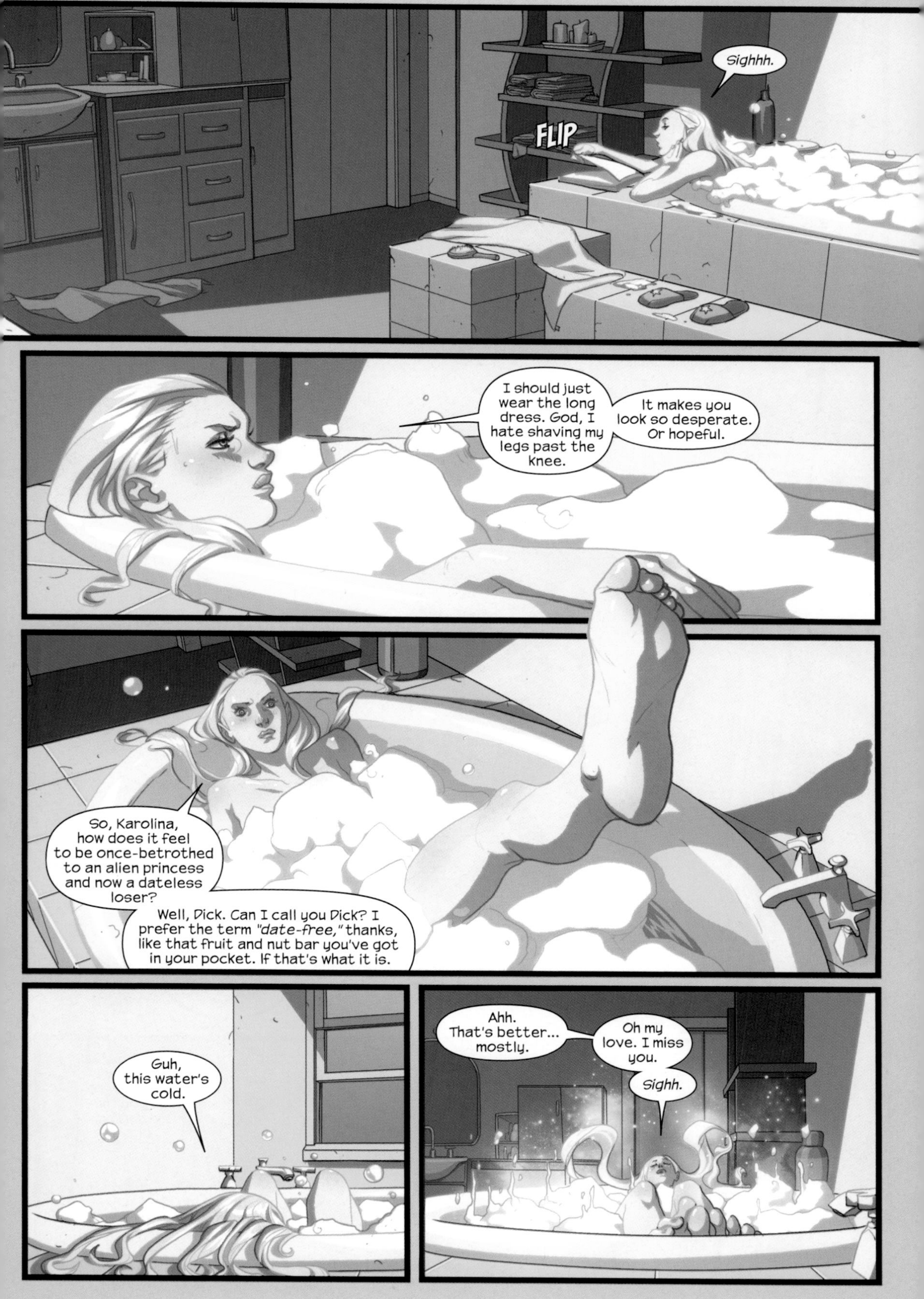
Sighhh.
FLIP
I should just wear the long dress. God, I hate shaving my legs past the knee.
It makes you look so desperate. Or hopeful.
So, Karolina, how does it feel to be once-betrothed to an alien princess and now a dateless loser?
Well, Dick. Can I call you Dick? I prefer the term "date-free," thanks, like that fruit and nut bar you've got in your pocket. If that's what it is.
Guh, this water's cold.
Ahh. That's better... mostly.
Oh my love. I miss you.
Sighh.

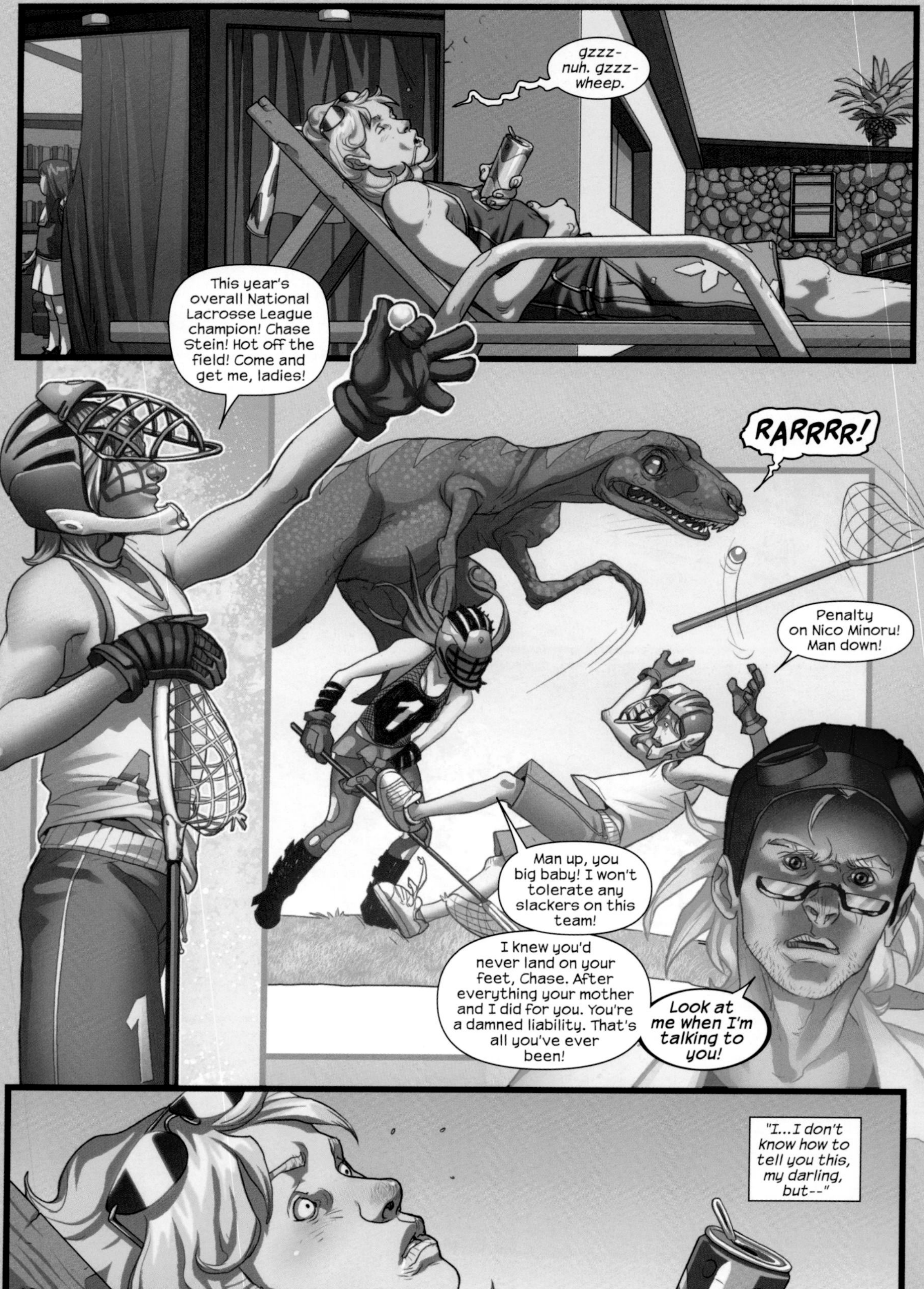
gzzz-
nuh. gzzz-
wheep.
This year's overall National Lacrosse League champion! Chase Stein! Hot off the field! Come and get me, ladies!
RARRRR!
Penalty on Nico Minoru! Man down!
Man up, you big baby! I won't tolerate any slackers on this team!
I knew you'd never land on your feet, Chase. After everything your mother and I did for you. You're a damned liability. That's all you've ever been!
Look at me when I'm talking to you!
"I...I don't know how to tell you this, my darling, but--"

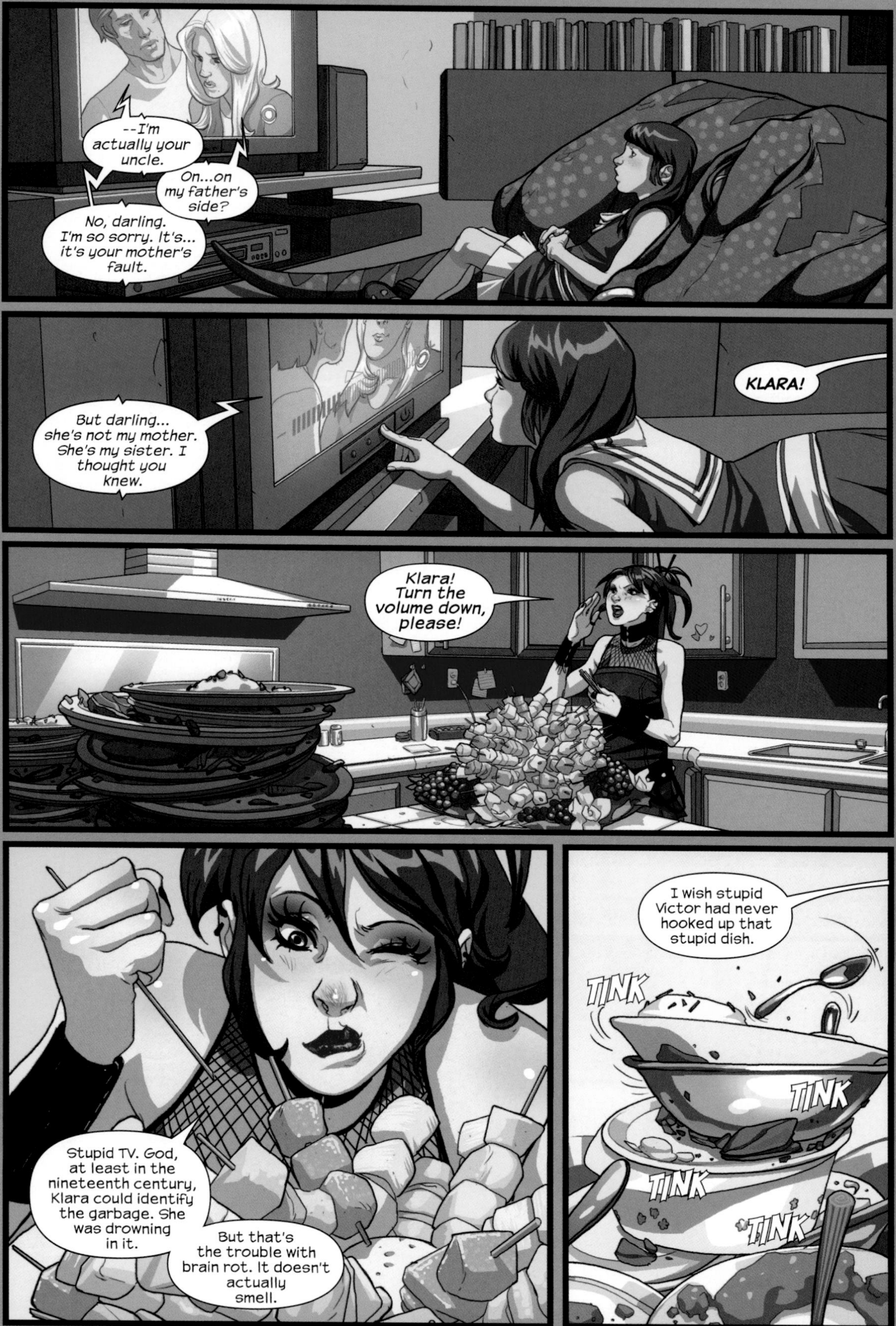
--I'm actually your uncle.
On...on my father's side?
No, darling. I'm so sorry. It's... it's your mother's fault.
But darling... she's not my mother. She's my sister. I thought you knew.
KLARA!
Klara! Turn the volume down, please!
Stupid TV. God, at least in the nineteenth century, Klara could identify the garbage. She was drowning in it.
But that's the trouble with brain rot. It doesn't actually smell.
I wish stupid Victor had never hooked up that stupid dish.
TINK
TINK
TINK
TINK

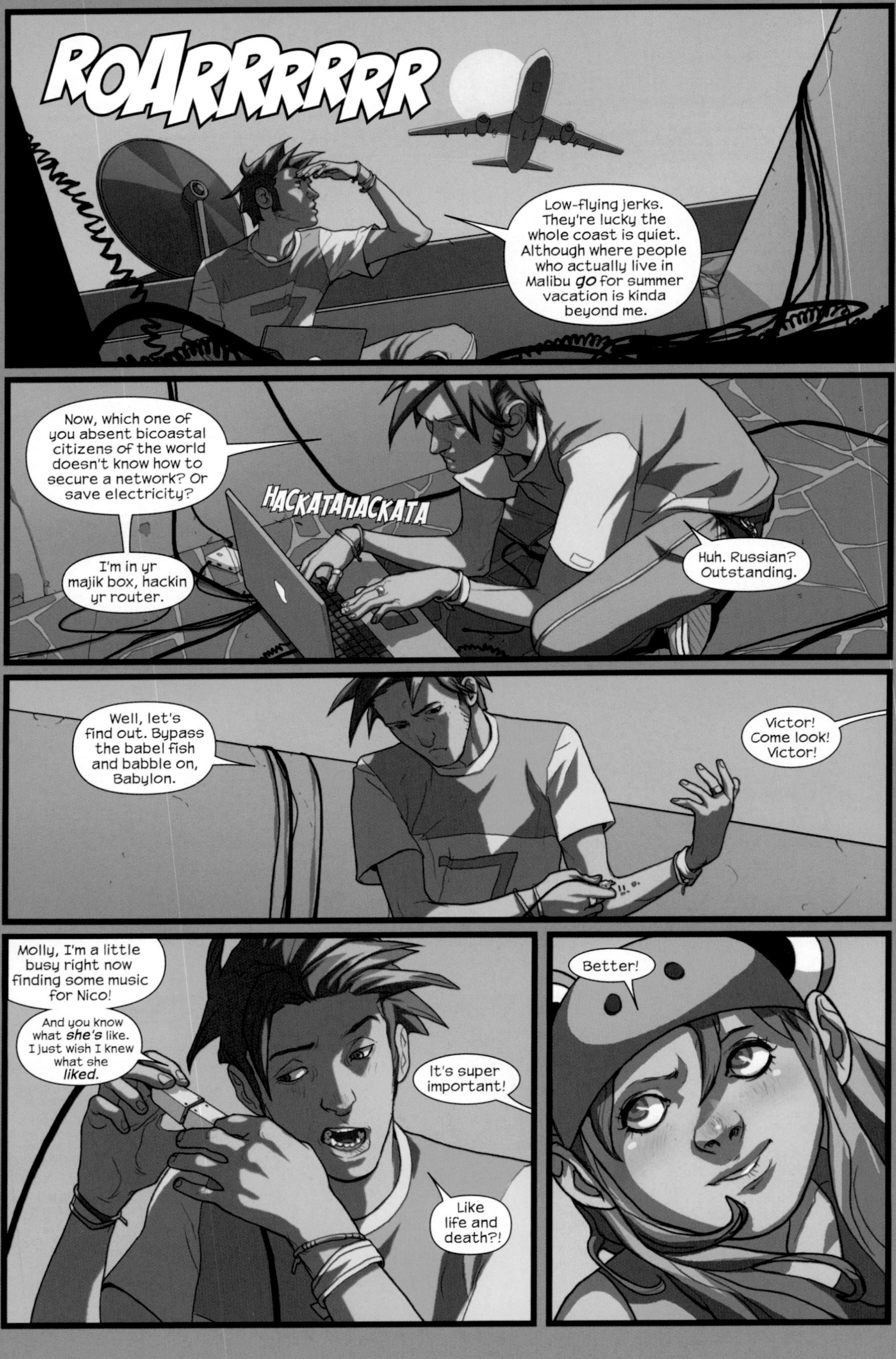
ROARRRRRR
Low-flying jerks. They're lucky the whole coast is quiet. Although where people who actually live in Malibu *go* for summer vacation is kinda beyond me.
Now, which one of you absent bicoastal citizens of the world doesn't know how to secure a network? Or save electricity?
HACKATAHACKATA
I'm in yr majik box, hackin yr router.
Huh. Russian? Outstanding.
Well, let's find out. Bypass the babel fish and babble on, Babylon.
Victor! Come look! Victor!
Molly, I'm a little busy right now finding some music for Nico!
And you know what *she's* like. I just wish I knew what she *liked.*
It's super important!
Like life and death?!
Better!

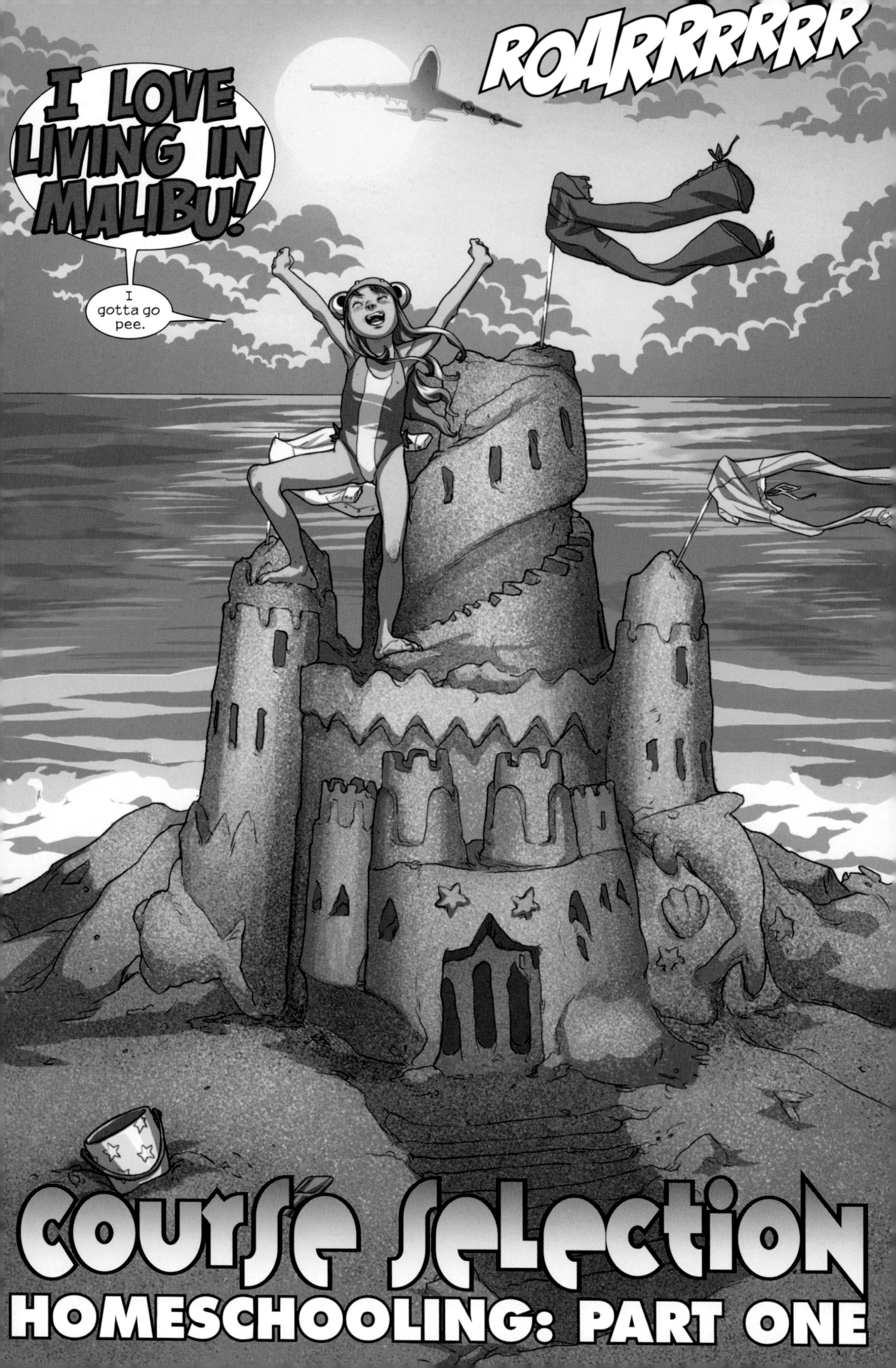

ROARRRRRR
I LOVE LIVING IN MALIBU!
I gotta go pee.
COURSE SELECTION
HOMESCHOOLING: PART ONE

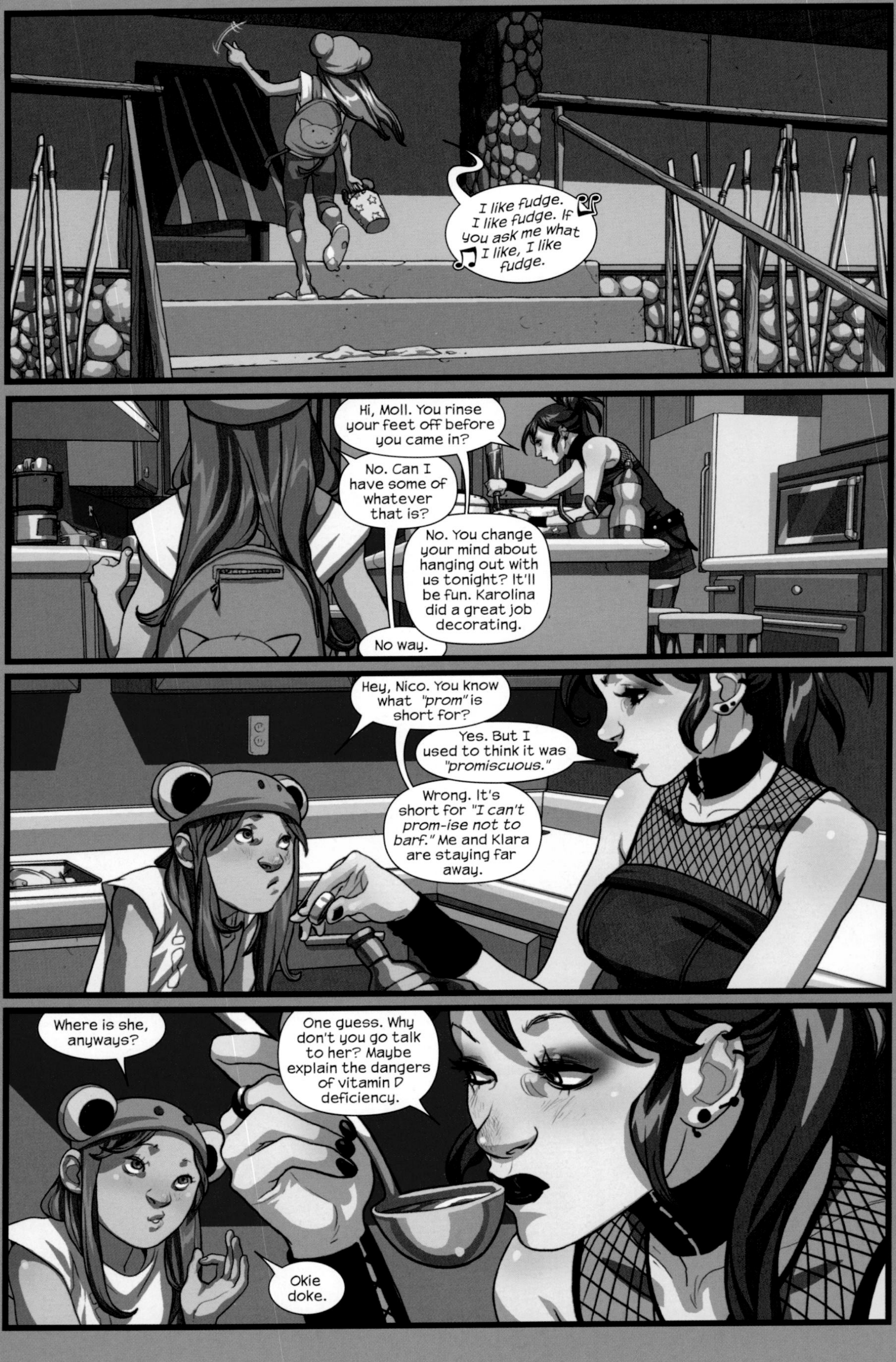
I like fudge. I like fudge. If you ask me what I like, I like fudge.
Hi, Moll. You rinse your feet off before you came in?
No. Can I have some of whatever that is?
No. You change your mind about hanging out with us tonight? It'll be fun. Karolina did a great job decorating.
No way.
Hey, Nico. You know what "prom" is short for?
Yes. But I used to think it was "promiscuous."
Wrong. It's short for "I can't prom-ise not to barf." Me and Klara are staying far away.
Where is she, anyways?
One guess. Why don't you go talk to her? Maybe explain the dangers of vitamin D deficiency.
Okie doke.

Hey, Klaaaraaaa!

Hey, Klara! Nico says you're deficient!

Shhhh...

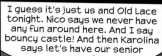

I guess it's just us and Old Lace tonight. Nico says we never have any fun around here. And I say bouncy castle! And then Karolina says let's have our senior prom!

Molly, please...

And I say I thought I never had to do school ever again. Dead parents equals no school. That was the deal!

And Victor gets all faraway-looking. And he's probably thinking about slow dancing. And tongues!

Oh Nico! You're so beautiful. Oh Chase! *Smooch smooch smooch.*

I don't think it's like that.

Klara, you have no idea what's gone on around here. **MWAH! MWAH! SMOOCH!**

Neither do you.

Hahahahahaha! I love you, Old Lace! Marry me!

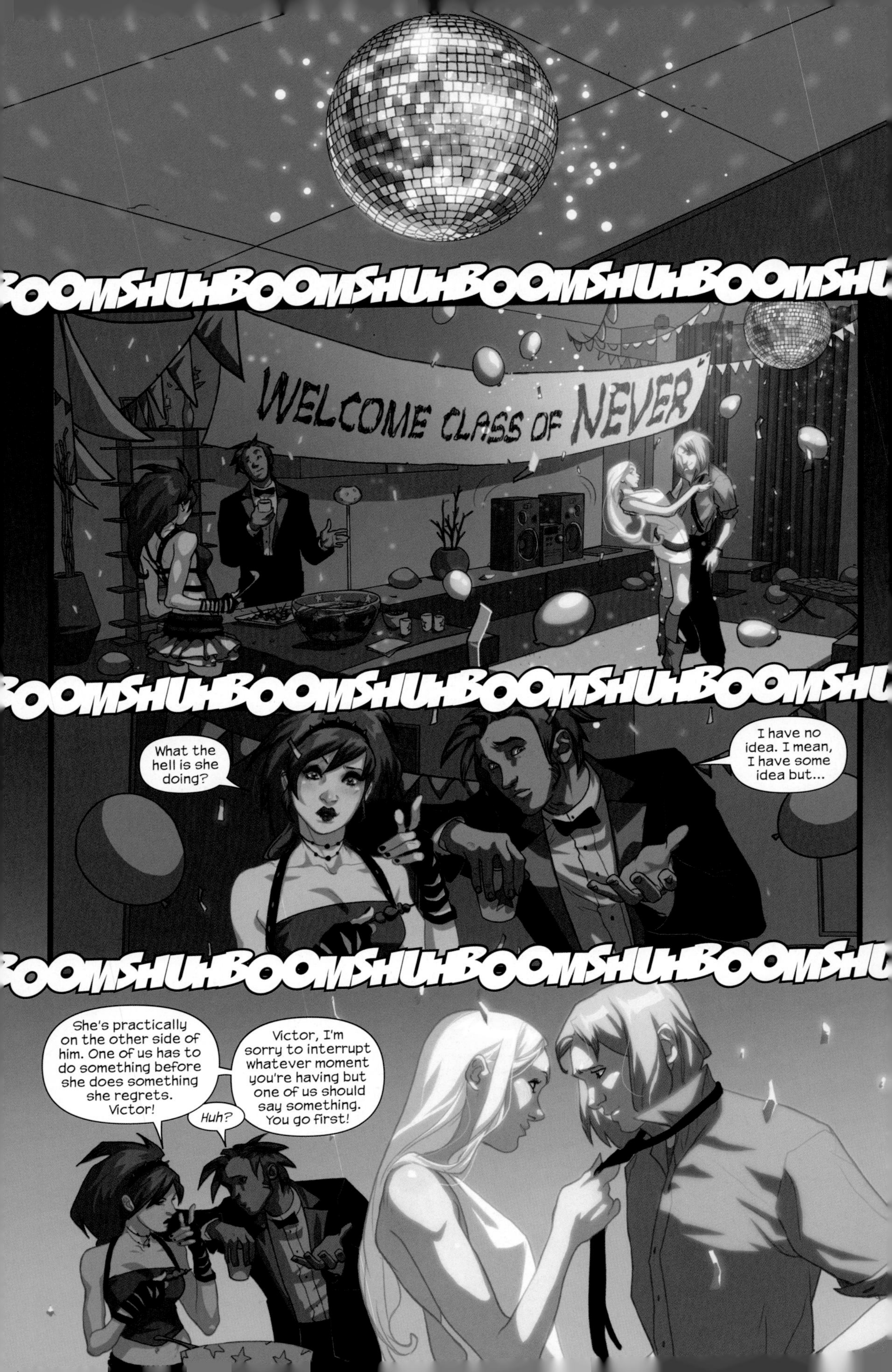
BOOMSHUHBOOMSHUHBOOMSHUHBOOMSHU
WELCOME CLASS OF NEVER
BOOMSHUHBOOMSHUHBOOMSHUHBOOMSHU
What the hell is she doing?
I have no idea. I mean, I have some idea but...
BOOMSHUHBOOMSHUHBOOMSHUHBOOMSHU
She's practically on the other side of him. One of us has to do something before she does something she regrets. Victor!
Huh?
Victor, I'm sorry to interrupt whatever moment you're having but one of us should say something. You go first!

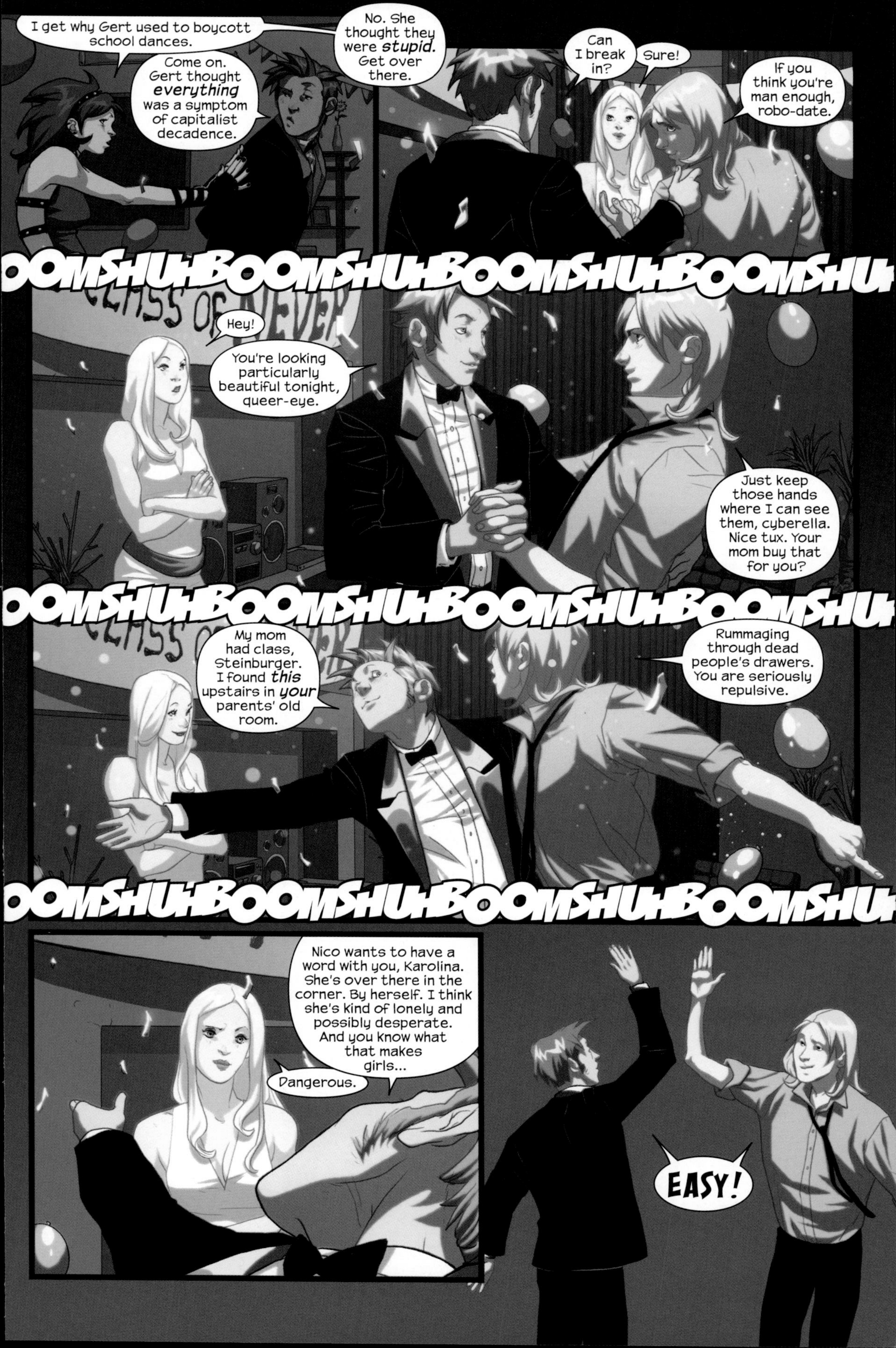

I get why Gert used to boycott school dances.
Come on. Gert thought *everything* was a symptom of capitalist decadence.
No. She thought they were *stupid.* Get over there.
Can I break in?
Sure!
If you think you're man enough, robo-date.
OOMSHUHBOOMSHUHBOOMSHUHBOOMSHU
CLASS OF NEVER
Hey!
You're looking particularly beautiful tonight, queer-eye.
Just keep those hands where I can see them, cyberella. Nice tux. Your mom buy that for you?
OOMSHUHBOOMSHUHBOOMSHUHBOOMSHU
My mom had class, Steinburger. I found *this* upstairs in *your* parents' old room.
Rummaging through dead people's drawers. You are seriously repulsive.
OOMSHUHBOOMSHUHBOOMSHUHBOOMSHU
Nico wants to have a word with you, Karolina. She's over there in the corner. By herself. I think she's kind of lonely and possibly desperate. And you know what that makes girls...
Dangerous.
EASY!

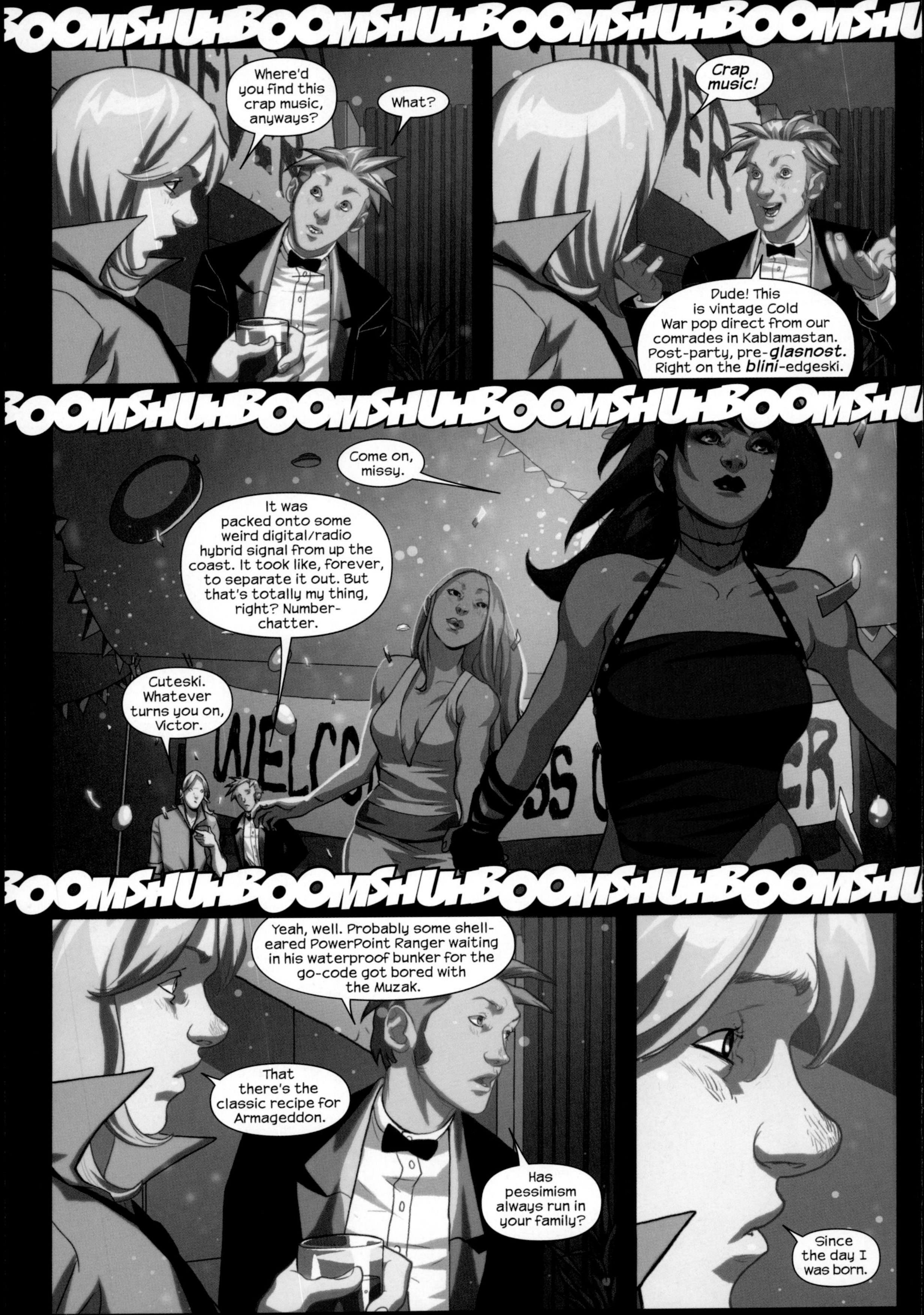
BOOMSHUHBOOMSHUHBOOMSHU
Where'd you find this crap music, anyways?
What?
Crap music!
Dude! This is vintage Cold War pop direct from our comrades in Kablamastan. Post-party, pre-glasnost. Right on the blini-edgeski.
BOOMSHUHBOOMSHUHBOOMSHU
Come on, missy.
It was packed onto some weird digital/radio hybrid signal from up the coast. It took like, forever, to separate it out. But that's totally my thing, right? Number-chatter.
Cuteski. Whatever turns you on, Victor.
BOOMSHUHBOOMSHUHBOOMSHU
Yeah, well. Probably some shell-eared PowerPoint Ranger waiting in his waterproof bunker for the go-code got bored with the Muzak.
That there's the classic recipe for Armageddon.
Has pessimism always run in your family?
Since the day I was born.

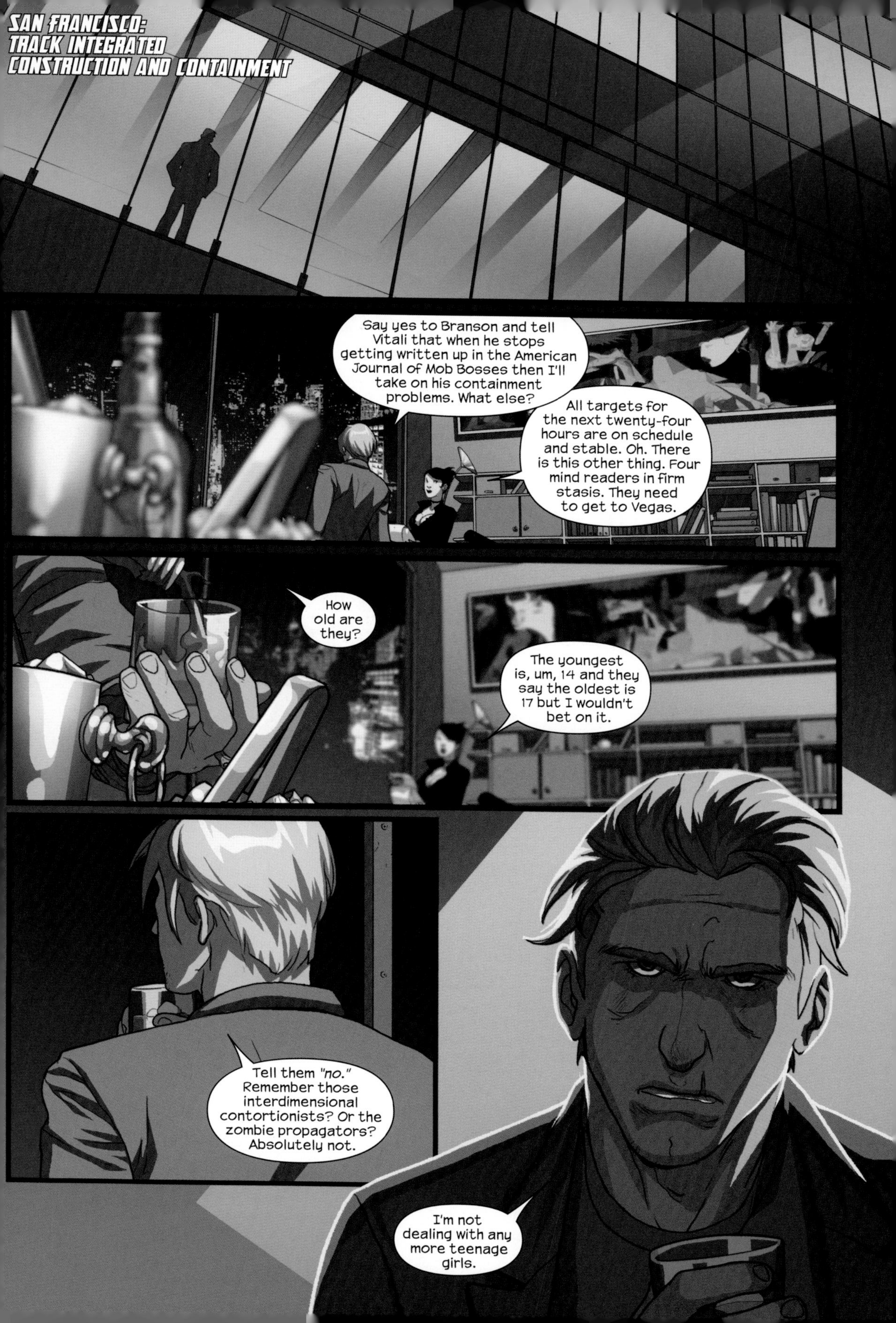
SAN FRANCISCO: TRACK INTEGRATED CONSTRUCTION AND CONTAINMENT
Say yes to Branson and tell Vitali that when he stops getting written up in the American Journal of Mob Bosses then I'll take on his containment problems. What else?
All targets for the next twenty-four hours are on schedule and stable. Oh. There is this other thing. Four mind readers in firm stasis. They need to get to Vegas.
How old are they?
The youngest is, um, 14 and they say the oldest is 17 but I wouldn't bet on it.
Tell them "no." Remember those interdimensional contortionists? Or the zombie propagators? Absolutely not.
I'm not dealing with any more teenage girls.

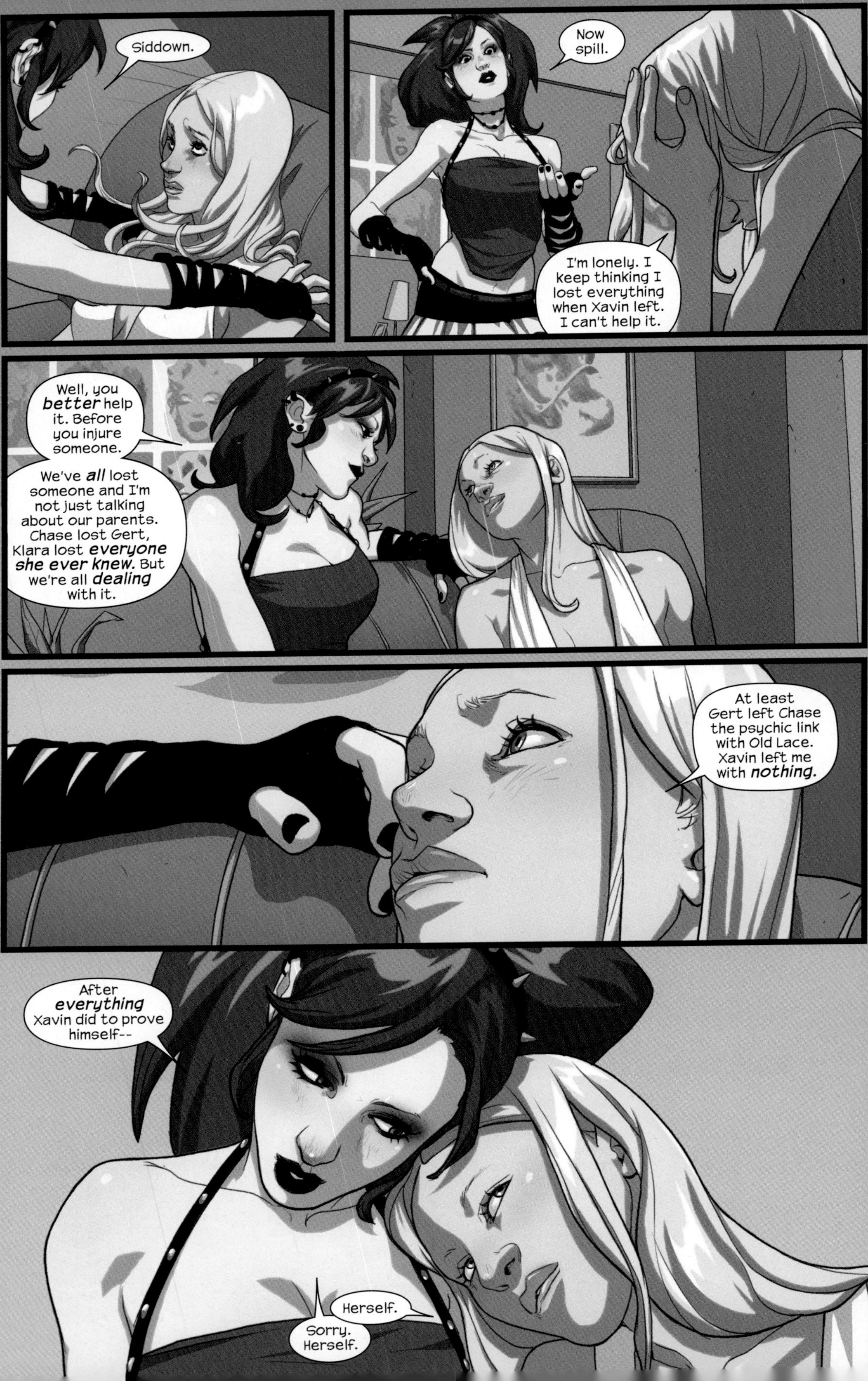
Siddown.
Now spill.
I'm lonely. I keep thinking I lost everything when Xavin left. I can't help it.
Well, you **better** help it. Before you injure someone.
We've **all** lost someone and I'm not just talking about our parents. Chase lost Gert, Klara lost **everyone she ever knew.** But we're all **dealing** with it.
At least Gert left Chase the psychic link with Old Lace. Xavin left me with **nothing.**
After **everything** Xavin did to prove himself--
Herself.
Sorry. Herself.

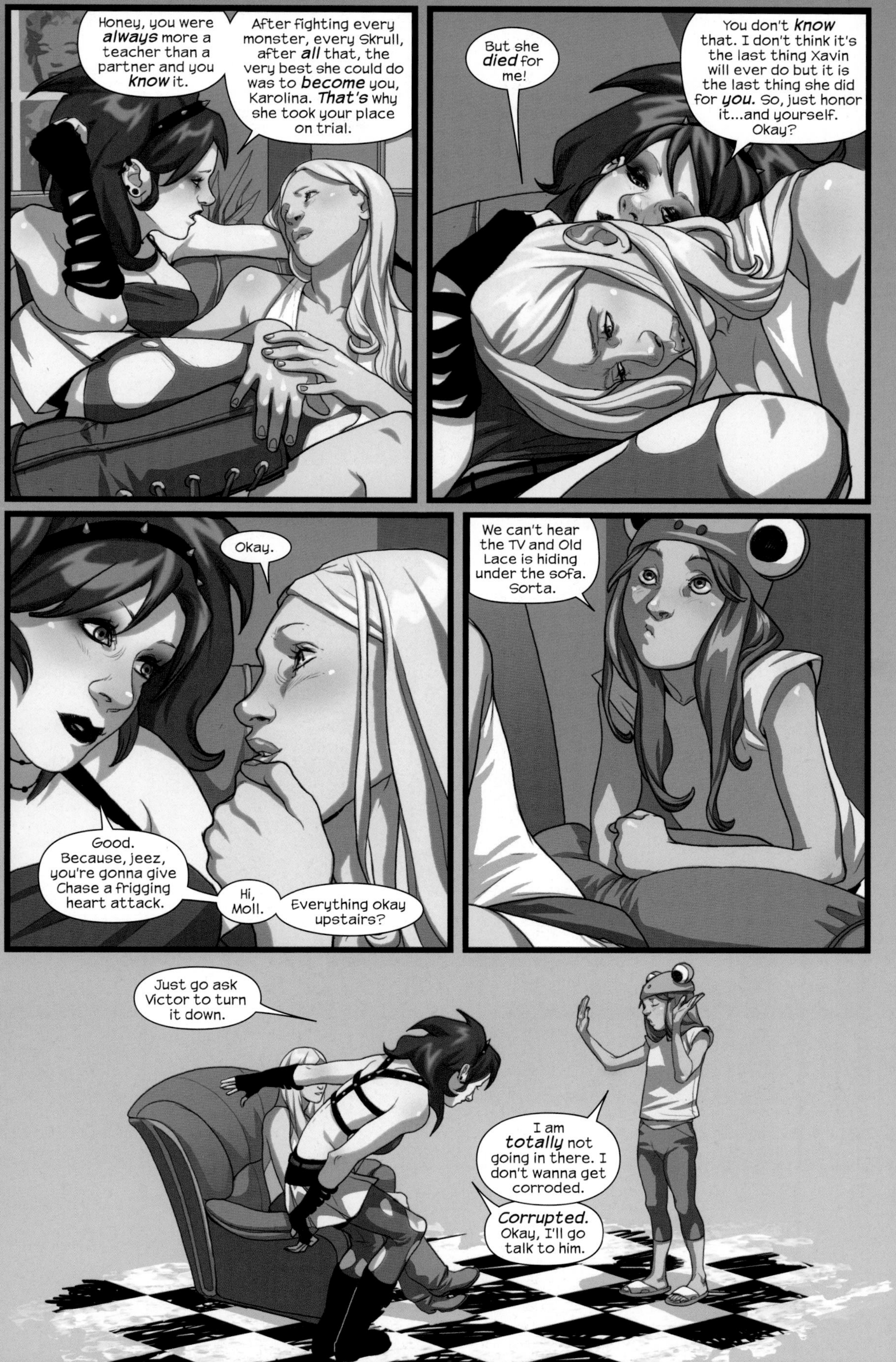
Honey, you were *always* more a teacher than a partner and you *know* it.
After fighting every monster, every Skrull, after *all* that, the very best she could do was to *become* you, Karolina. *That's* why she took your place on trial.
But she *died* for me!
You don't *know* that. I don't think it's the last thing Xavin will ever do but it is the last thing she did for *you.* So, just honor it...and yourself. Okay?
Okay.
Good. Because, jeez, you're gonna give Chase a frigging heart attack.
Hi, Moll.
Everything okay upstairs?
We can't hear the TV and Old Lace is hiding under the sofa. Sorta.
Just go ask Victor to turn it down.
I am *totally* not going in there. I don't wanna get corroded.
Corrupted. Okay, I'll go talk to him.

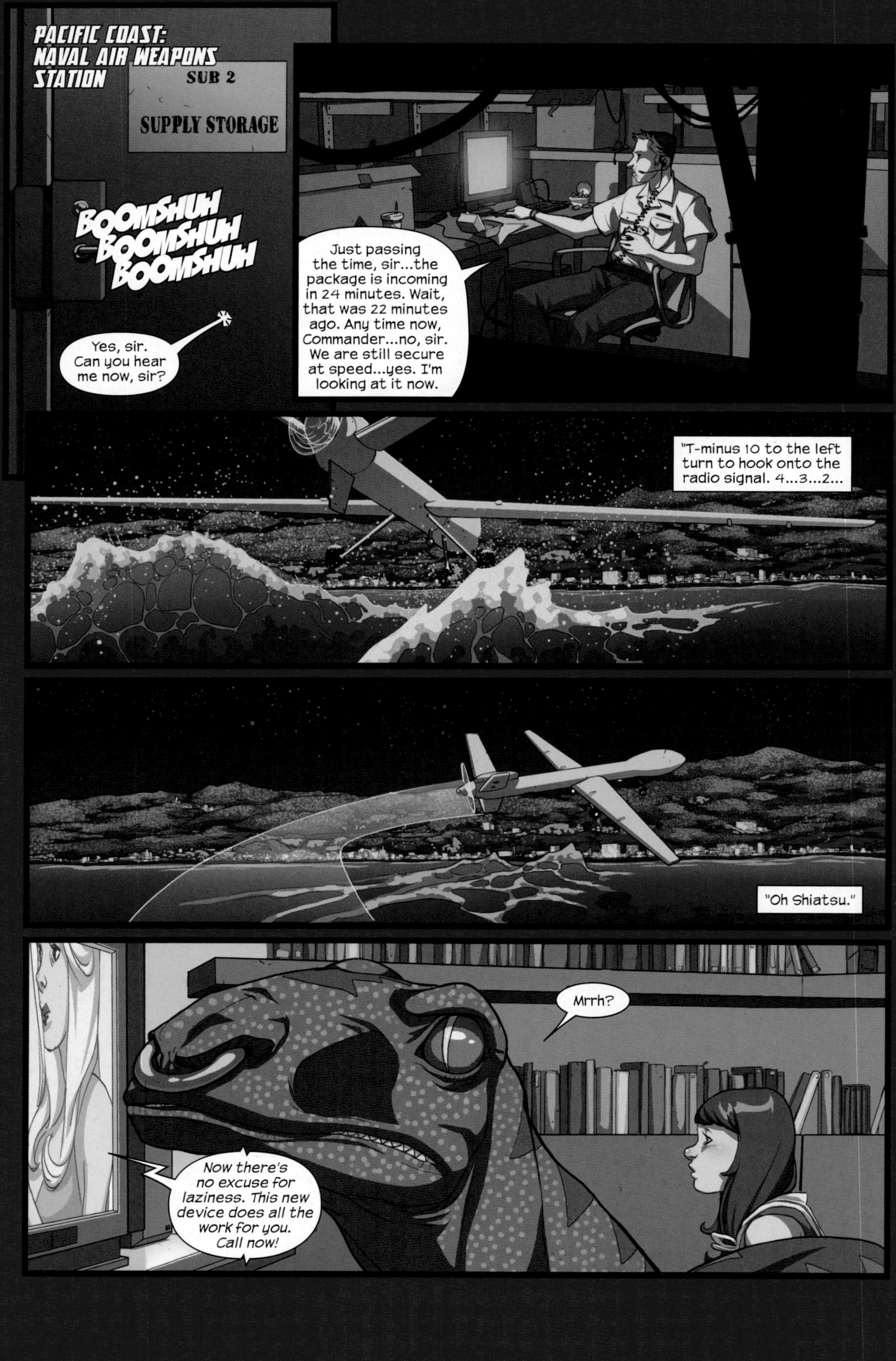
PACIFIC COAST: NAVAL AIR WEAPONS STATION
SUB 2
SUPPLY STORAGE
BOOMSHUH BOOMSHUH BOOMSHUH
Yes, sir. Can you hear me now, sir?
Just passing the time, sir...the package is incoming in 24 minutes. Wait, that was 22 minutes ago. Any time now, Commander...no, sir. We are still secure at speed...yes. I'm looking at it now.
"T-minus 10 to the left turn to hook onto the radio signal. 4...3...2...
"Oh Shiatsu."
Mrrh?
Now there's no excuse for laziness. This new device does all the work for you. Call now!

RUUHHHHHH

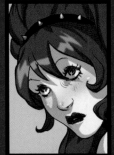

SKREEEEEEEEEEEEEEEE

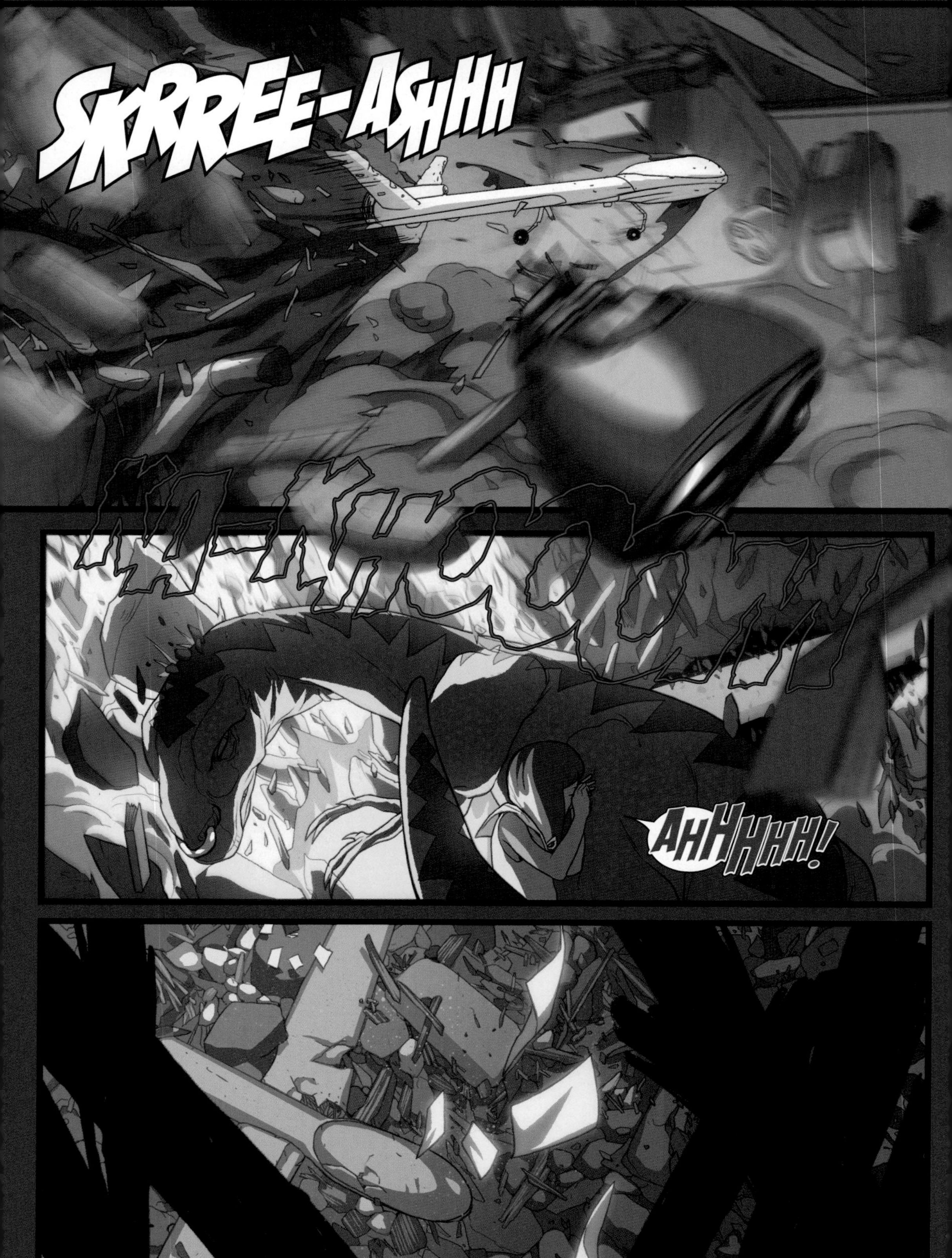
SKRREE-ASHHH
AHHHHH!

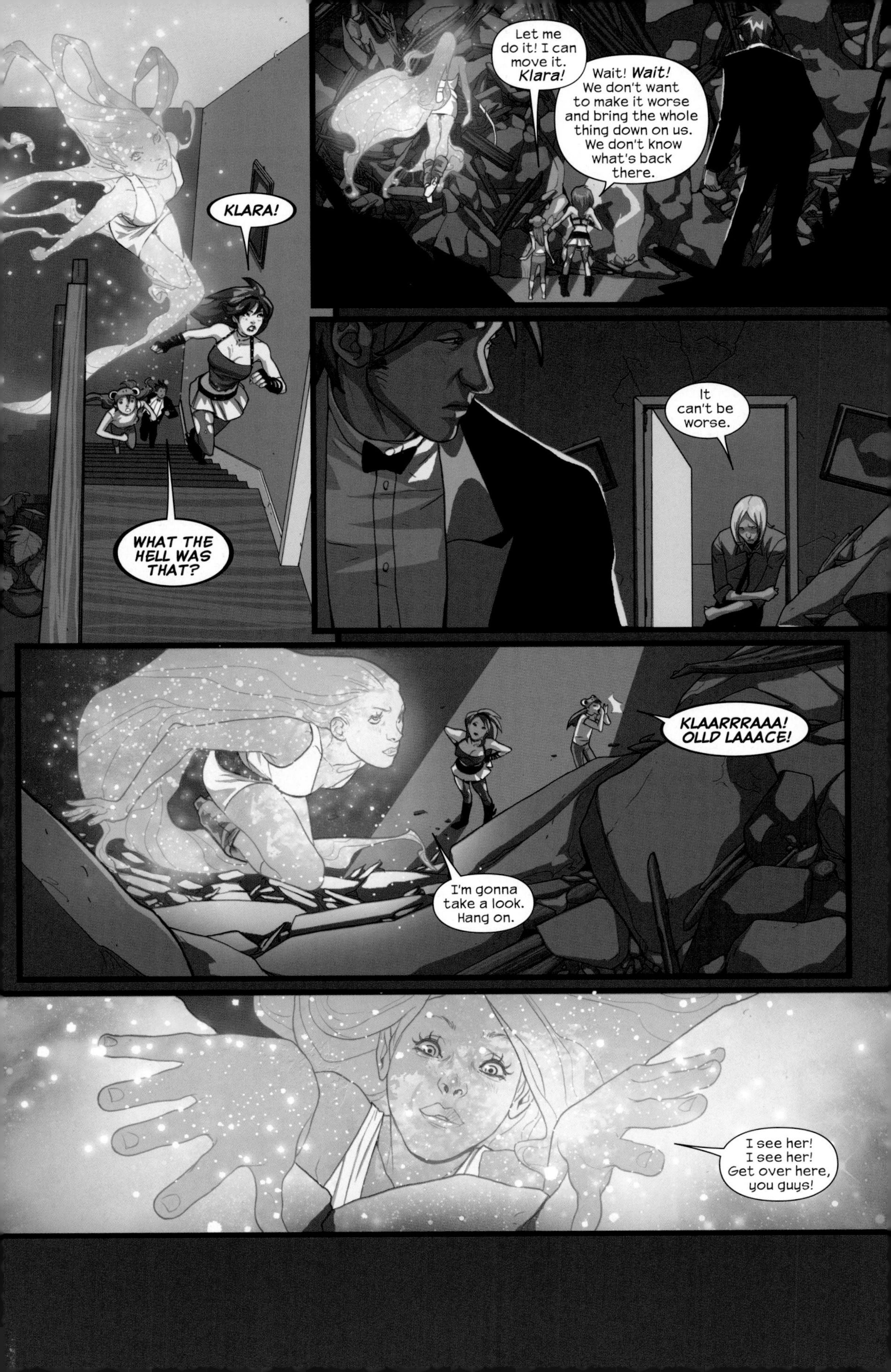
KLARA!
WHAT THE HELL WAS THAT?
Let me do it! I can move it. Klara!
Wait! Wait! We don't want to make it worse and bring the whole thing down on us. We don't know what's back there.
It can't be worse.
KLAARRRAAA! OLLD LAAACE!
I'm gonna take a look. Hang on.
I see her! I see her! Get over here, you guys!

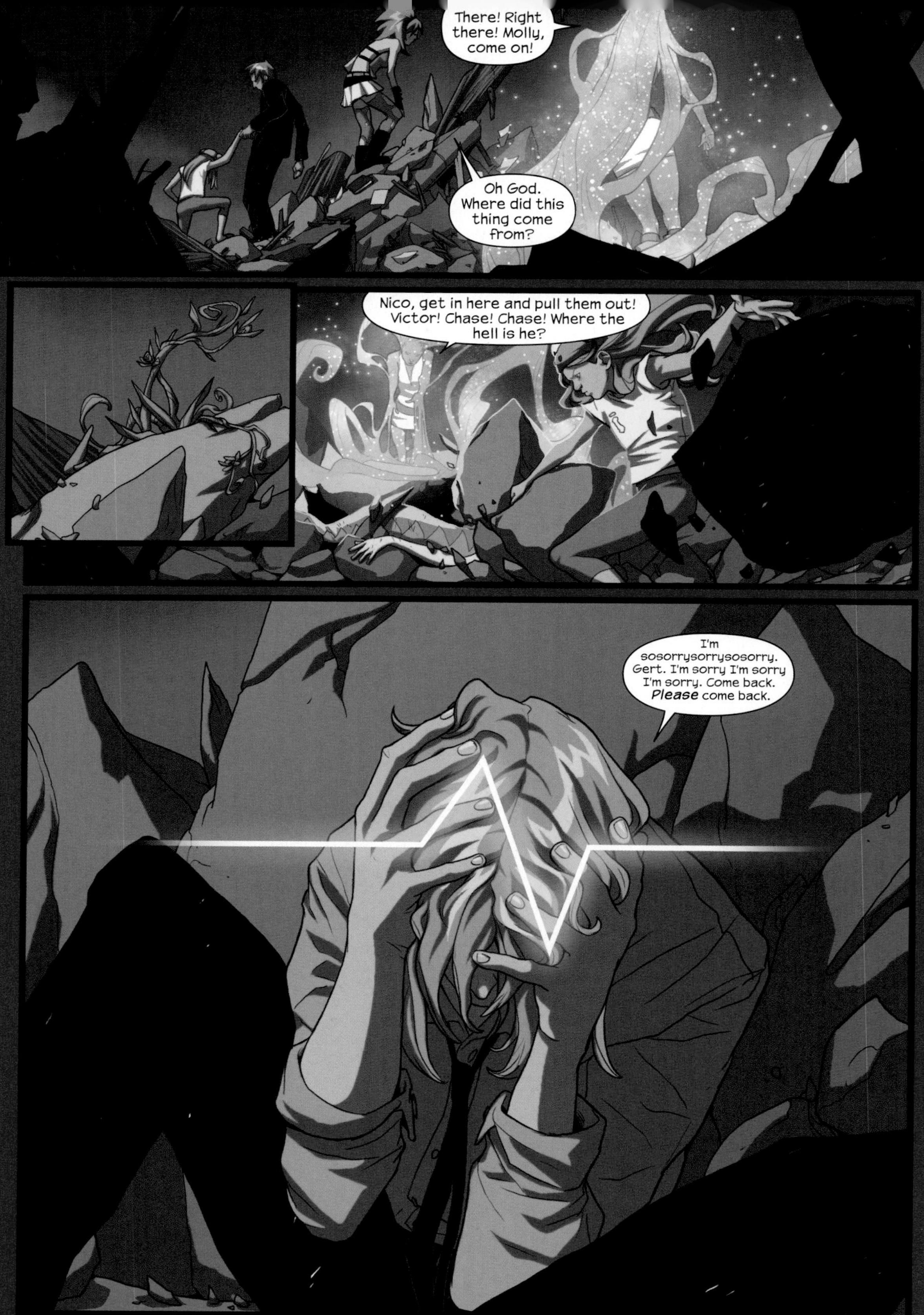

There! Right there! Molly, come on!
Oh God. Where did this thing come from?
Nico, get in here and pull them out! Victor! Chase! Chase! Where the hell is he?
I'm sosorrysorrysosorry. Gert. I'm sorry I'm sorry I'm sorry. Come back. *Please* come back.

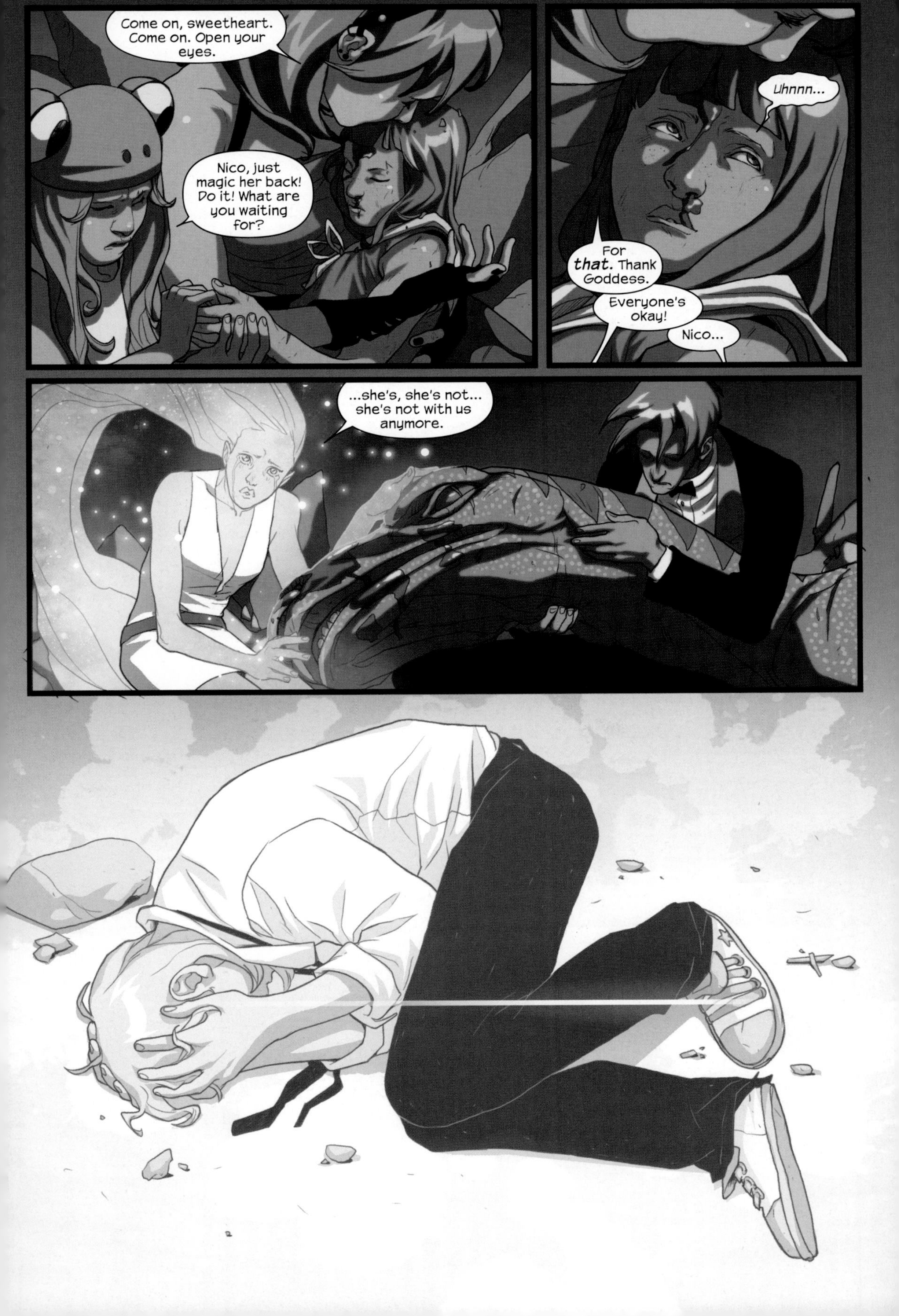
Come on, sweetheart. Come on. Open your eyes.
Nico, just magic her back! Do it! What are you waiting for?
Uhnnn...
For *that.* Thank Goddess.
Everyone's okay!
Nico...
...she's, she's not... she's not with us anymore.

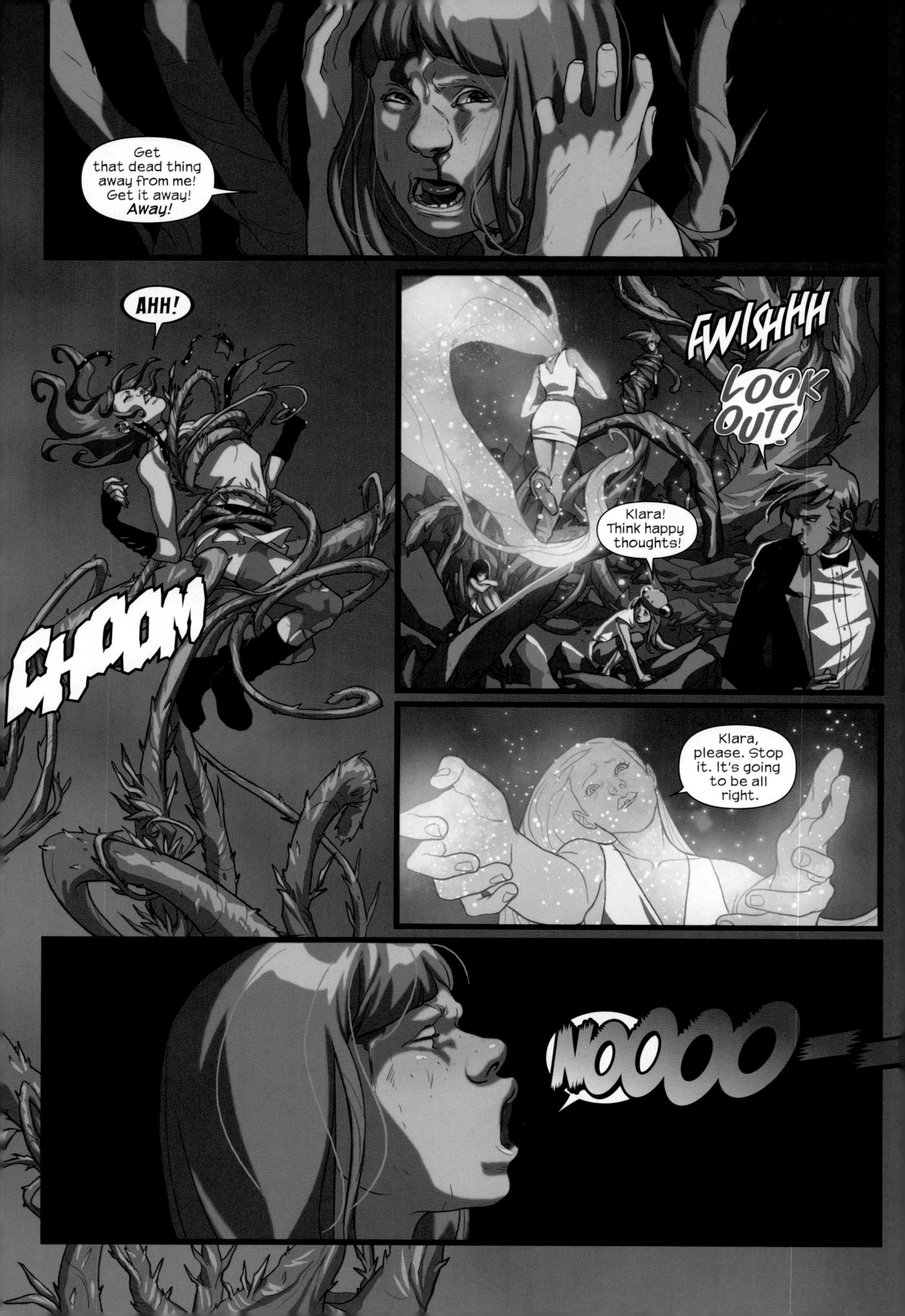
Get
that dead thing
away from me!
Get it away!
Away!
AHH!
CHOOM
FWISHHH
LOOK OUT!
Klara! Think happy thoughts!
Klara, please. Stop it. It's going to be all right.
NOOOO

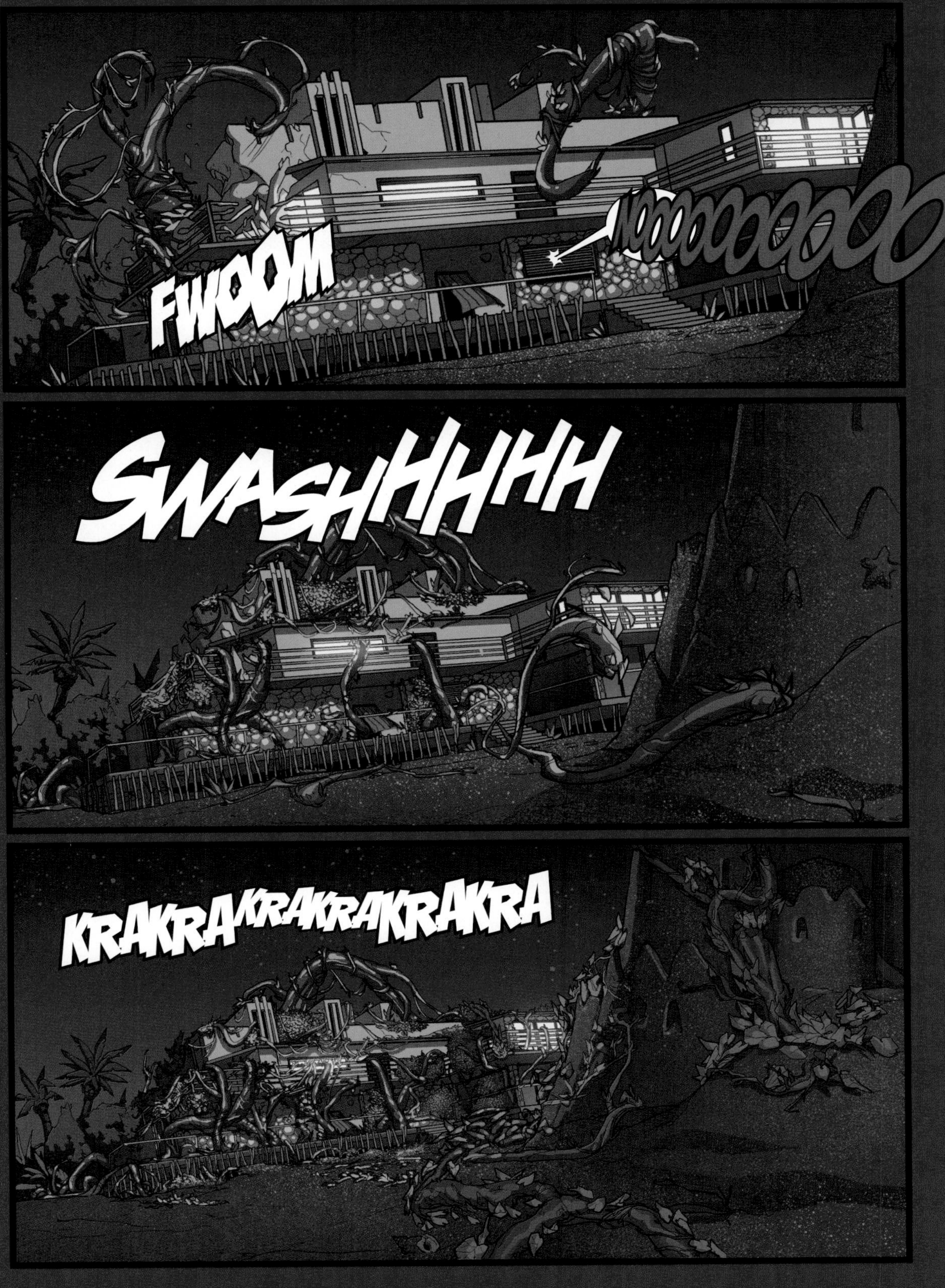
FWOOM
NOOOOOOOOOOO
SWASHHHHH
KRAKRAKRAKRAKRAKRAKRA

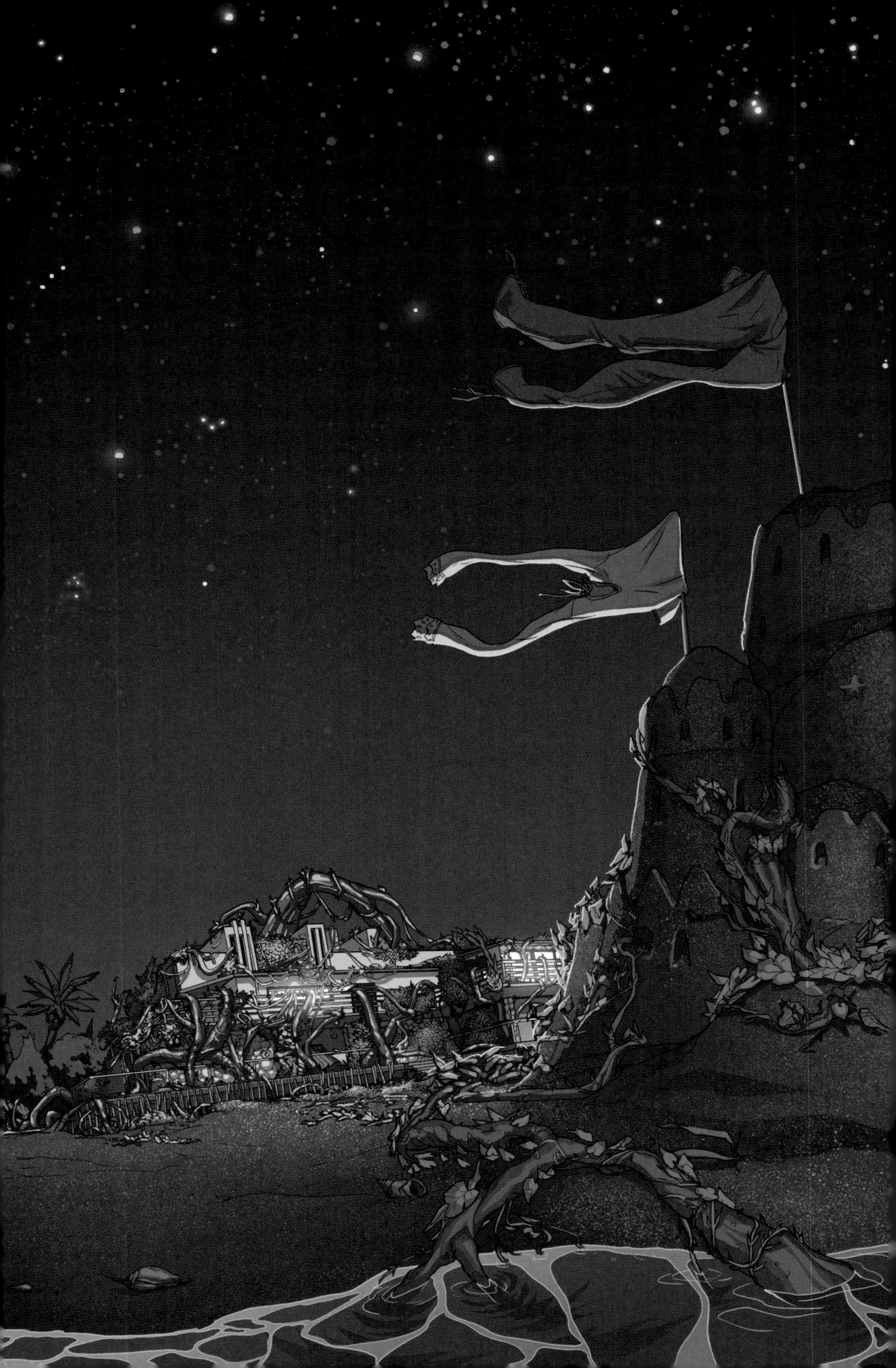

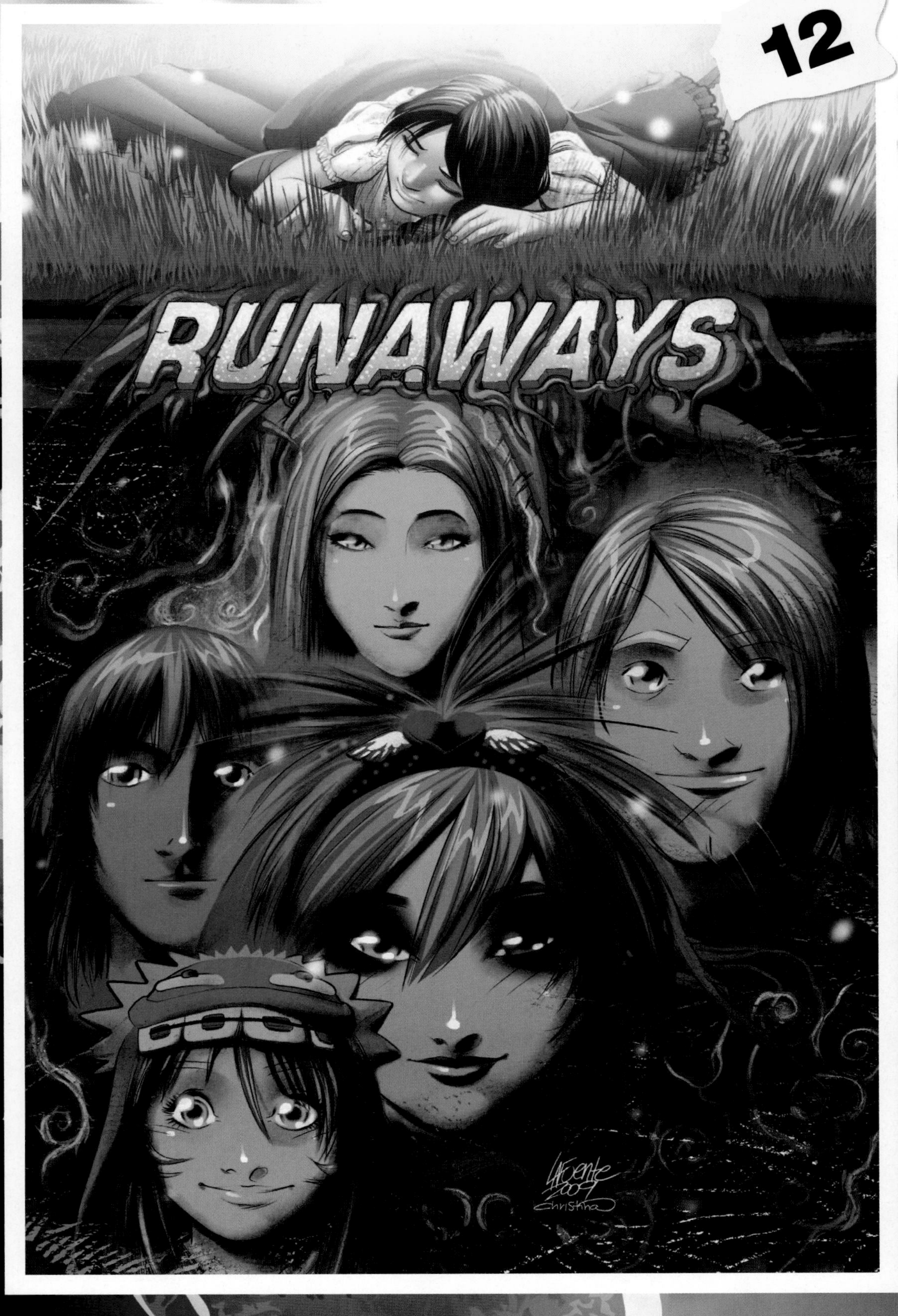
12
RUNAWAYS
LAFuente 2009 Christina

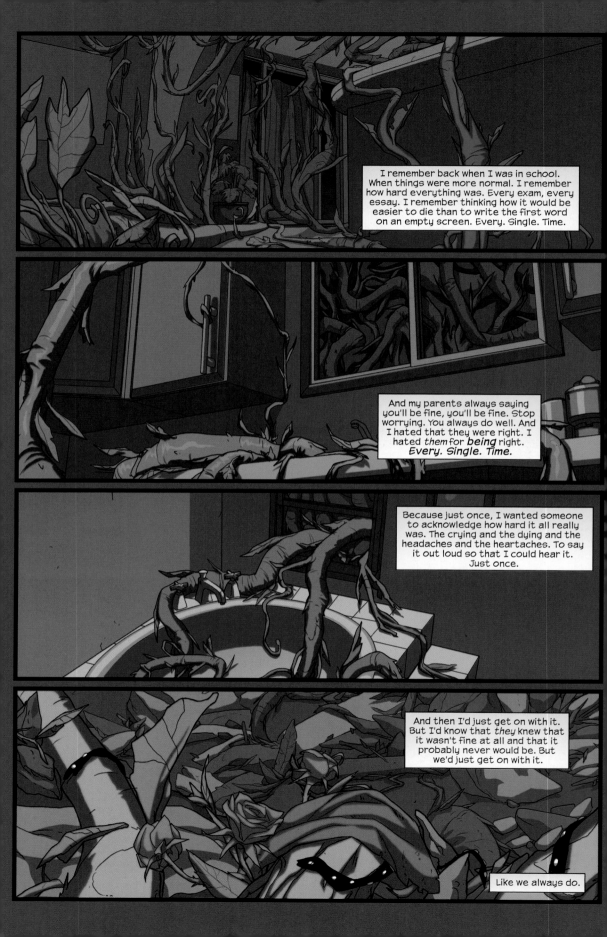

I remember back when I was in school. When things were more normal. I remember how hard everything was. Every exam, every essay. I remember thinking how it would be easier to die than to write the first word on an empty screen. Every. Single. Time.

And my parents always saying you'll be fine, you'll be fine. Stop worrying. You always do well. And I hated that they were right. I hated *them* for *being* right. *Every. Single. Time.*

Because just once, I wanted someone to acknowledge how hard it all really was. The crying and the dying and the headaches and the heartaches. To say it out loud so that I could hear it. Just once.

And then I'd just get on with it. But I'd know that *they* knew that it wasn't fine at all and that it probably never would be. But we'd just get on with it.

Like we always do.

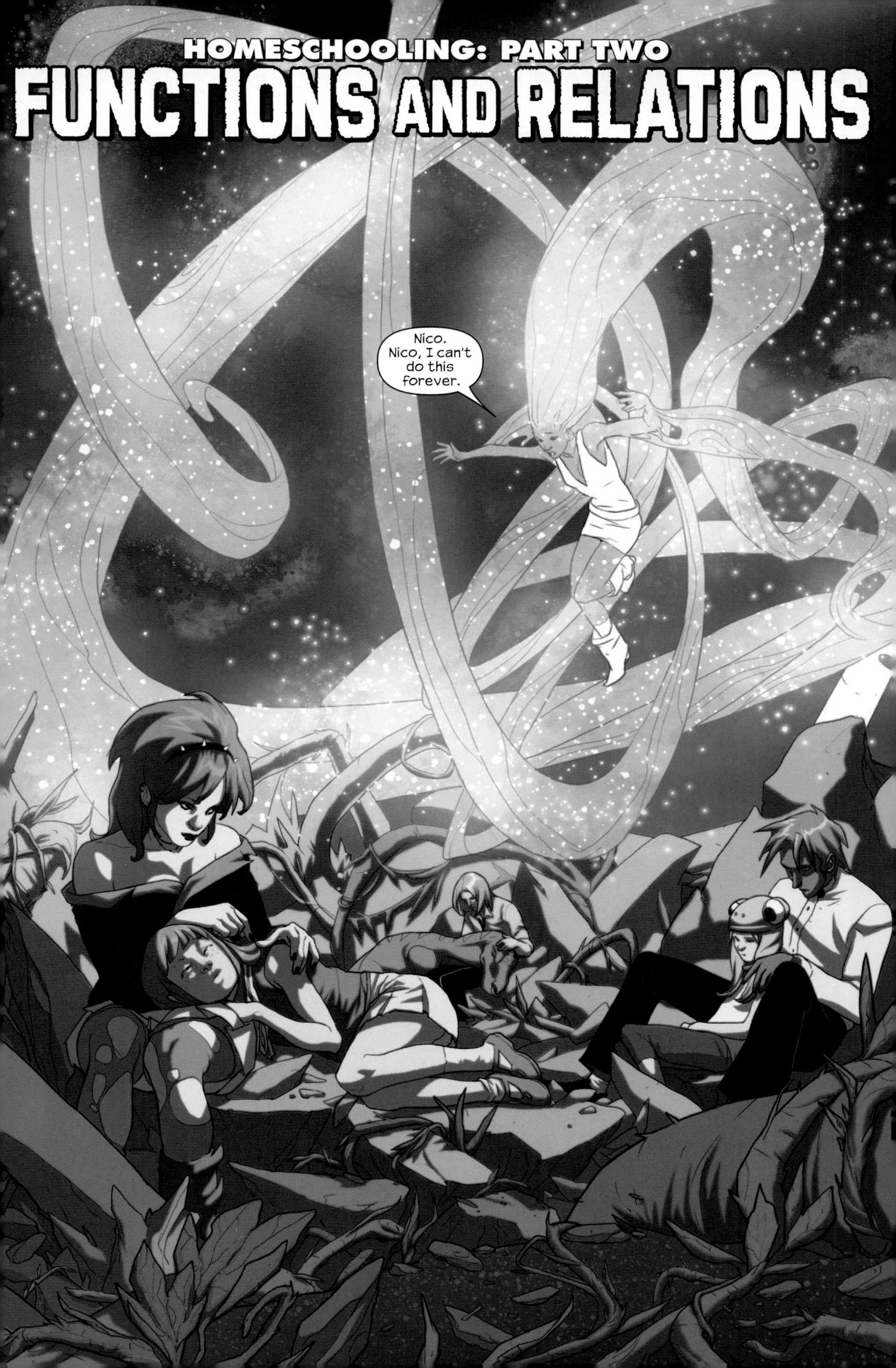
HOMESCHOOLING: PART TWO
FUNCTIONS AND RELATIONS
Nico.
Nico, I can't
do this
forever.

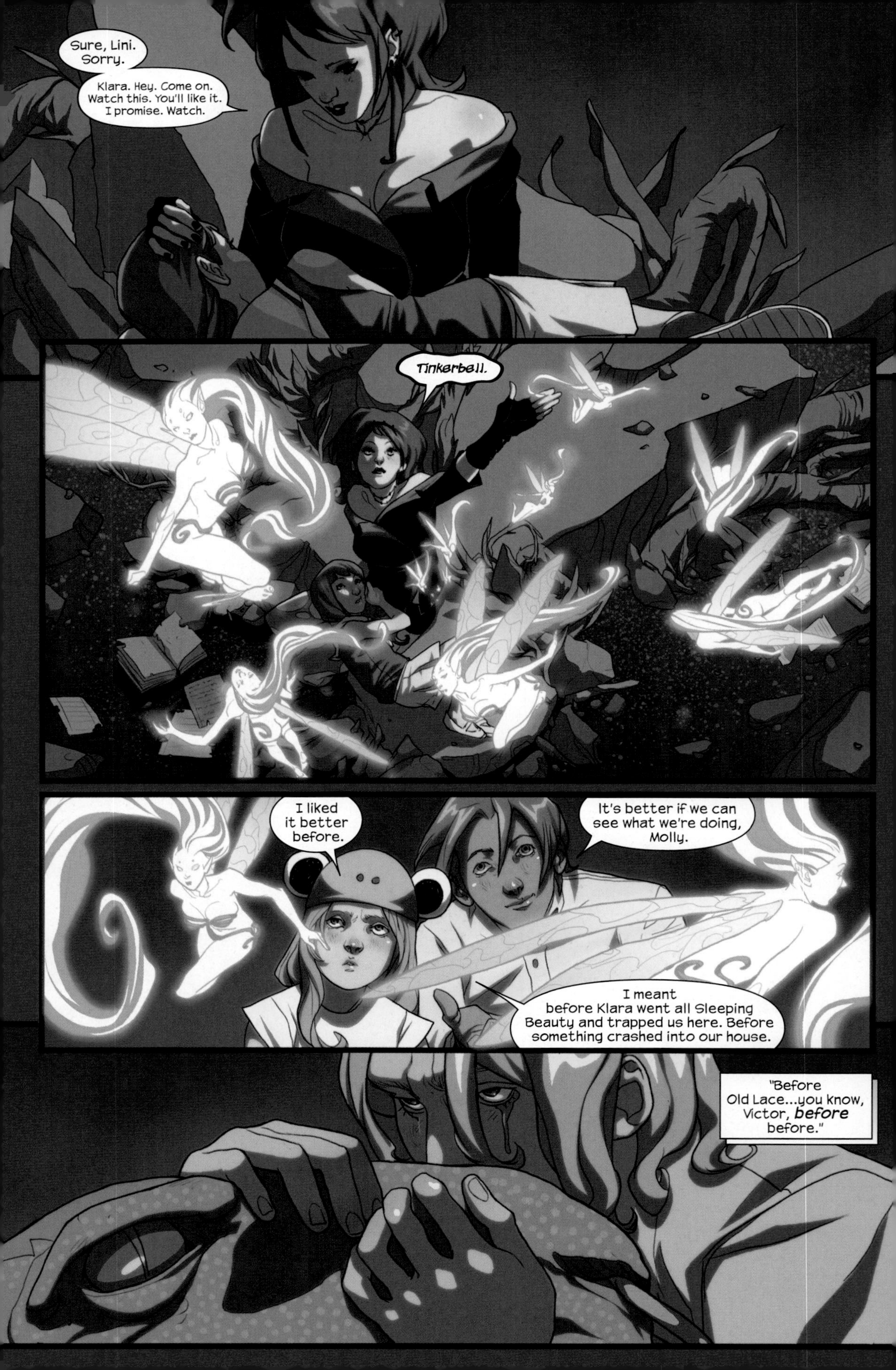
Sure, Lini. Sorry.
Klara. Hey. Come on. Watch this. You'll like it. I promise. Watch.
Tinkerbell.
I liked it better before.
It's better if we can see what we're doing, Molly.
I meant before Klara went all Sleeping Beauty and trapped us here. Before something crashed into our house.
"Before Old Lace...you know, Victor, *before* before."

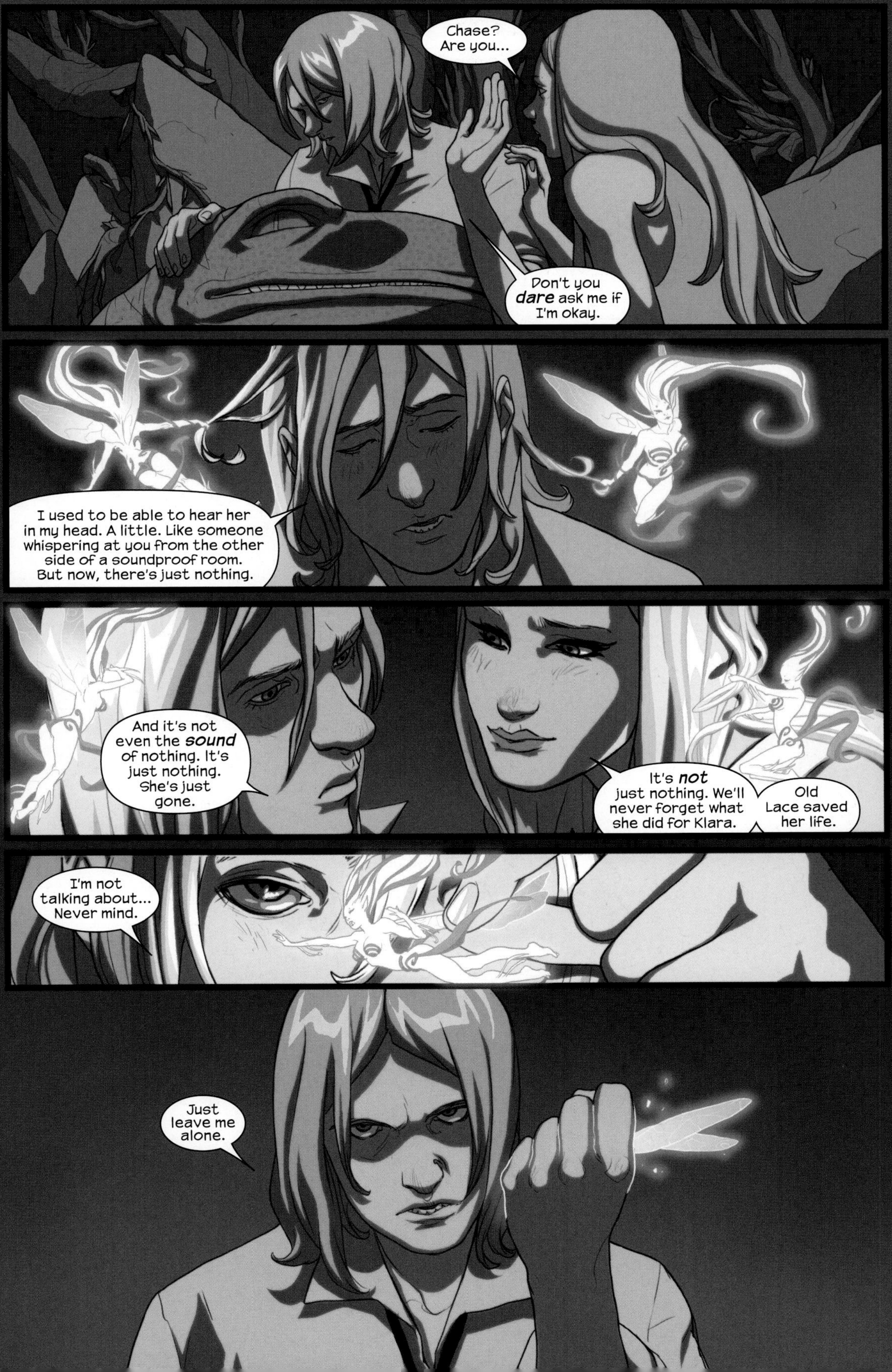
Chase? Are you...
Don't you *dare* ask me if I'm okay.
I used to be able to hear her in my head. A little. Like someone whispering at you from the other side of a soundproof room. But now, there's just nothing.
And it's not even the *sound* of nothing. It's just nothing. She's just gone.
It's *not* just nothing. We'll never forget what she did for Klara.
Old Lace saved her life.
I'm not talking about... Never mind.
Just leave me alone.

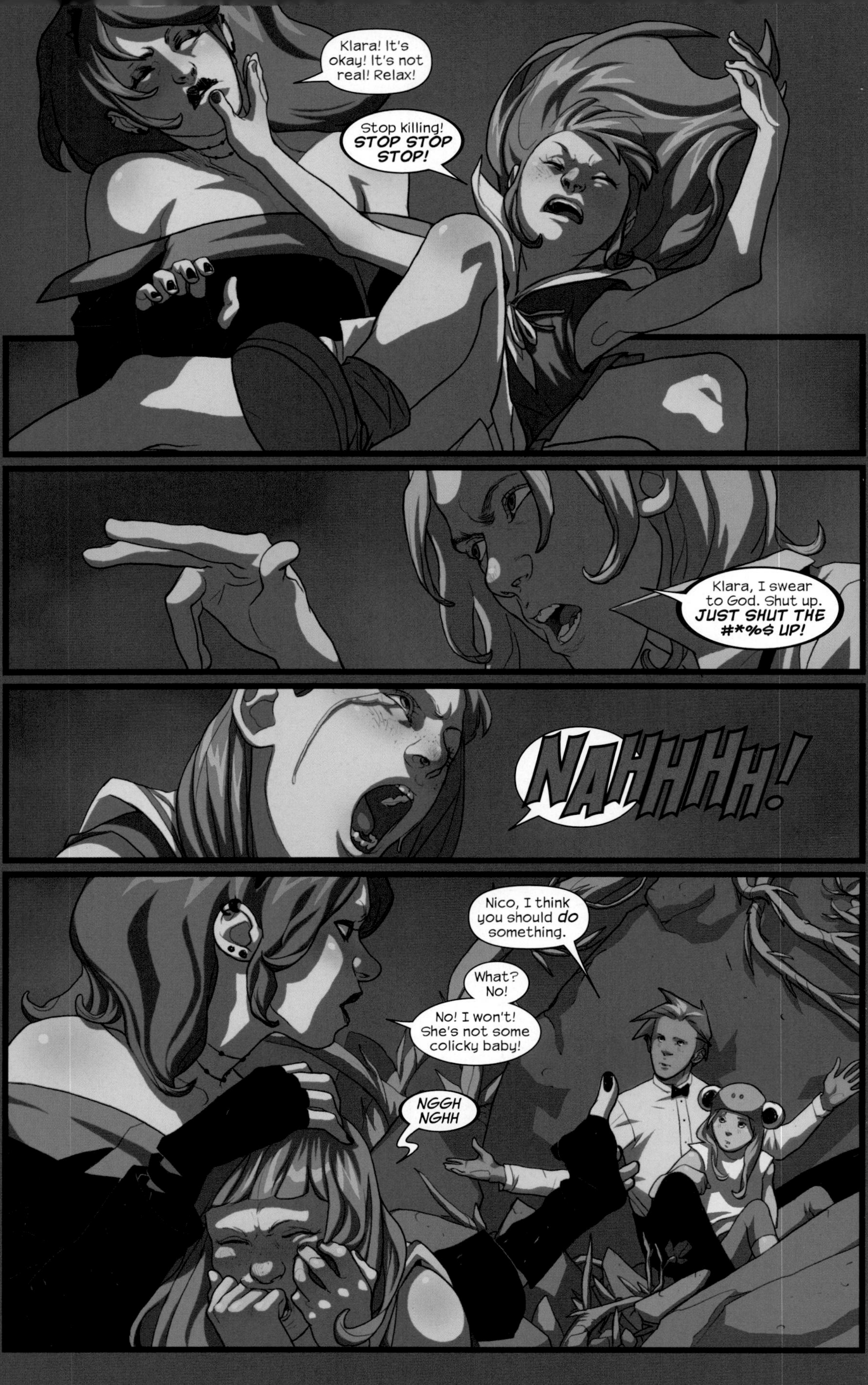

Klara! It's okay! It's not real! Relax!
Stop killing! STOP STOP STOP!
Klara, I swear to God. Shut up. JUST SHUT THE #*%$ UP!
NAHHHH!
Nico, I think you should do something.
What? No!
No! I won't! She's not some colicky baby!
NGGH NGHH

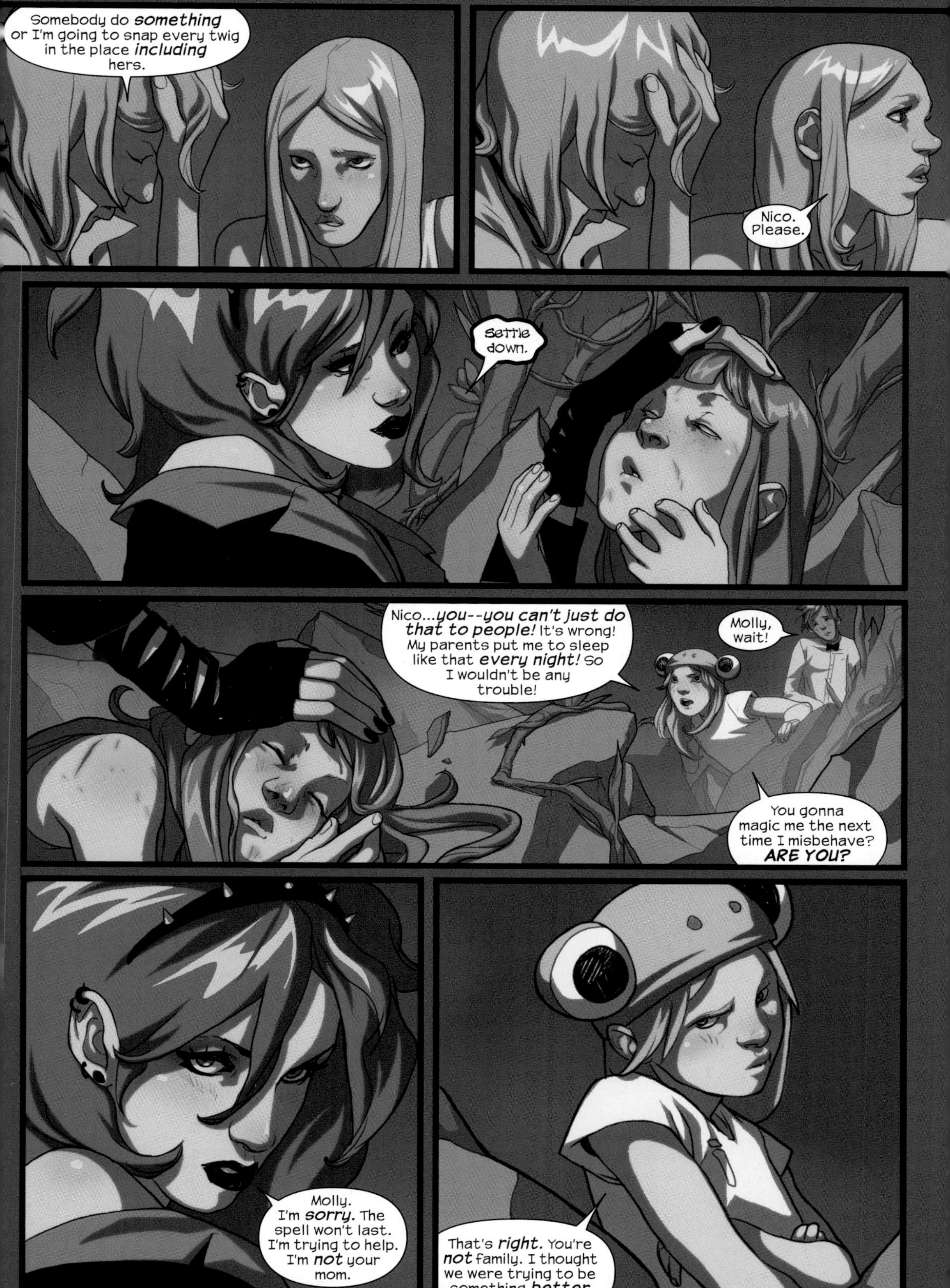
Somebody do something or I'm going to snap every twig in the place including hers.
Nico. Please.
Settle down.
Nico...you--you can't just do that to people! It's wrong! My parents put me to sleep like that every night! So I wouldn't be any trouble!
Molly, wait!
You gonna magic me the next time I misbehave? ARE YOU?
Molly. I'm sorry. The spell won't last. I'm trying to help. I'm not your mom.
That's right. You're not family. I thought we were trying to be something better.

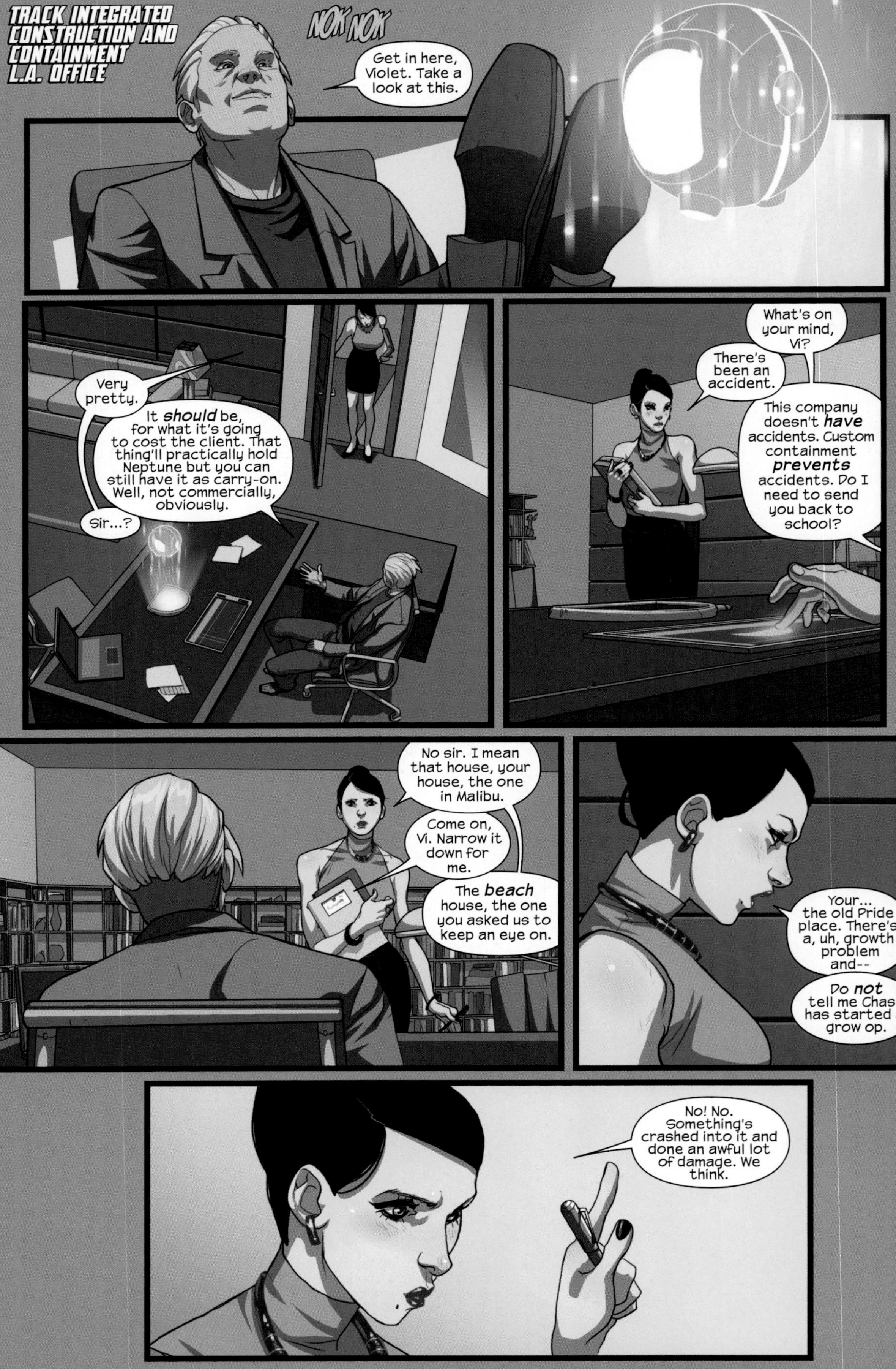
TRACK INTEGRATED CONSTRUCTION AND CONTAINMENT L.A. OFFICE
NOK NOK
Get in here, Violet. Take a look at this.
Very pretty.
It should be, for what it's going to cost the client. That thing'll practically hold Neptune but you can still have it as carry-on. Well, not commercially, obviously.
Sir...?
What's on your mind, Vi?
There's been an accident.
This company doesn't have accidents. Custom containment prevents accidents. Do I need to send you back to school?
No sir. I mean that house, your house, the one in Malibu.
Come on, Vi. Narrow it down for me.
The beach house, the one you asked us to keep an eye on.
Your... the old Pride place. There's a, uh, growth problem and--
Do not tell me Chase has started a grow op.
No! No. Something's crashed into it and done an awful lot of damage. We think.

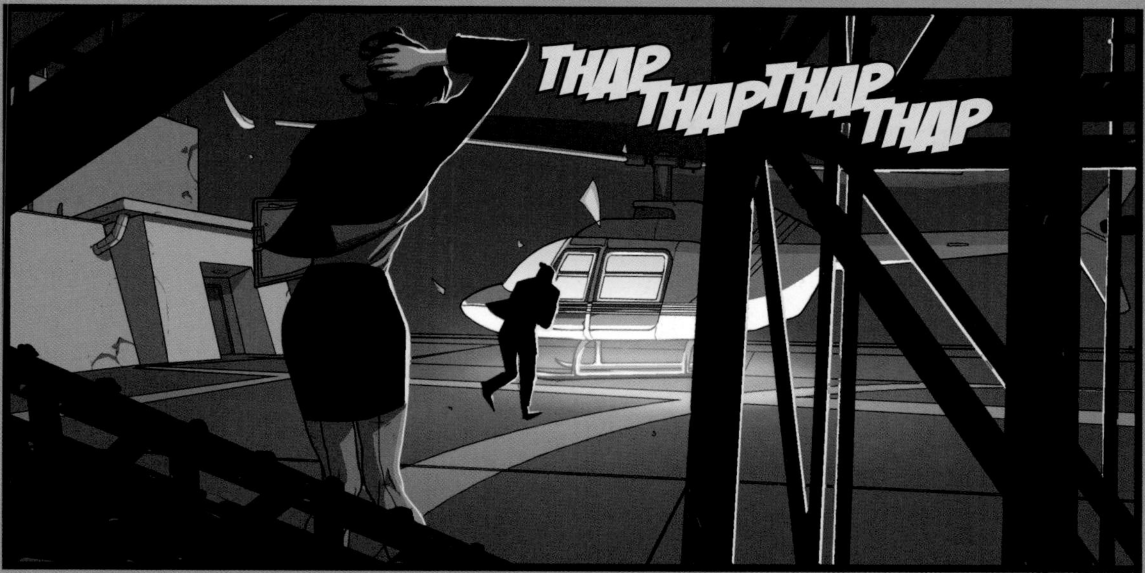
THAP THAP THAP THAP

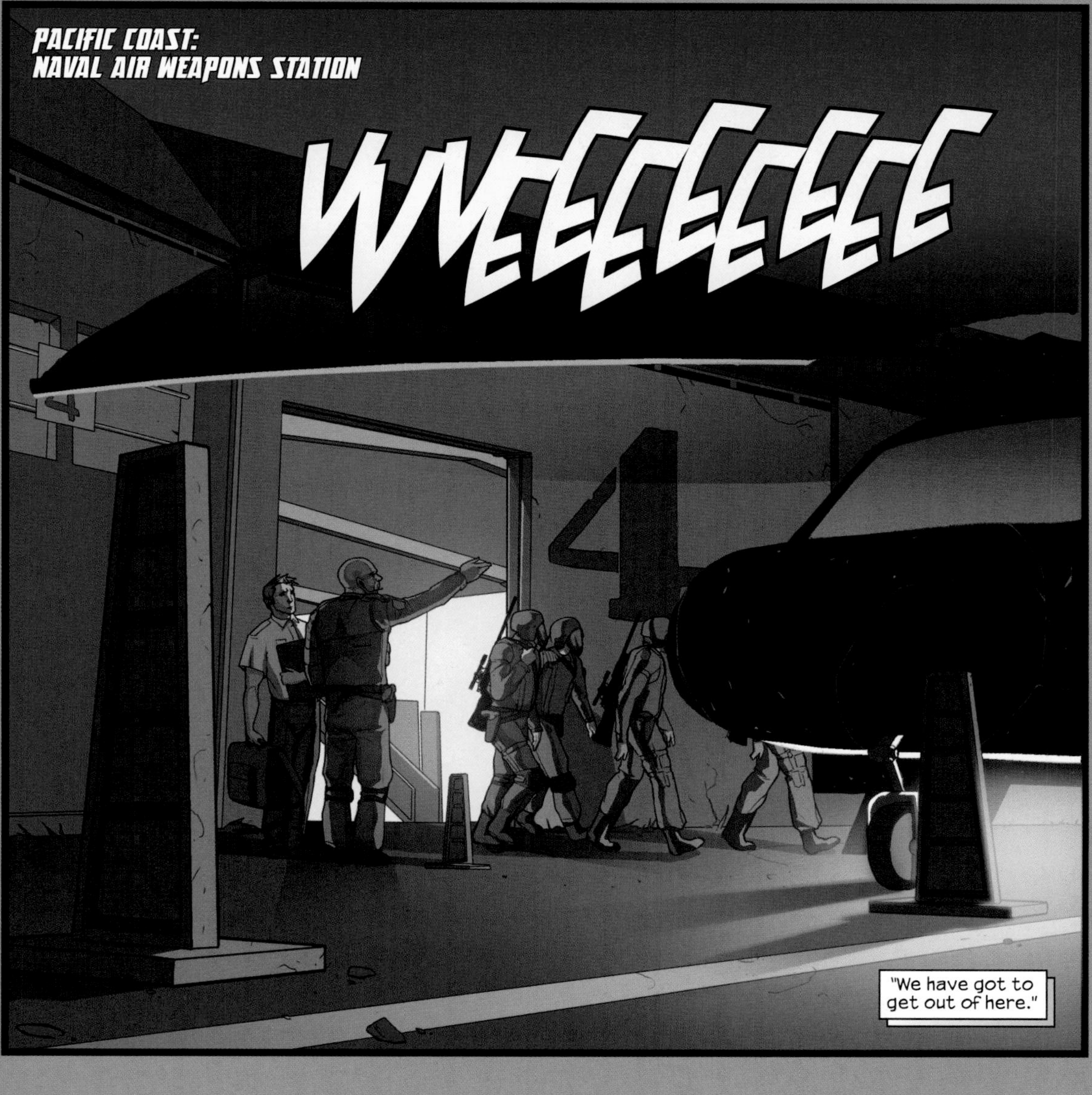
PACIFIC COAST:
NAVAL AIR WEAPONS STATION
WVEEEEEEEEE
"We have got to get out of here."

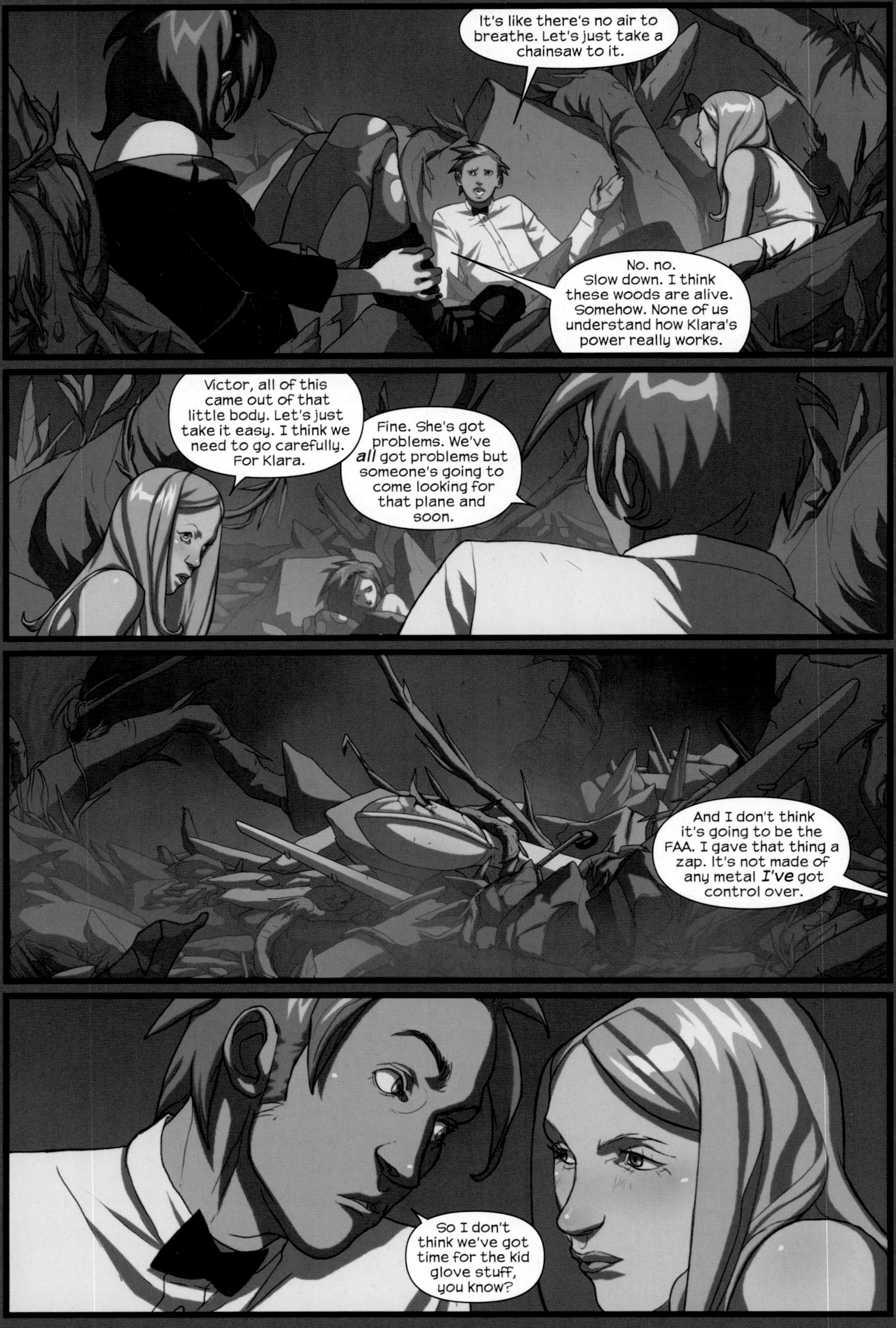
It's like there's no air to breathe. Let's just take a chainsaw to it.
No. no. Slow down. I think these woods are alive. Somehow. None of us understand how Klara's power really works.
Victor, all of this came out of that little body. Let's just take it easy. I think we need to go carefully. For Klara.
Fine. She's got problems. We've *all* got problems but someone's going to come looking for that plane and soon.
And I don't think it's going to be the FAA. I gave that thing a zap. It's not made of any metal *I've* got control over.
So I don't think we've got time for the kid glove stuff, you know?

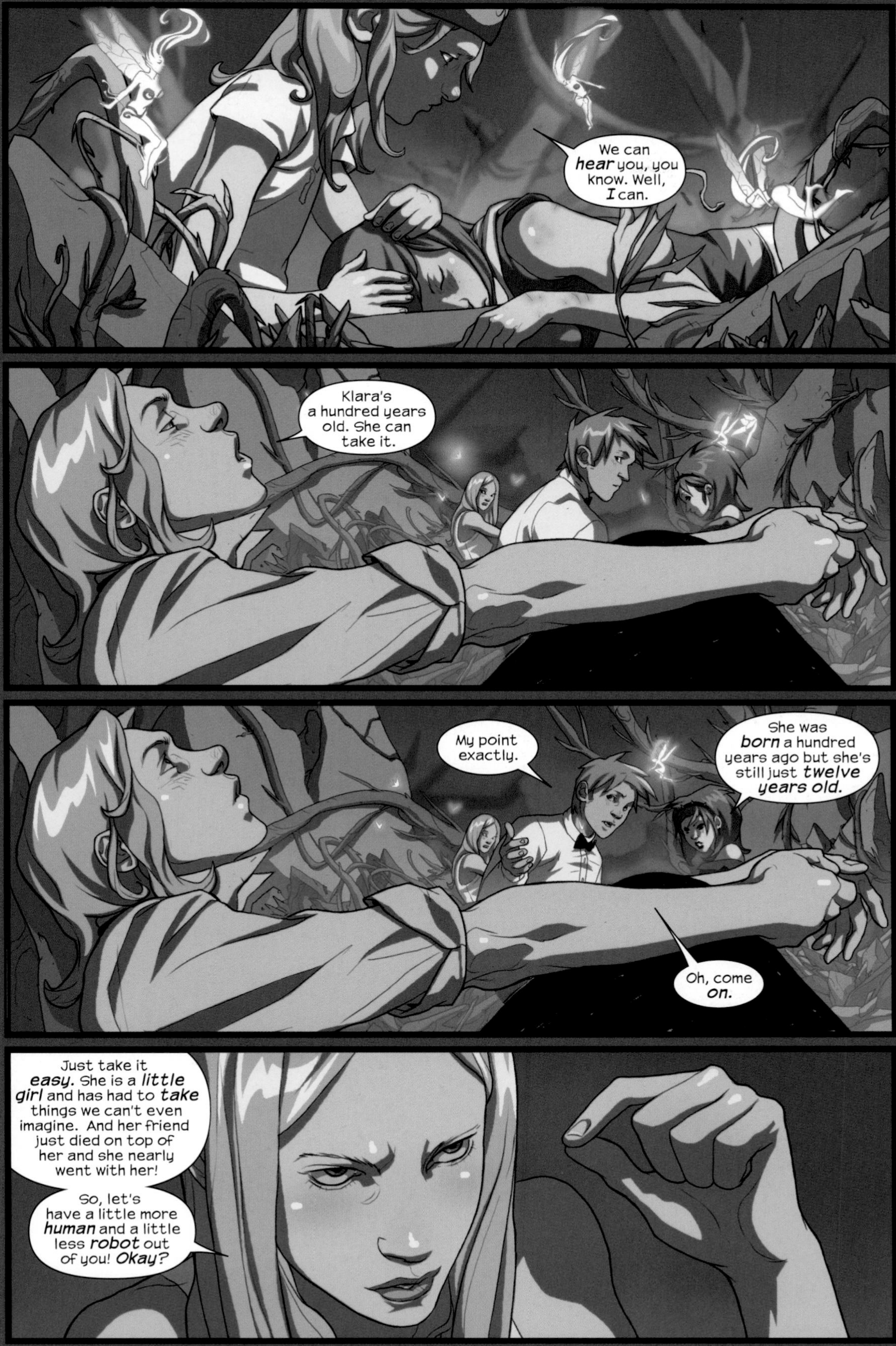
We can *hear* you, you know. Well, *I* can.
Klara's a hundred years old. She can take it.
My point exactly.
She was *born* a hundred years ago but she's still just *twelve years old.*
Oh, come *on.*
Just take it *easy.* She is a *little girl* and has had to *take* things we can't even imagine. And her friend just died on top of her and she nearly went with her!
So, let's have a little more *human* and a little less *robot* out of you! *Okay?*

What the hell? Walton! I want to hear that *we* are not responsible for *that* and I want to hear it *now.*

No, *Sir!* Readings indicate there is no breach. Repeat, no containment breach and we have a full mile empty radius.

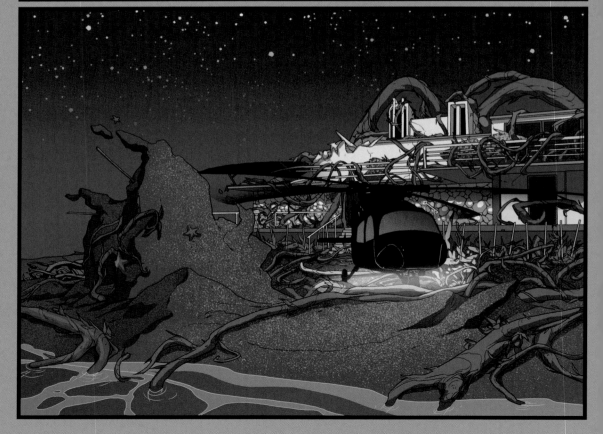

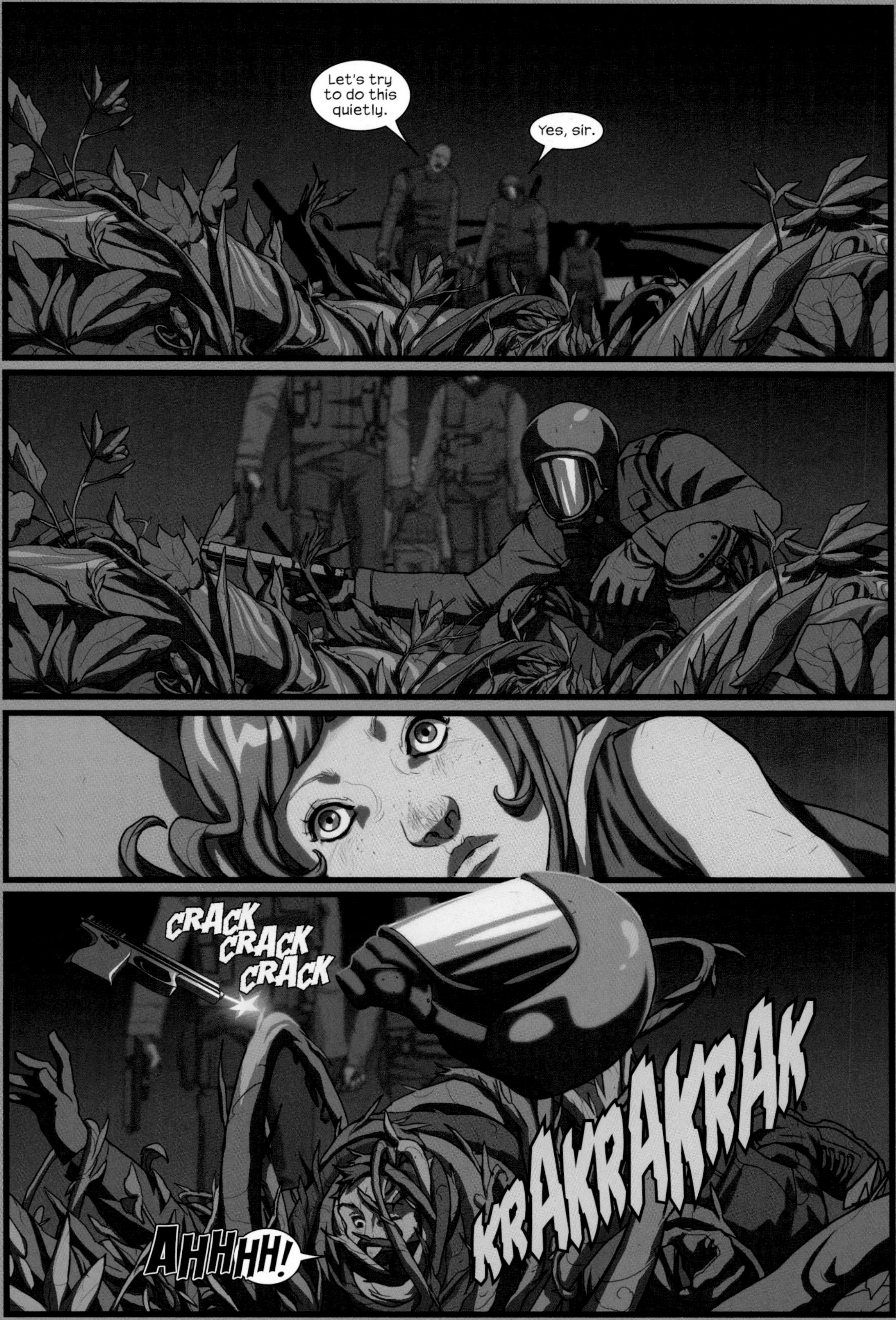

Let's try to do this quietly.
Yes, sir.
CRACK CRACK CRACK
KRAKRAKRAK
AHHHH!

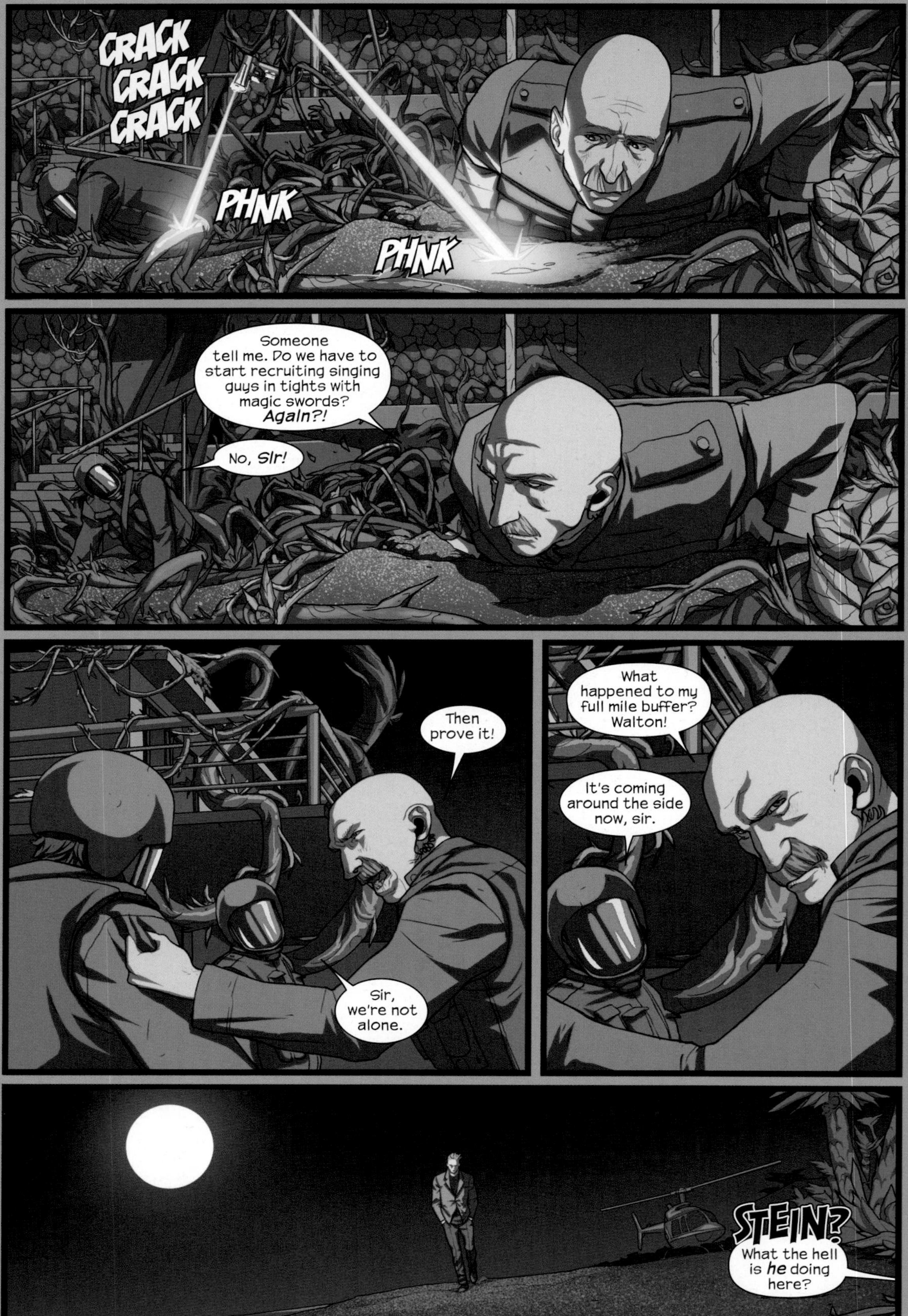
CRACK
CRACK
CRACK
PHNK
PHNK
Someone tell me. Do we have to start recruiting singing guys in tights with magic swords? *Again?!*
No, *Sir!*
Then prove it!
Sir, we're not alone.
What happened to my full mile buffer? Walton!
It's coming around the side now, sir.
STEIN?
What the hell is *he* doing here?

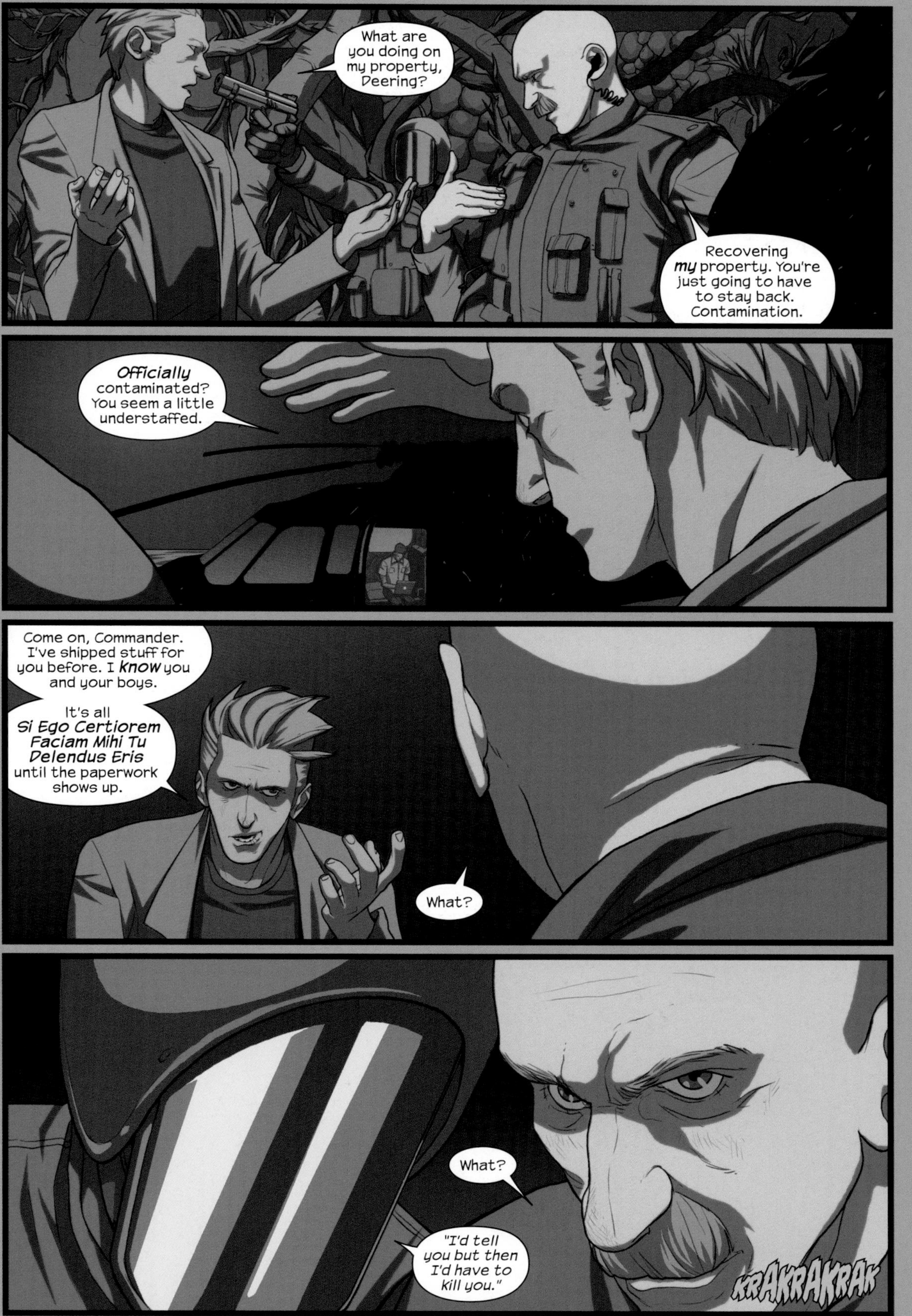

What are you doing on my property, Deering?
Recovering *my* property. You're just going to have to stay back. Contamination.
Officially contaminated? You seem a little understaffed.
Come on, Commander. I've shipped stuff for you before. I **know** you and your boys.
It's all ***Si Ego Certiorem Faciam Mihi Tu Delendus Eris*** until the paperwork shows up.
What?
What?
"I'd tell you but then I'd have to kill you."
KRAKRAKRAK

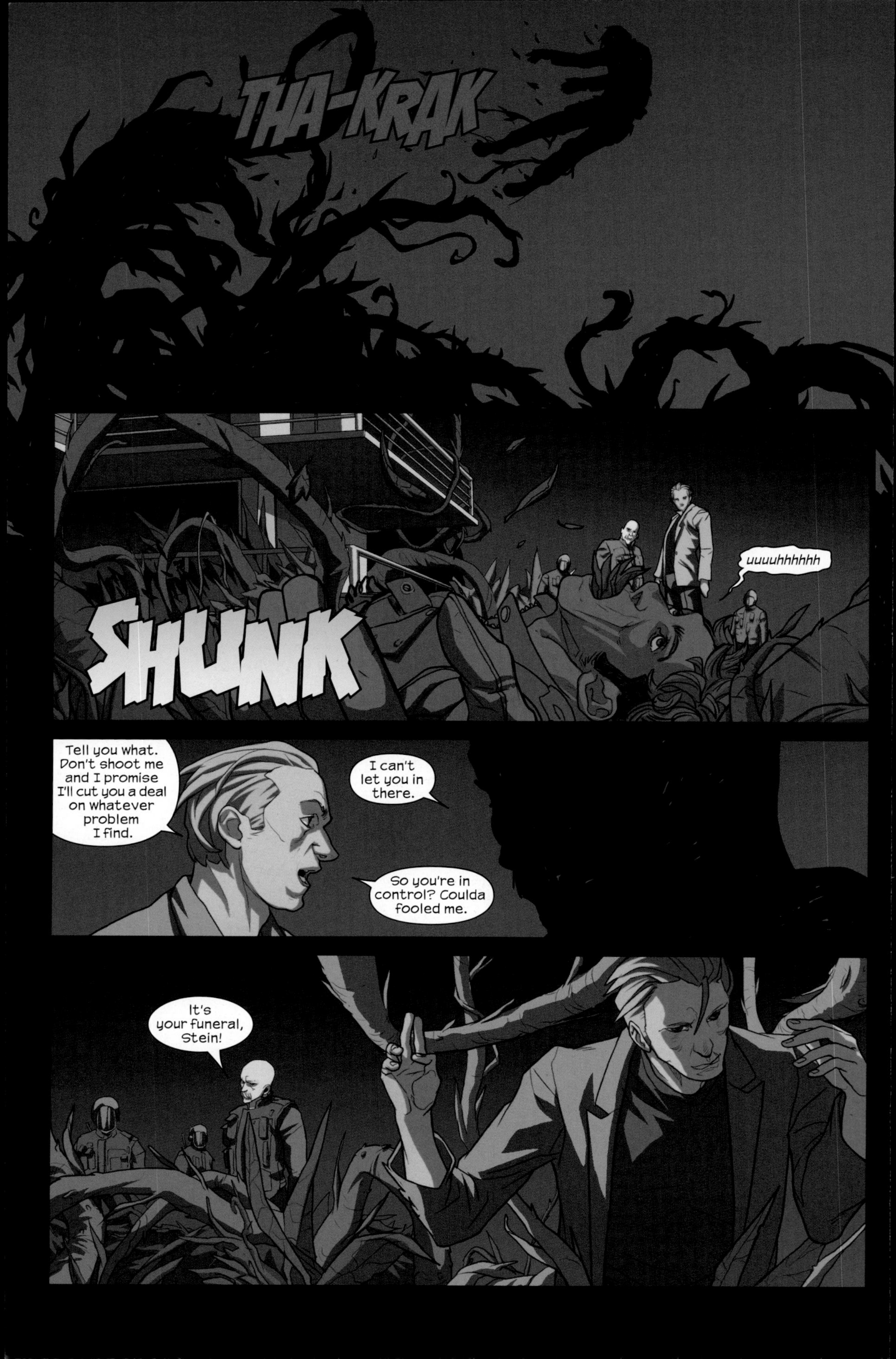

THA-KRAK
SHUNK
uuuuhhhhhh
Tell you what. Don't shoot me and I promise I'll cut you a deal on whatever problem I find.
I can't let you in there.
So you're in control? Coulda fooled me.
It's your funeral, Stein!

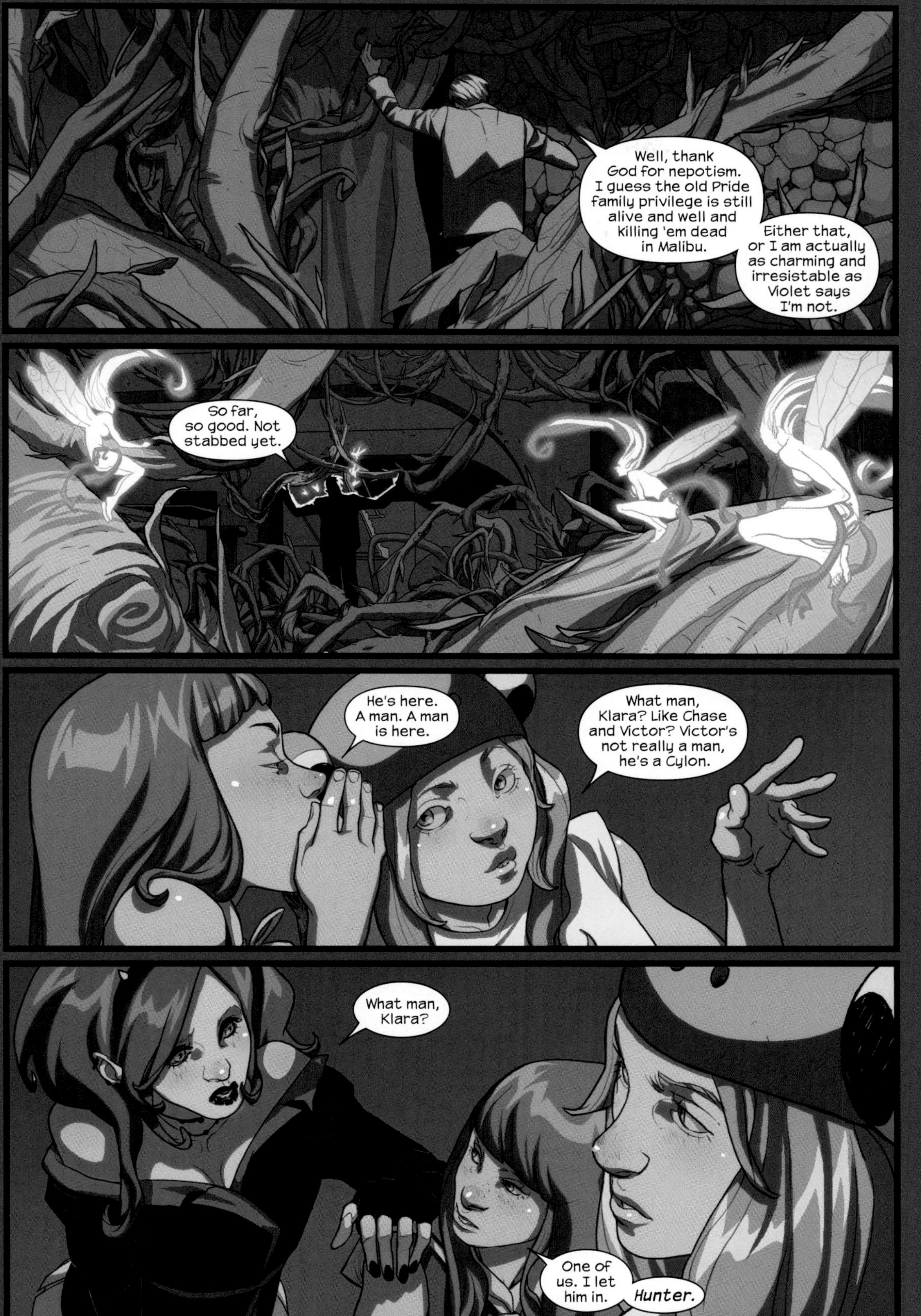
Well, thank God for nepotism. I guess the old Pride family privilege is still alive and well and killing 'em dead in Malibu.
Either that, or I am actually as charming and irresistable as Violet says I'm not.
So far, so good. Not stabbed yet.
He's here. A man. A man is here.
What man, Klara? Like Chase and Victor? Victor's not really a man, he's a Cylon.
What man, Klara?
One of us. I let him in.
Hunter.

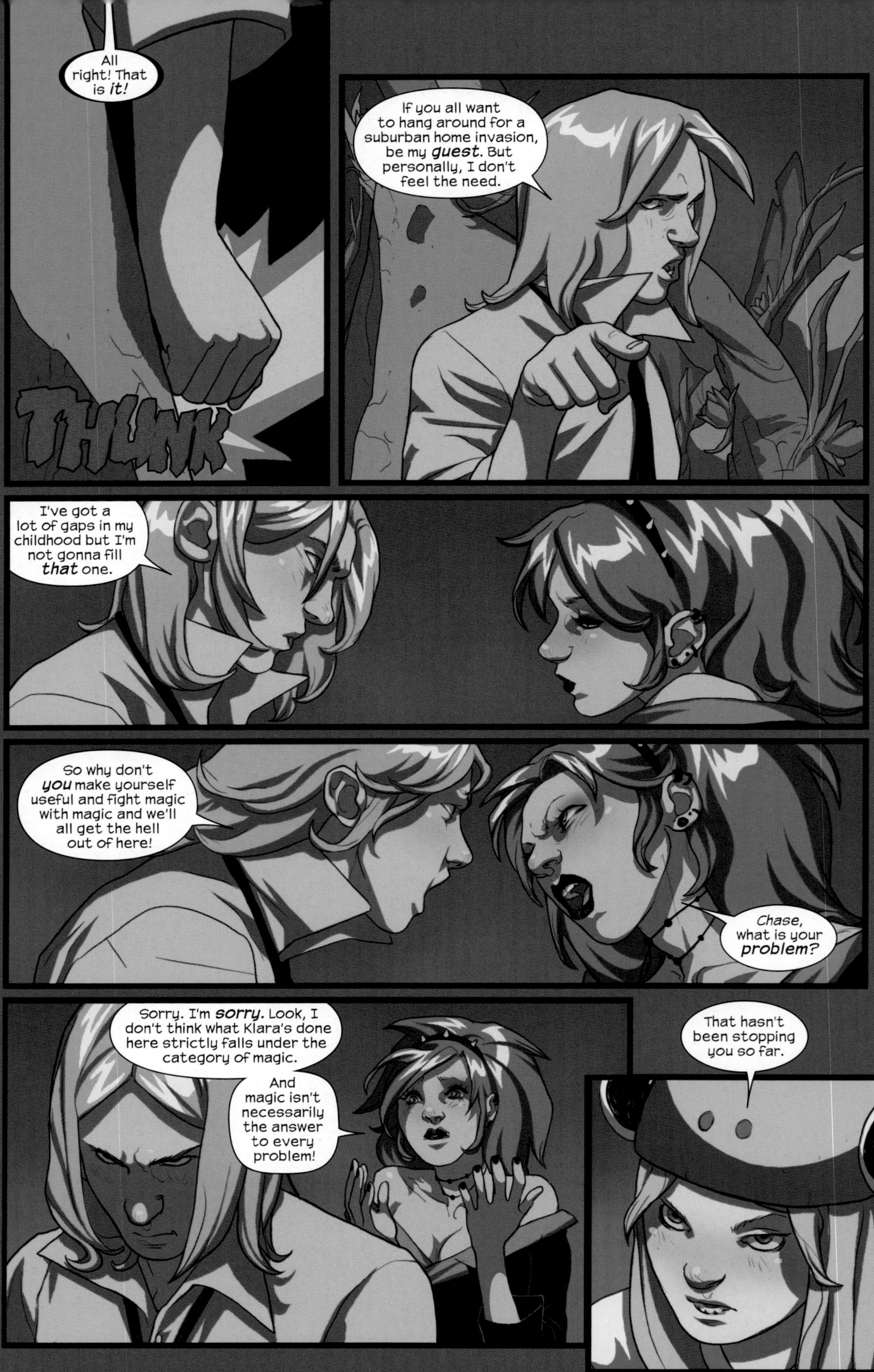
All right! That is *it!*
THUNK
If you all want to hang around for a suburban home invasion, be my **guest**. But personally, I don't feel the need.
I've got a lot of gaps in my childhood but I'm not gonna fill **that** one.
So why don't **you** make yourself useful and fight magic with magic and we'll all get the hell out of here!
Chase, what is your **problem?**
Sorry. I'm **sorry.** Look, I don't think what Klara's done here strictly falls under the category of magic.
And magic isn't necessarily the answer to every problem!
That hasn't been stopping you so far.

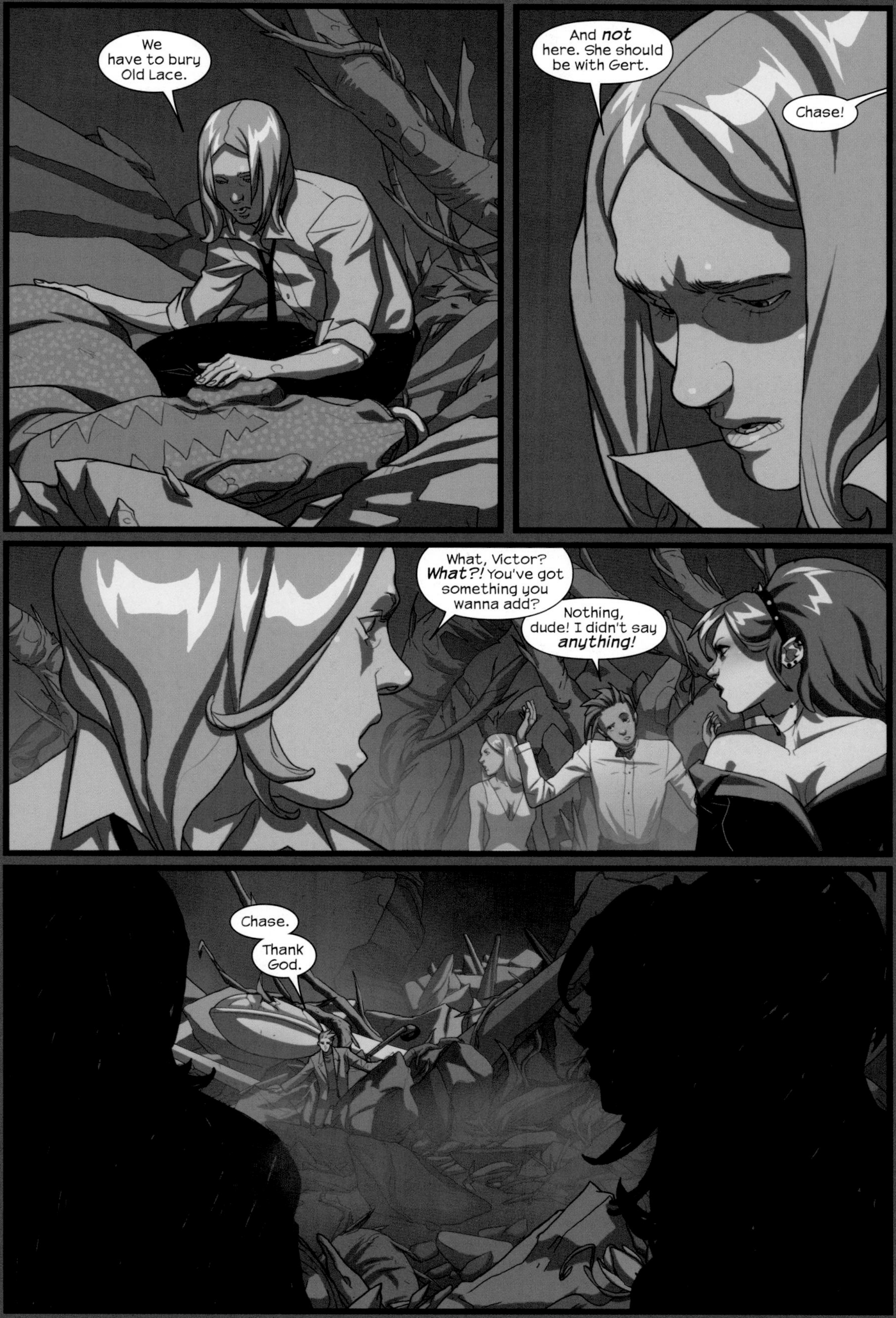
We have to bury Old Lace.
And *not* here. She should be with Gert.
Chase!
What, Victor? *What?!* You've got something you wanna add?
Nothing, dude! I didn't say *anything!*
Chase.
Thank God.

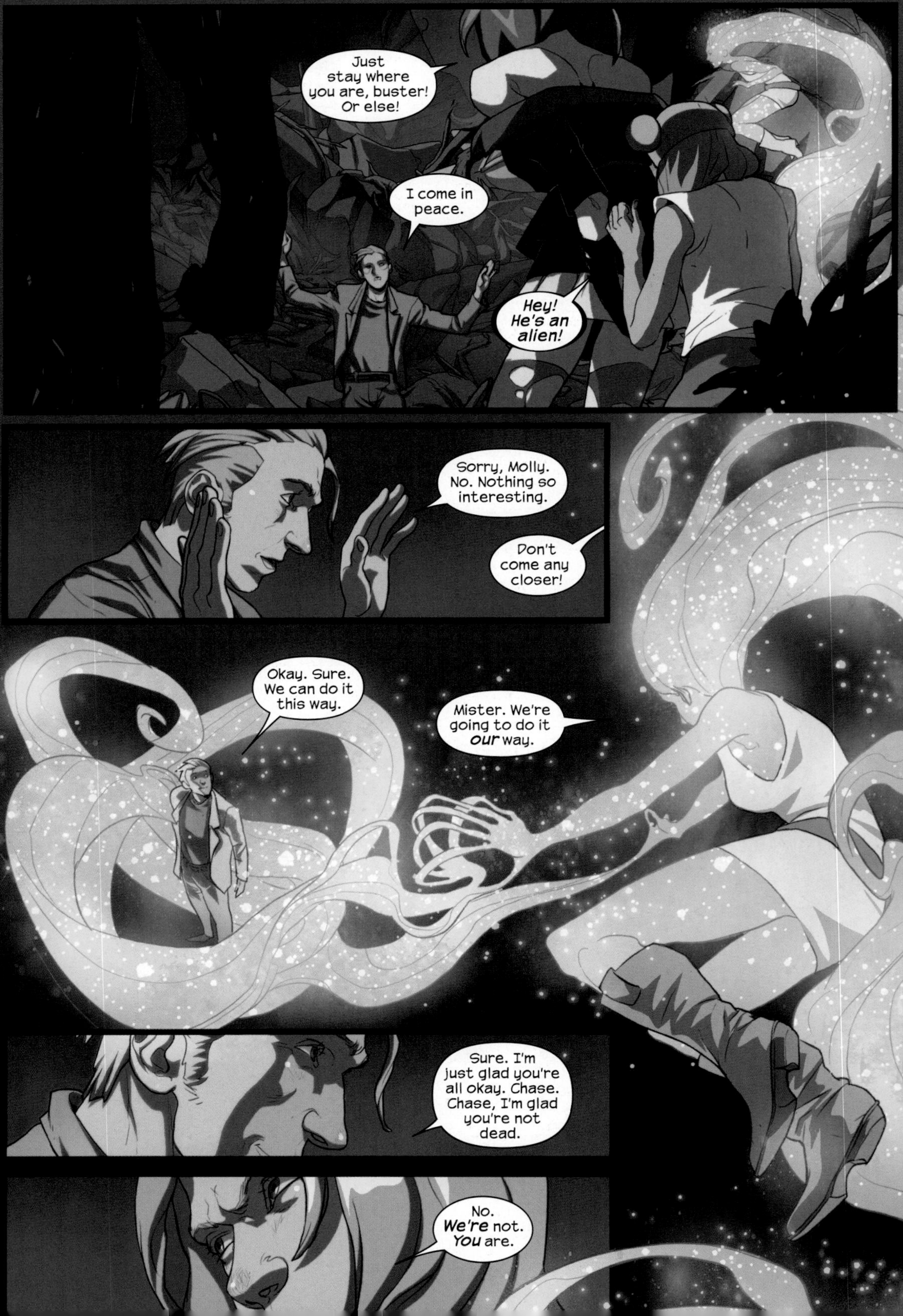
Just stay where you are, buster! Or else!
I come in peace.
Hey! He's an alien!
Sorry, Molly. No. Nothing so interesting.
Don't come any closer!
Okay. Sure. We can do it this way.
Mister. We're going to do it *our* way.
Sure. I'm just glad you're all okay. Chase. Chase, I'm glad you're not dead.
No. *We're* not. *You* are.

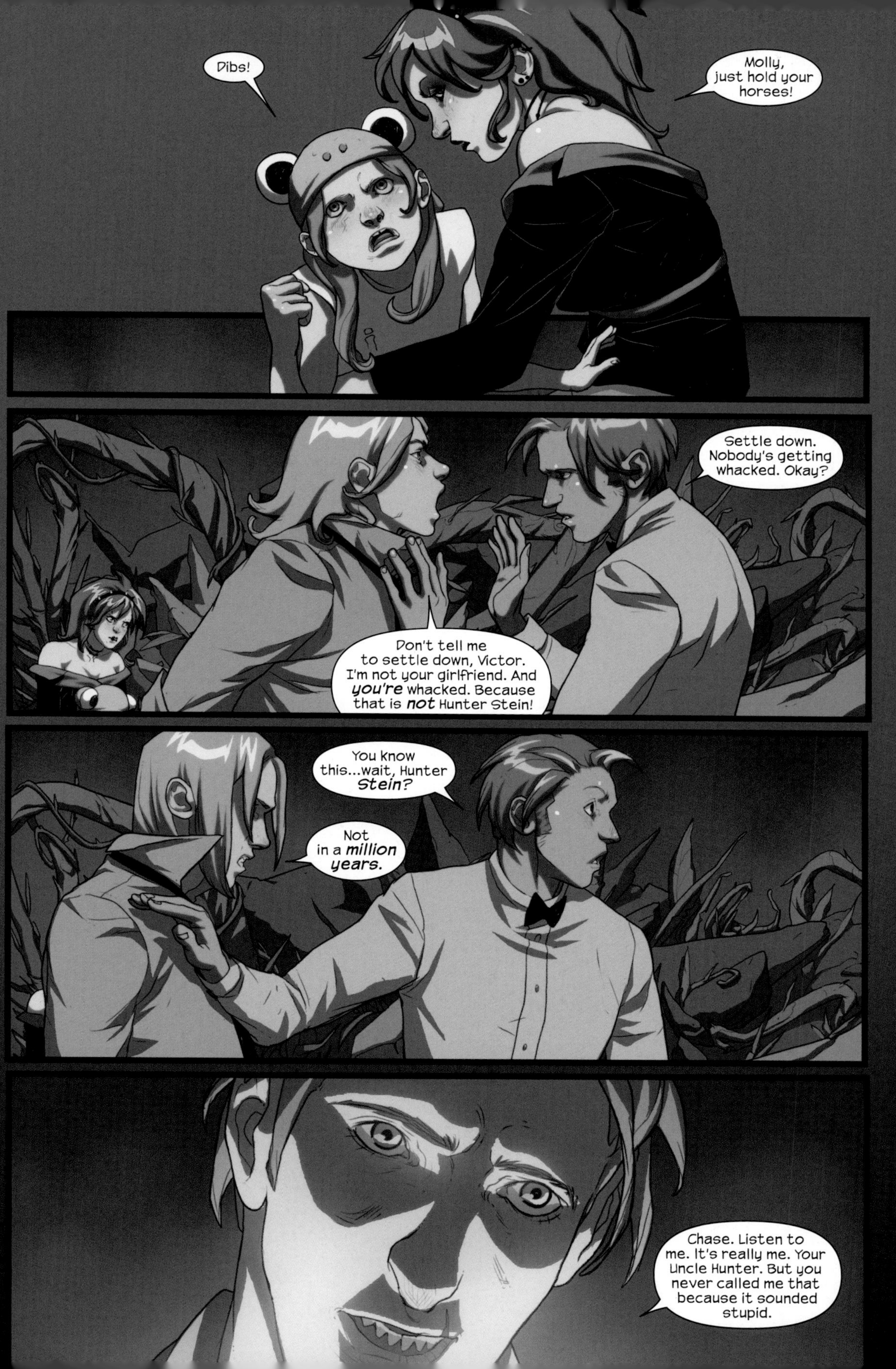
Dibs!
Molly, just hold your horses!
Settle down. Nobody's getting whacked. Okay?
Don't tell me to settle down, Victor. I'm not your girlfriend. And *you're* whacked. Because that is *not* Hunter Stein!
You know this...wait, Hunter *Stein*?
Not in a **million years.**
Chase. Listen to me. It's really me. Your Uncle Hunter. But you never called me that because it sounded stupid.

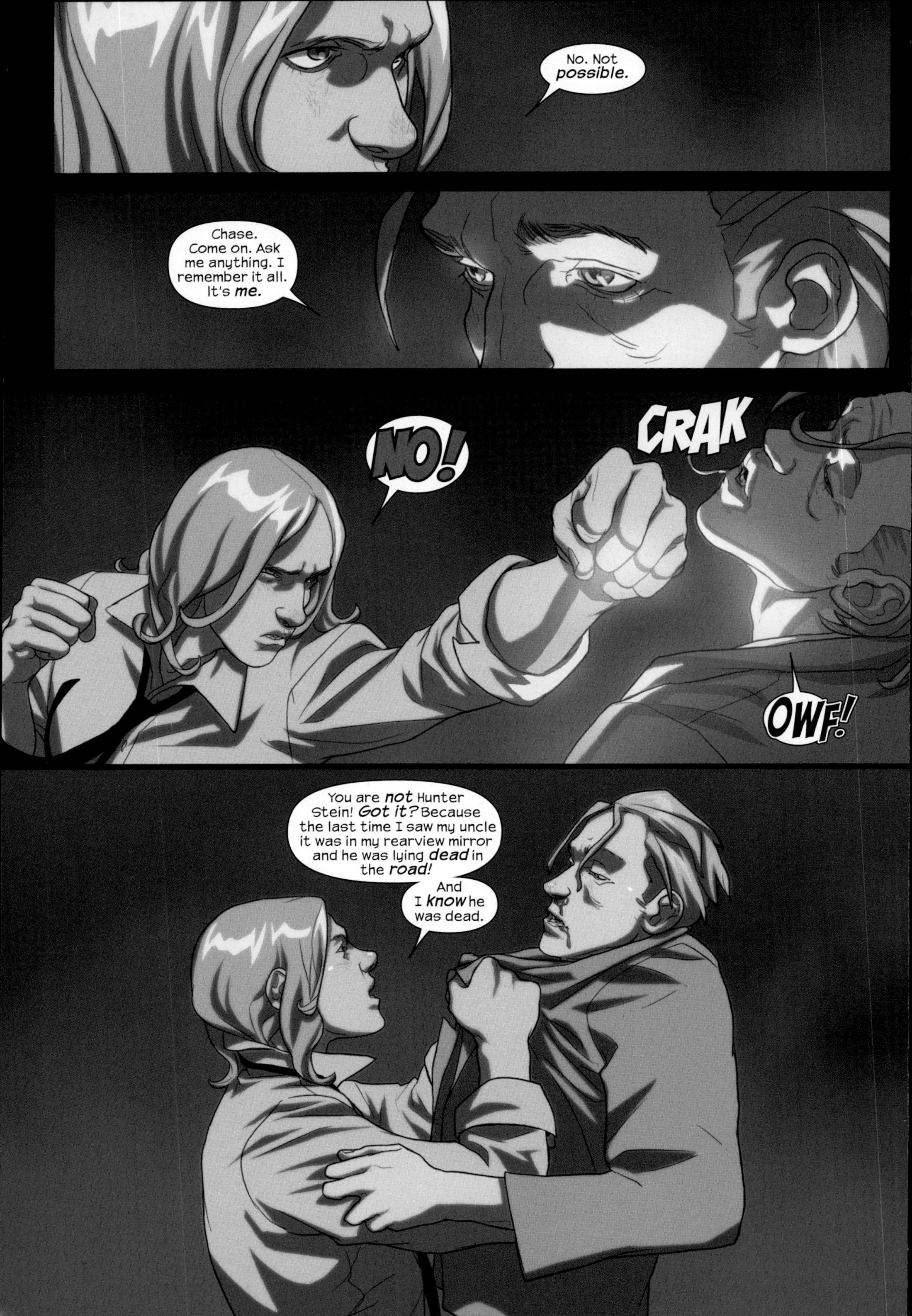
No. Not *possible.*
Chase. Come on. Ask me anything. I remember it all. It's *me.*
NO!
CRAK
OWF!
You are *not* Hunter Stein! *Got it?* Because the last time I saw my uncle it was in my rearview mirror and he was lying *dead* in the *road!*
And I *know* he was dead.

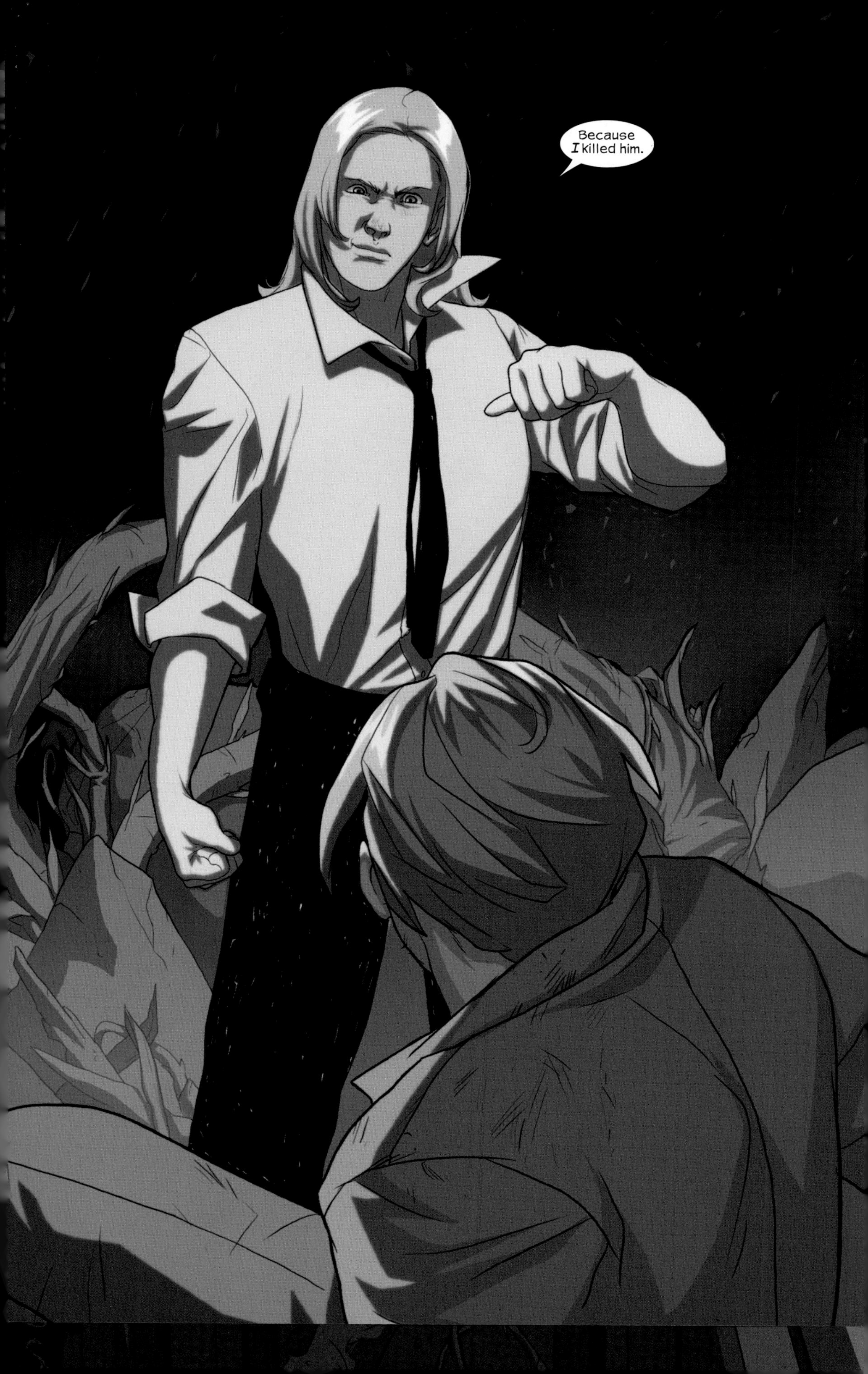
Because I killed him.

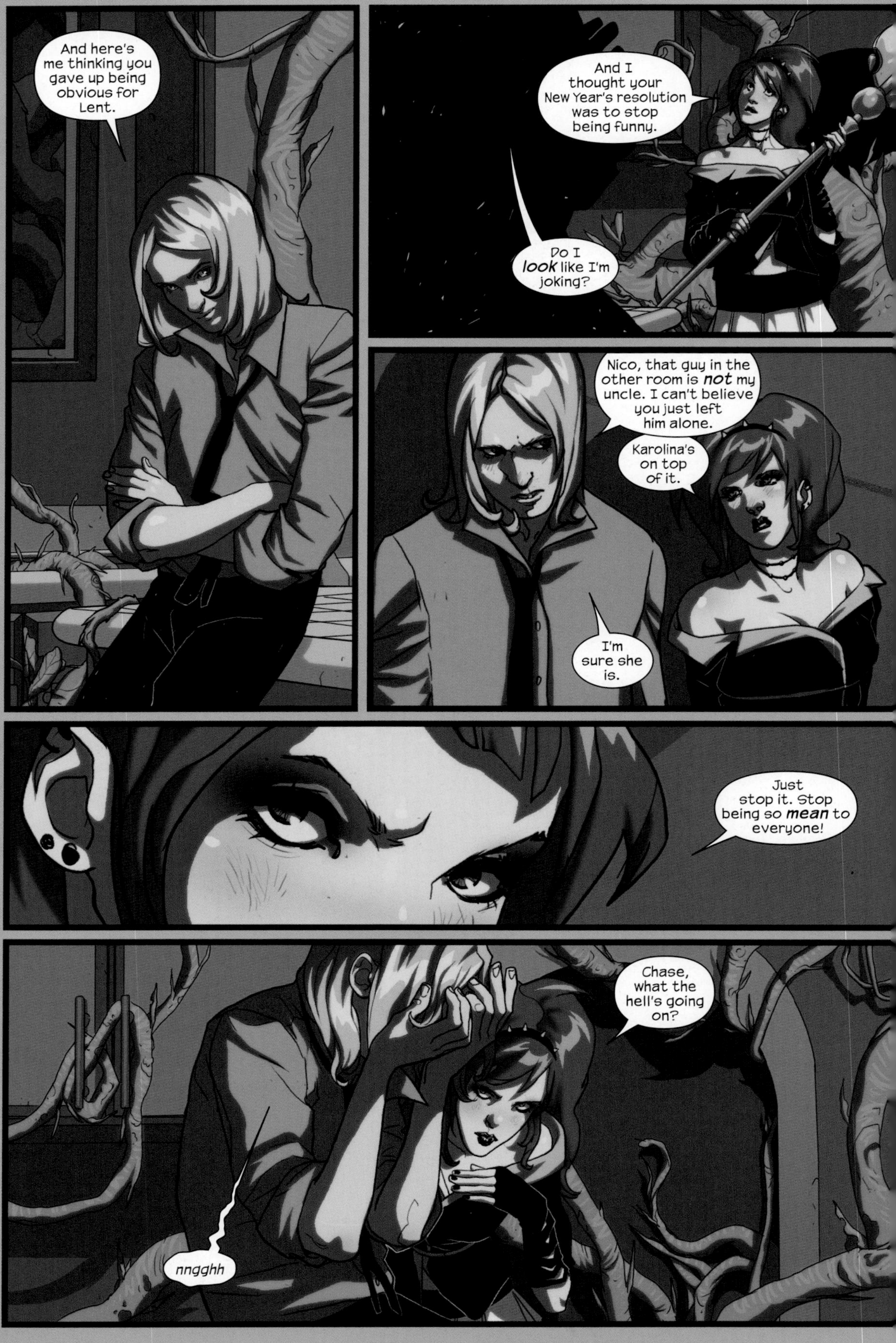
And here's me thinking you gave up being obvious for Lent.
And I thought your New Year's resolution was to stop being funny.
Do I *look* like I'm joking?
Nico, that guy in the other room is *not* my uncle. I can't believe you just left him alone.
Karolina's on top of it.
I'm sure she is.
Just stop it. Stop being so *mean* to everyone!
Chase, what the hell's going on?
nngghh

Sighh.

Remember that story I told... about how back in the day I killed some hobo who tried to jack my van?

You've told a couple of versions of that story, dude.

Yeah, well. In this one it wasn't some hobo. It was my uncle.

"I used to never see him. But the guy started coming around more and more and the fighting between him and my parents got worse and worse."

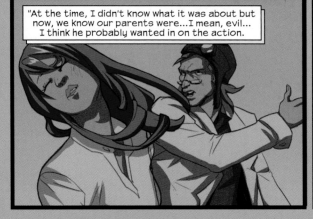

"At the time, I didn't know what it was about but now, we know our parents were...I mean, evil... I think he probably wanted in on the action."

"And then one night, things just got even worse and I knew I didn't want to be around for whatever was coming down the pipe."

"And I swear to God. It was pouring rain and I just didn't see him. I don't know if he was trying to stop me... or come with me."

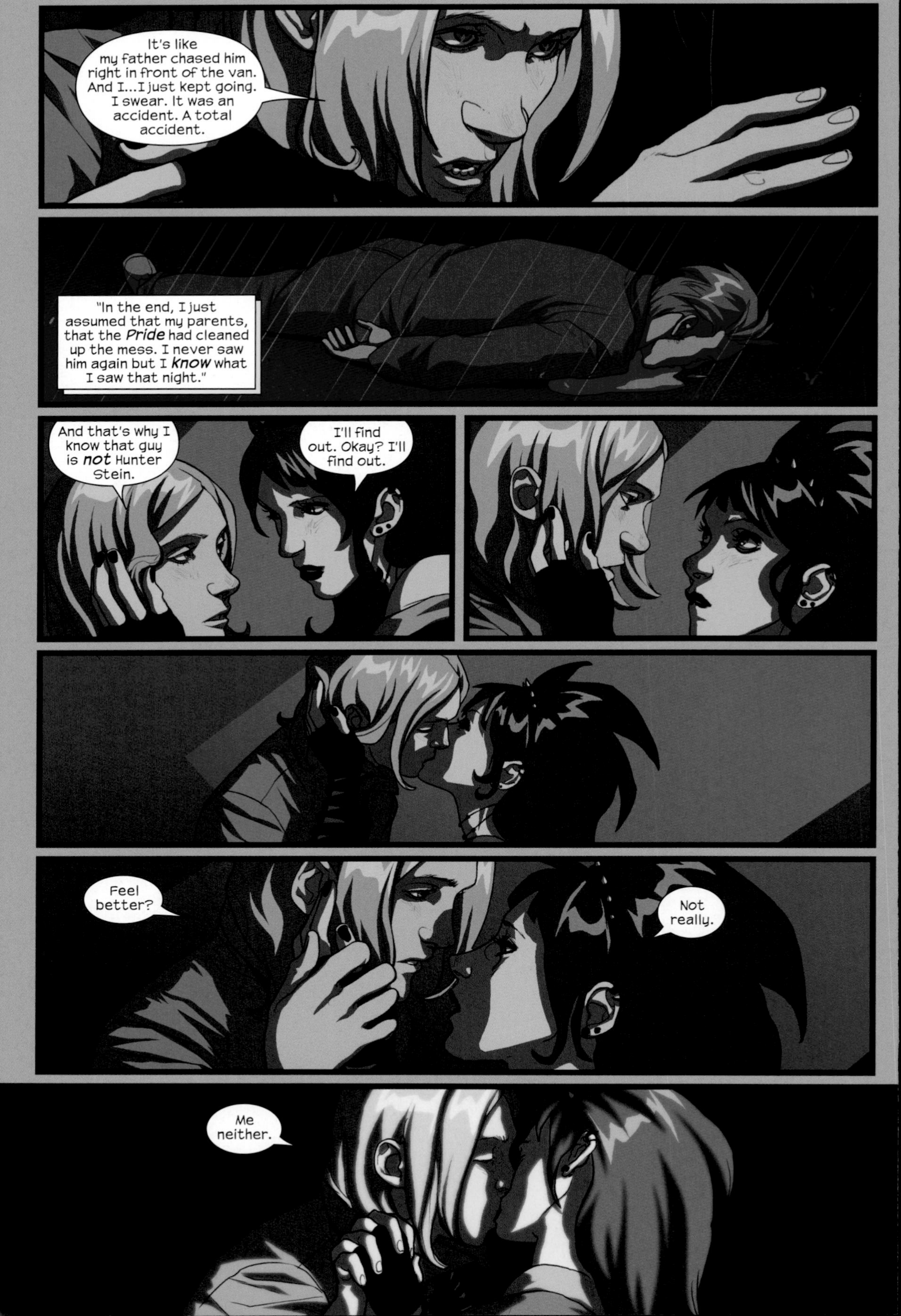
It's like my father chased him right in front of the van. And I...I just kept going. I swear. It was an accident. A total accident.
"In the end, I just assumed that my parents, that the *Pride* had cleaned up the mess. I never saw him again but I ***know*** what I saw that night."
And that's why I know that guy is ***not*** Hunter Stein.
I'll find out. Okay? I'll find out.
Feel better?
Not really.
Me neither.

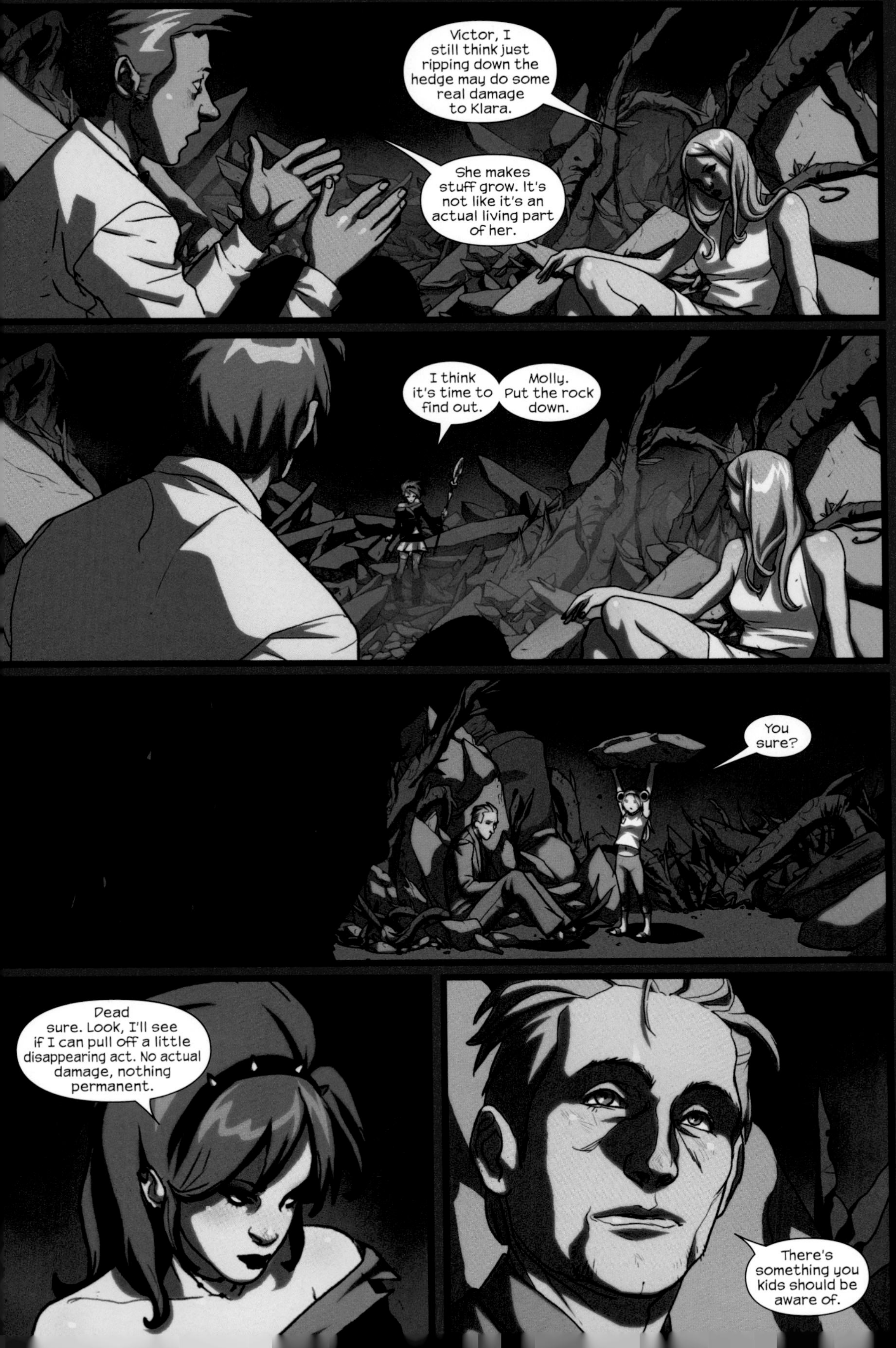
Victor, I still think just ripping down the hedge may do some real damage to Klara.
She makes stuff grow. It's not like it's an actual living part of her.
I think it's time to find out.
Molly. Put the rock down.
You sure?
Dead sure. Look, I'll see if I can pull off a little disappearing act. No actual damage, nothing permanent.
There's something you kids should be aware of.

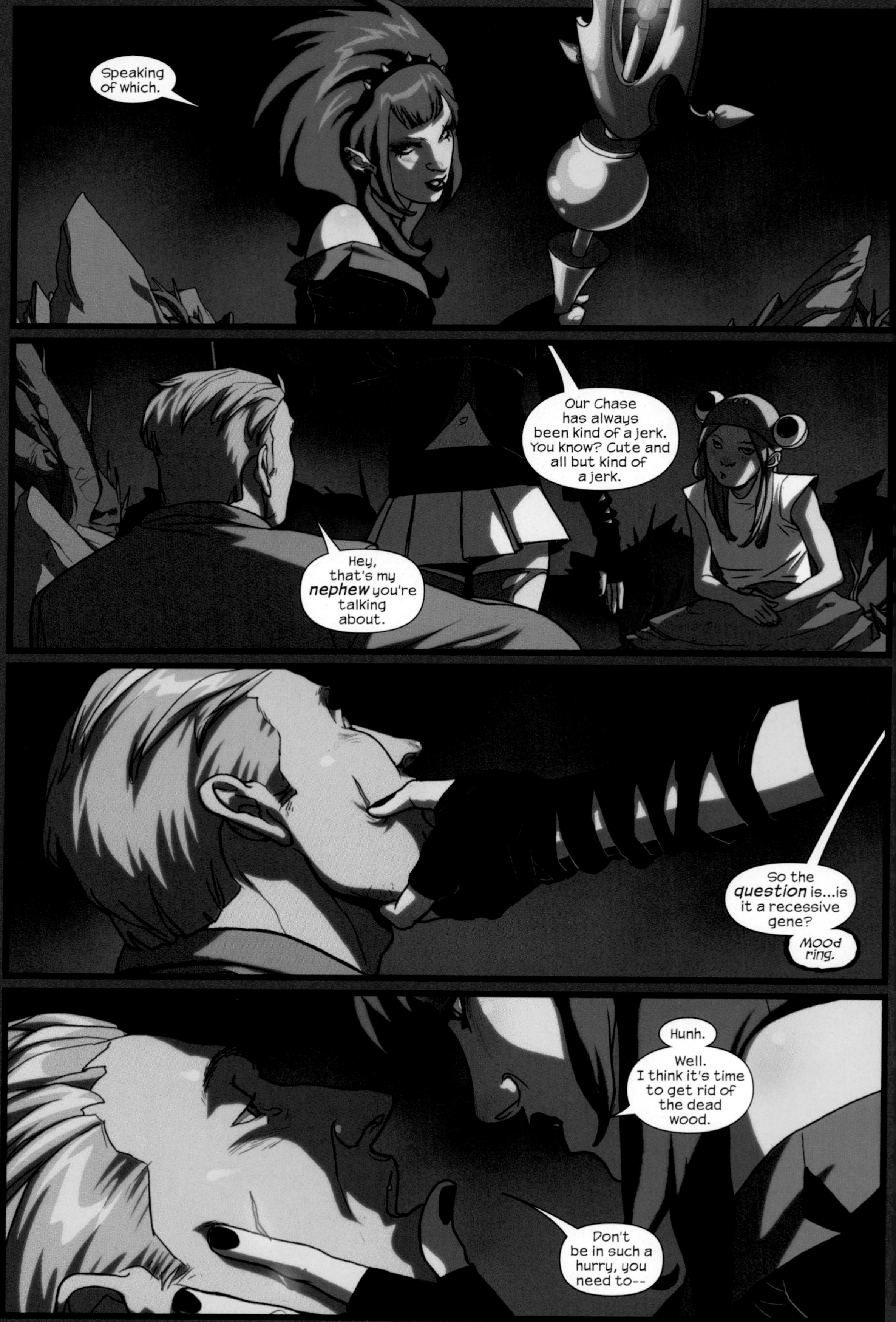
Speaking of which.
Our Chase has always been kind of a jerk. You know? Cute and all but kind of a jerk.
Hey, that's my *nephew* you're talking about.
So the *question* is...is it a recessive gene?
Mood ring.
Hunh.
Well. I think it's time to get rid of the dead wood.
Don't be in such a hurry, you need to--

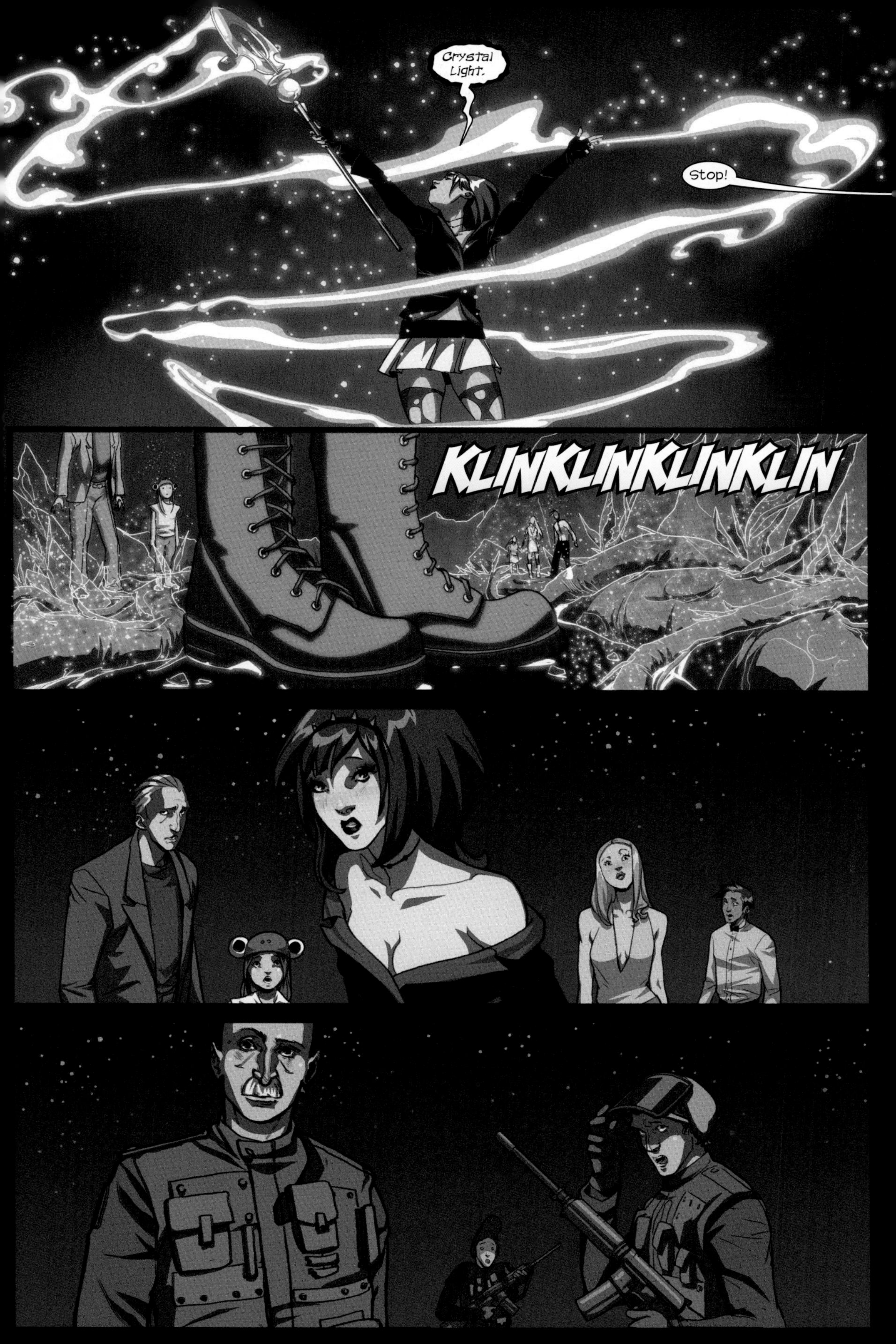
Crystal Light.
Stop!
KLINKLINKLINKLIN

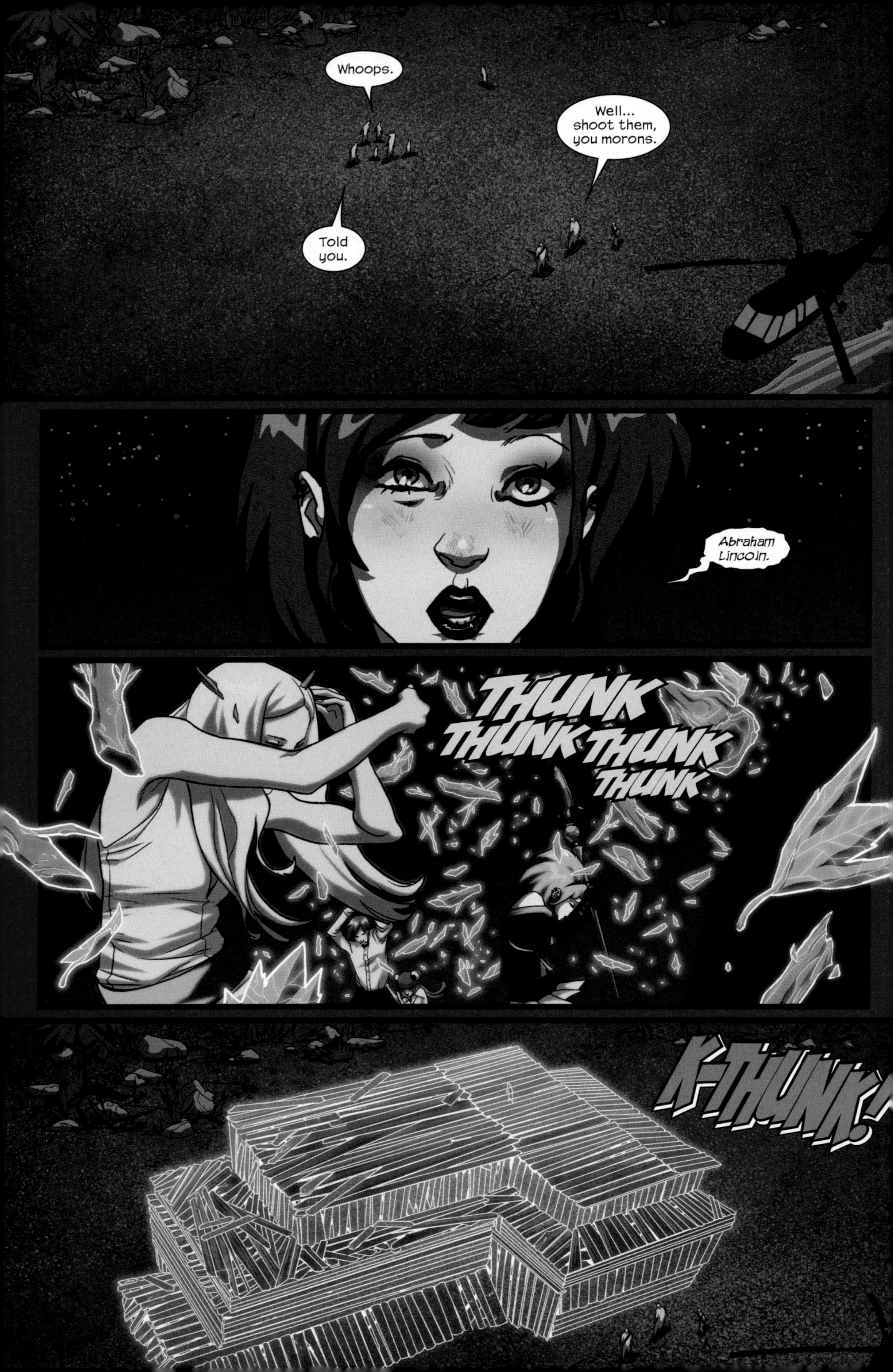
Whoops.
Well... shoot them, you morons.
Told you.
Abraham Lincoln.
THUNK THUNK THUNK THUNK
K-THUNK!

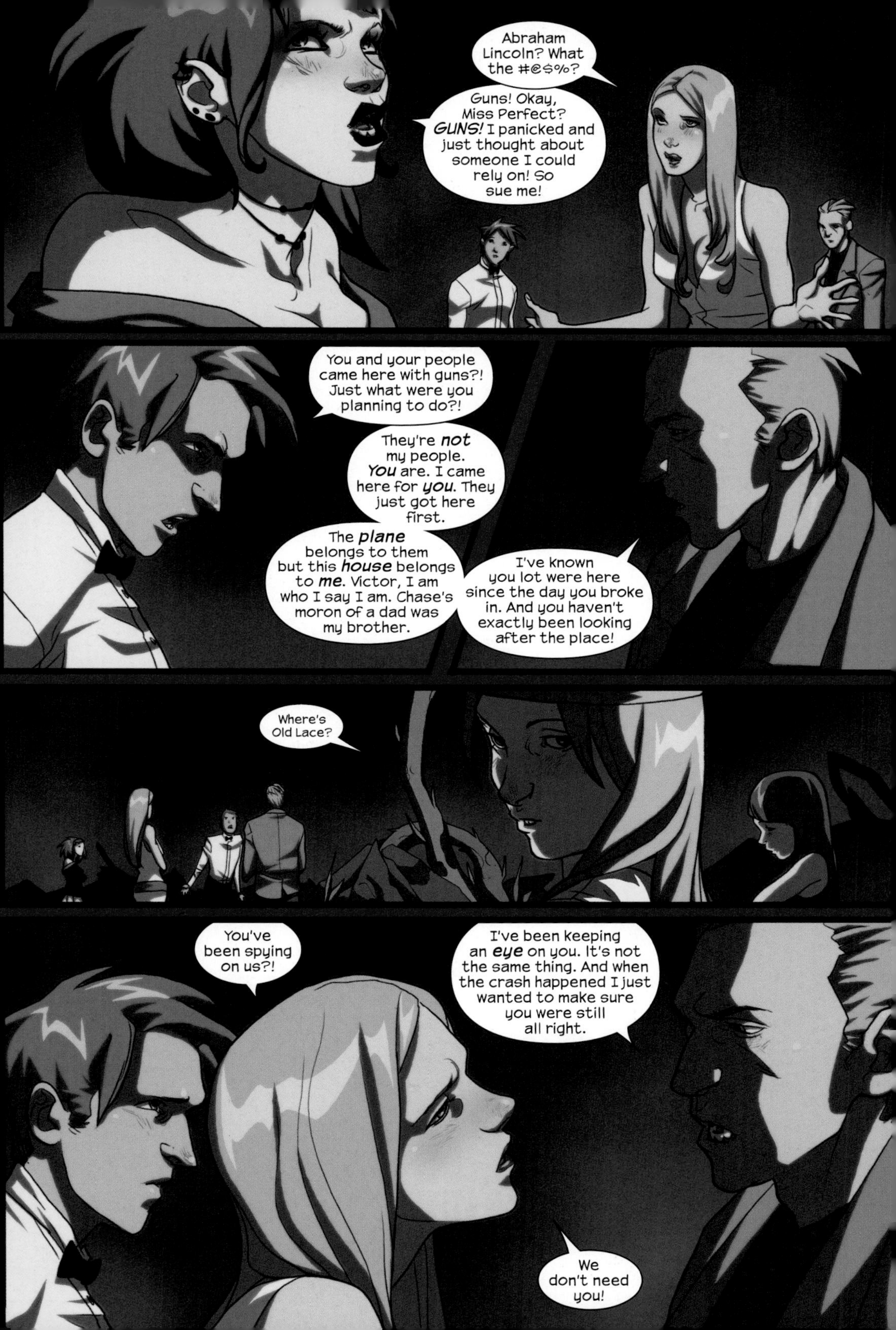
Abraham Lincoln? What the #@$%?
Guns! Okay, Miss Perfect? GUNS! I panicked and just thought about someone I could rely on! So sue me!
You and your people came here with guns?! Just what were you planning to do?!
They're not my people. You are. I came here for you. They just got here first.
The plane belongs to them but this house belongs to me. Victor, I am who I say I am. Chase's moron of a dad was my brother.
I've known you lot were here since the day you broke in. And you haven't exactly been looking after the place!
Where's Old Lace?
You've been spying on us?!
I've been keeping an eye on you. It's not the same thing. And when the crash happened I just wanted to make sure you were still all right.
We don't need you!

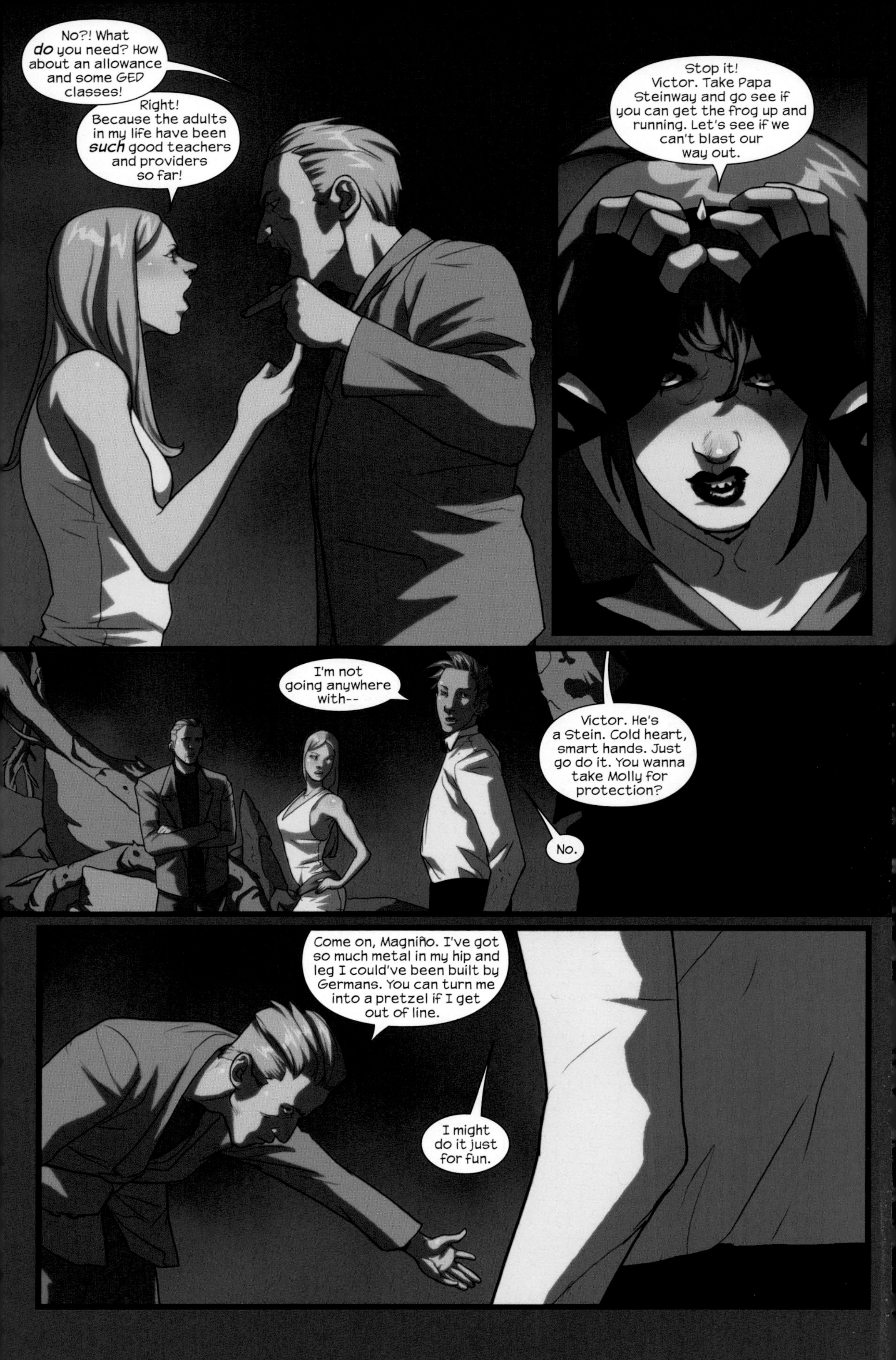

No?! What do you need? How about an allowance and some GED classes!
Right! Because the adults in my life have been *such* good teachers and providers so far!
Stop it! Victor. Take Papa Steinway and go see if you can get the frog up and running. Let's see if we can't blast our way out.
I'm not going anywhere with--
Victor. He's a Stein. Cold heart, smart hands. Just go do it. You wanna take Molly for protection?
No.
Come on, Magniño. I've got so much metal in my hip and leg I could've been built by Germans. You can turn me into a pretzel if I get out of line.
I might do it just for fun.

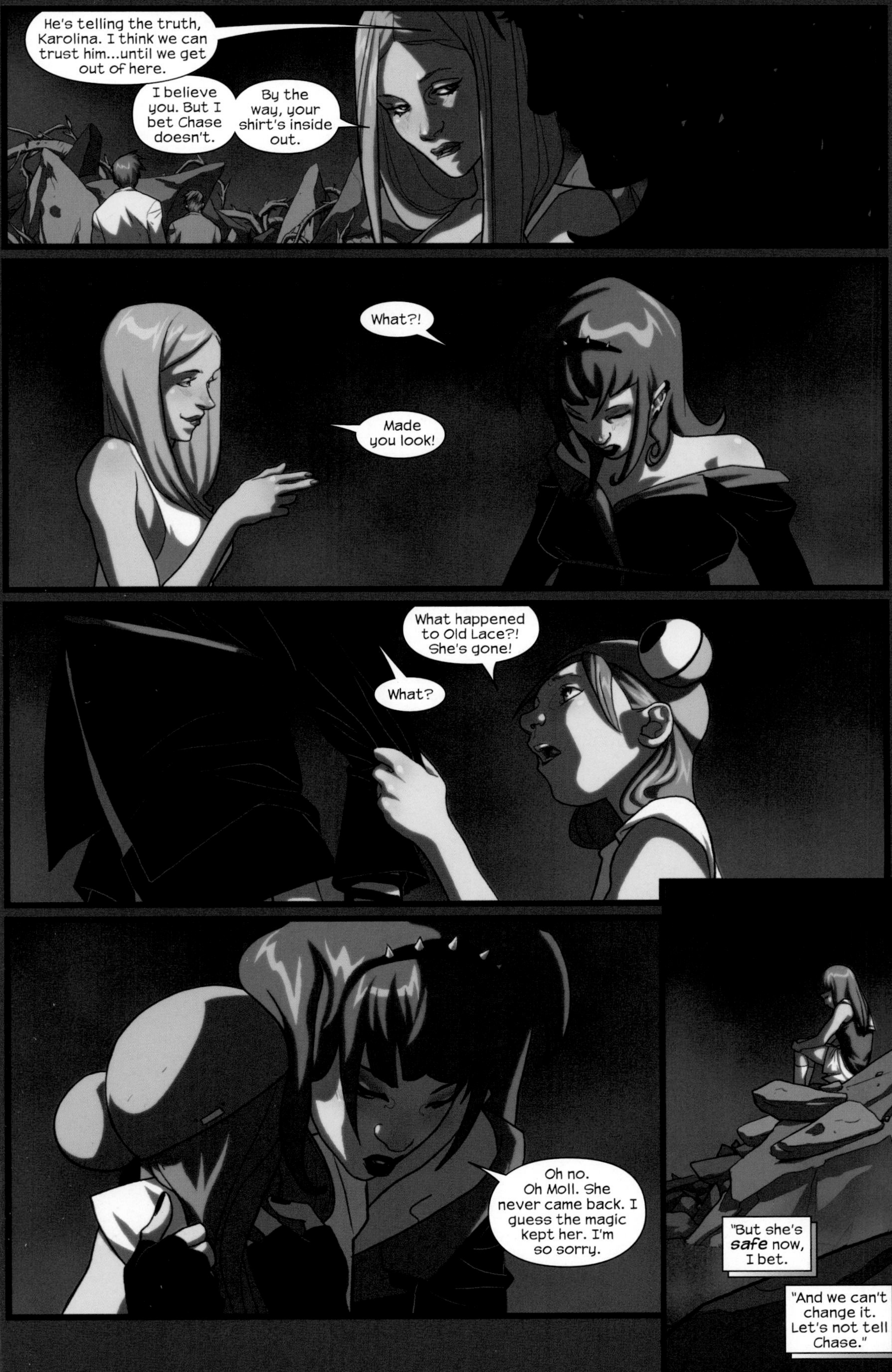
He's telling the truth, Karolina. I think we can trust him...until we get out of here.
I believe you. But I bet Chase doesn't.
By the way, your shirt's inside out.
What?!
Made you look!
What happened to Old Lace?! She's gone!
What?
Oh no. Oh Moll. She never came back. I guess the magic kept her. I'm so sorry.
"But she's *safe* now, I bet.
"And we can't change it. Let's not tell Chase."

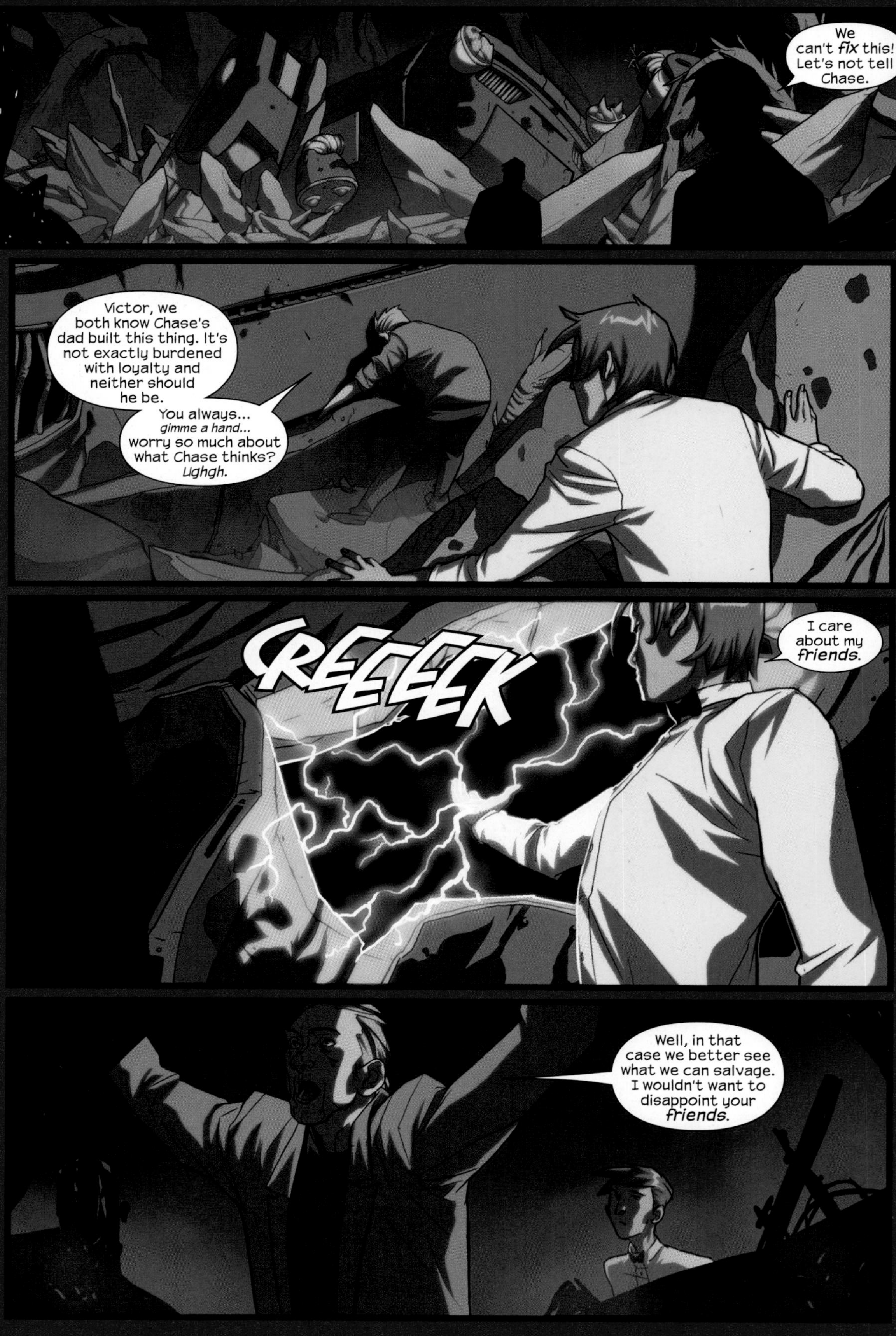

We can't fix this! Let's not tell Chase.
Victor, we both know Chase's dad built this thing. It's not exactly burdened with loyalty and neither should he be.
You always... gimme a hand... worry so much about what Chase thinks? Ughgh.
CREEEEK
I care about my friends.
Well, in that case we better see what we can salvage. I wouldn't want to disappoint your friends.

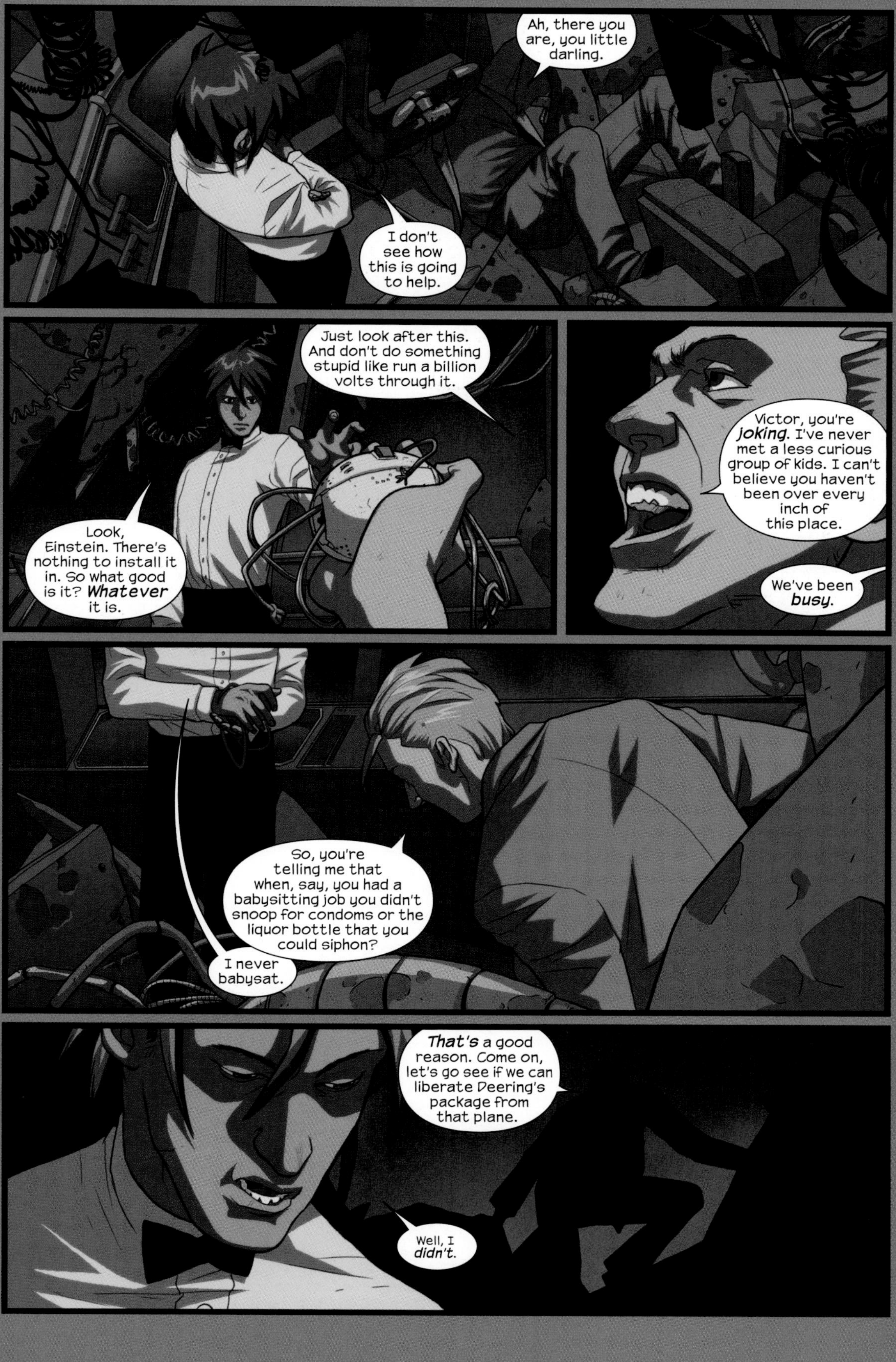

Ah, there you are, you little darling.
I don't see how this is going to help.
Just look after this. And don't do something stupid like run a billion volts through it.
Look, Einstein. There's nothing to install it in. So what good is it? *Whatever* it is.
Victor, you're *joking*. I've never met a less curious group of kids. I can't believe you haven't been over every inch of this place.
We've been *busy*.
So, you're telling me that when, say, you had a babysitting job you didn't snoop for condoms or the liquor bottle that you could siphon?
I never babysat.
That's a good reason. Come on, let's go see if we can liberate Deering's package from that plane.
Well, I *didn't*.

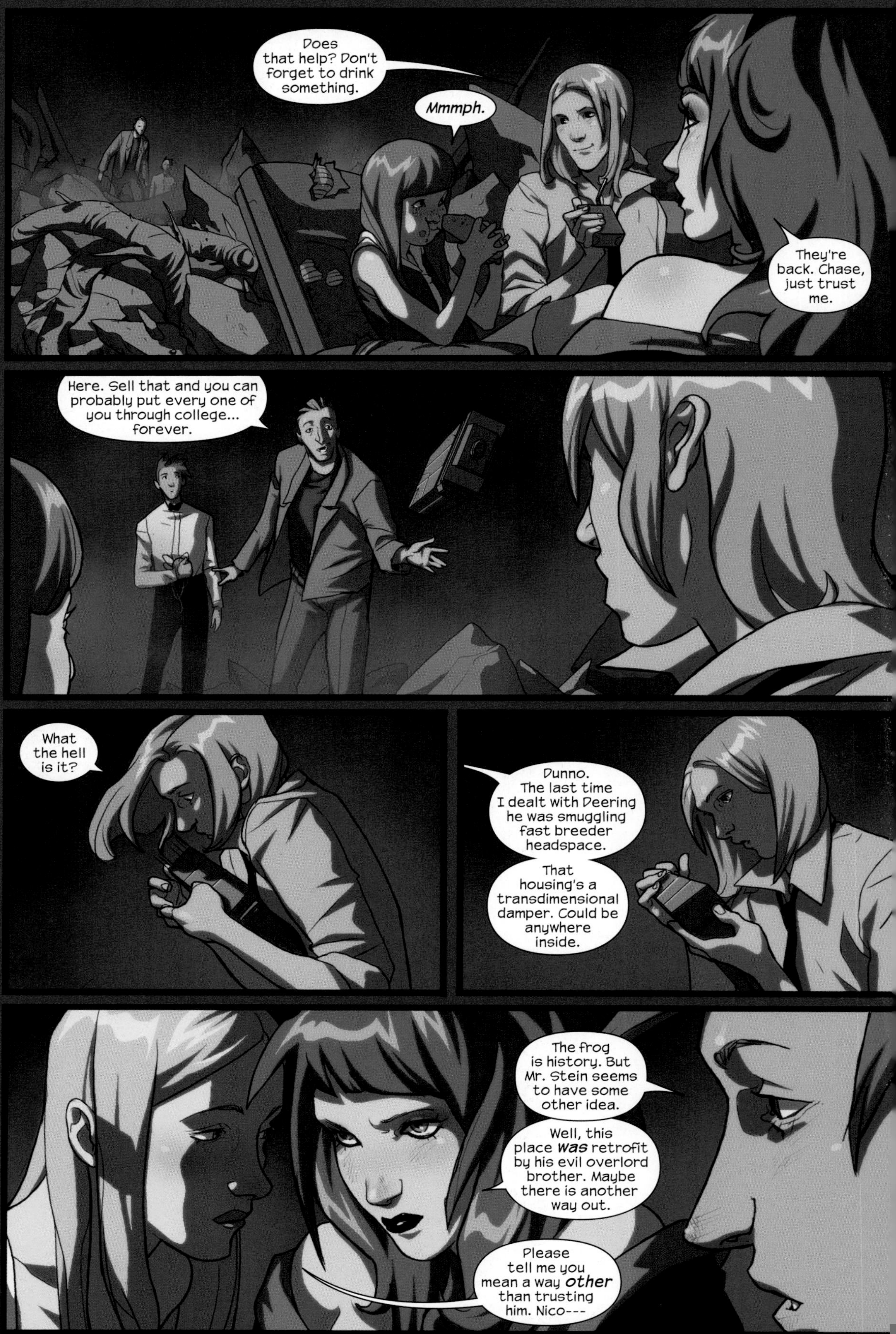
Does that help? Don't forget to drink something.
Mmmph.
They're back. Chase, just trust me.
Here. Sell that and you can probably put every one of you through college... forever.
What the hell is it?
Dunno. The last time I dealt with Deering he was smuggling fast breeder headspace.
That housing's a transdimensional damper. Could be anywhere inside.
The frog is history. But Mr. Stein seems to have some other idea.
Well, this place *was* retrofit by his evil overlord brother. Maybe there is another way out.
Please tell me you mean a way *other* than trusting him. Nico---

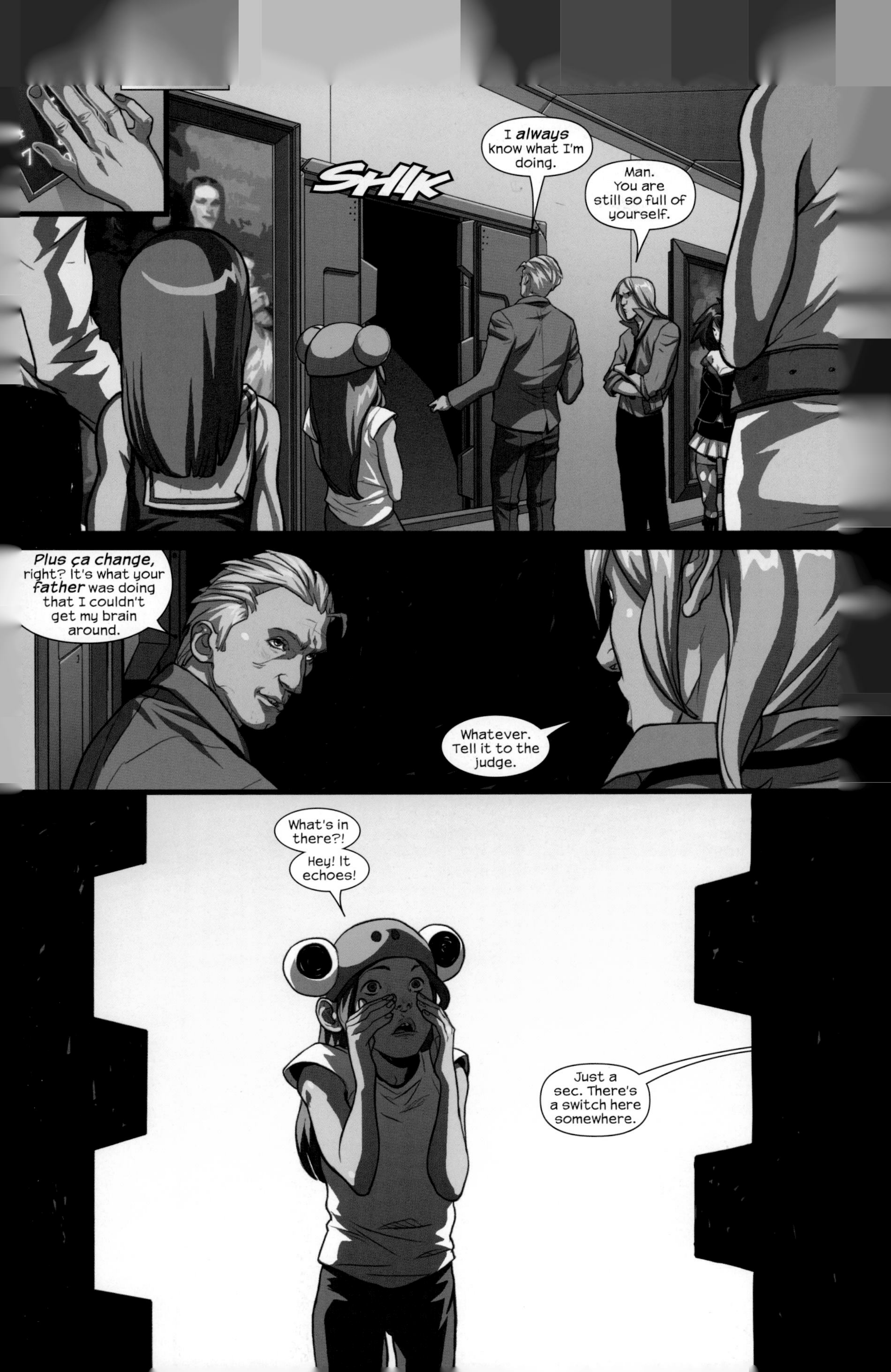

SHIK
I *always* know what I'm doing.
Man. You are still so full of yourself.
Plus ça change, right? It's what your *father* was doing that I couldn't get my brain around.
Whatever. Tell it to the judge.
What's in there?!
Hey! It echoes!
Just a sec. There's a switch here somewhere.

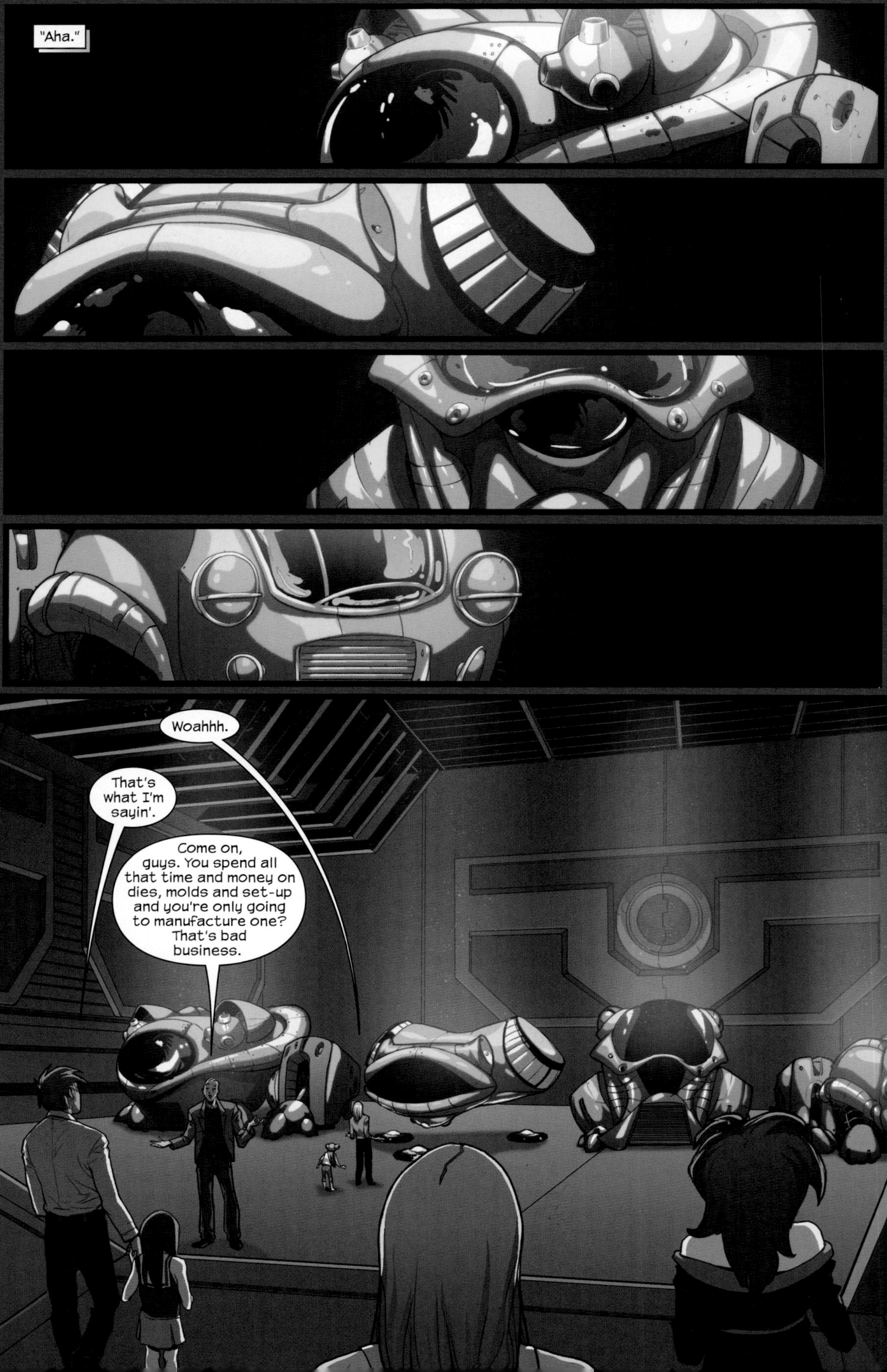
"Aha."
Woahhh.
That's what I'm sayin'.
Come on, guys. You spend all that time and money on dies, molds and set-up and you're only going to manufacture one? That's bad business.

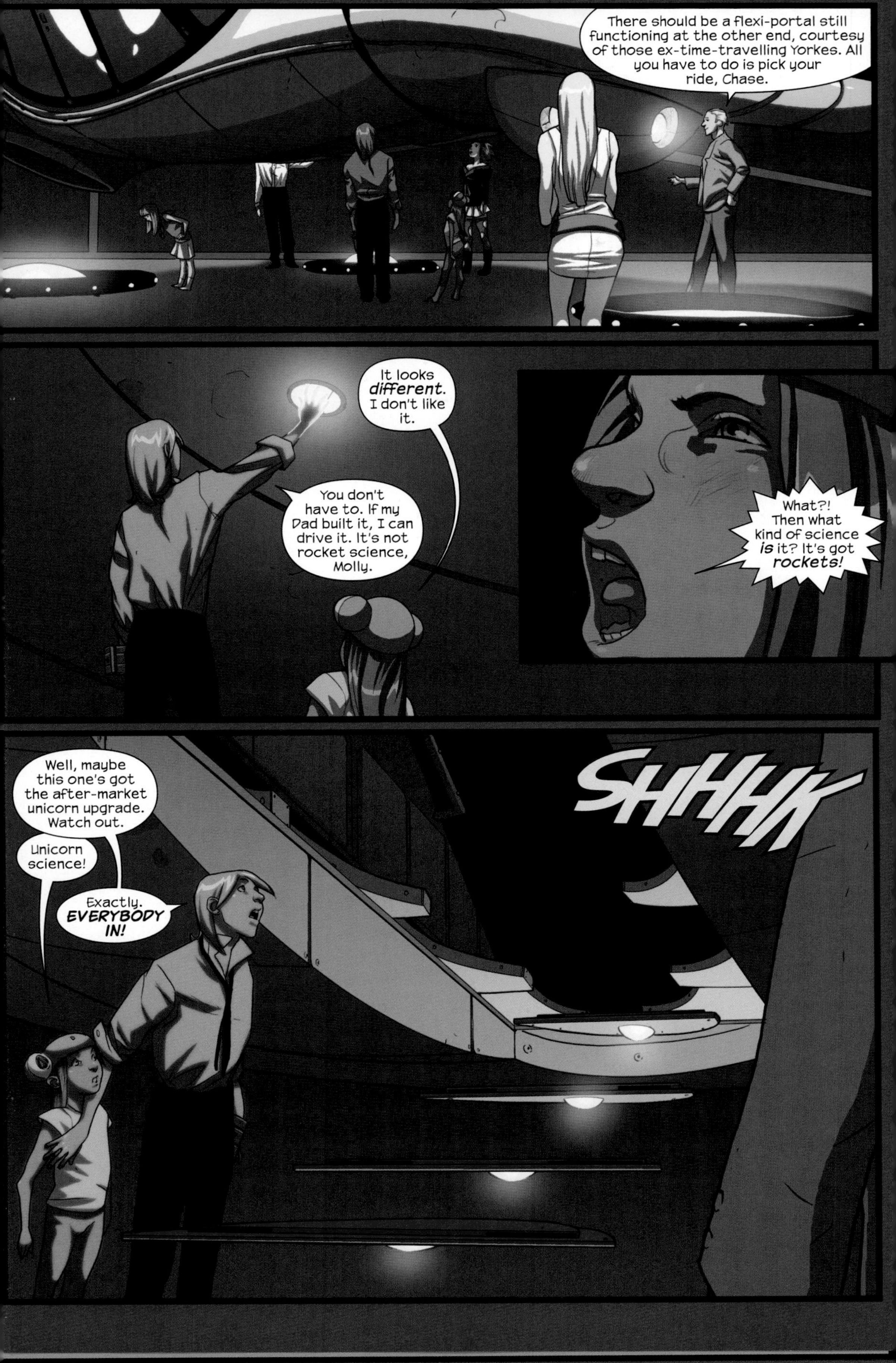
There should be a flexi-portal still functioning at the other end, courtesy of those ex-time-travelling Yorkes. All you have to do is pick your ride, Chase.
It looks *different*. I don't like it.
You don't have to. If my Dad built it, I can drive it. It's not rocket science, Molly.
What?! Then what kind of science *is* it? It's got *rockets!*
Well, maybe this one's got the after-market unicorn upgrade. Watch out.
Unicorn science!
Exactly. **EVERYBODY IN!**
SHHHK

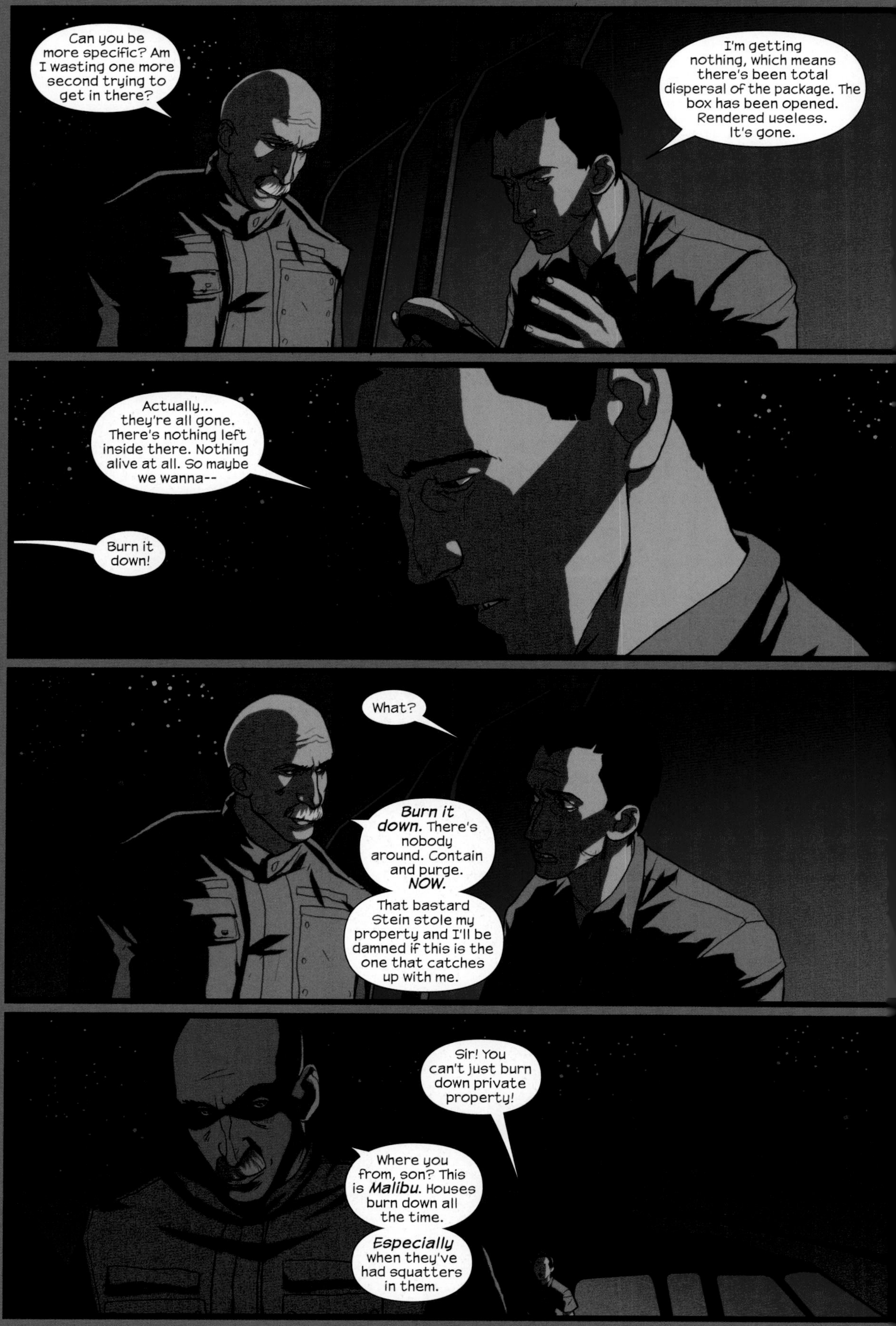
Can you be more specific? Am I wasting one more second trying to get in there?
I'm getting nothing, which means there's been total dispersal of the package. The box has been opened. Rendered useless. It's gone.
Actually... they're all gone. There's nothing left inside there. Nothing alive at all. So maybe we wanna--
Burn it down!
What?
Burn it down. There's nobody around. Contain and purge. *NOW.*
That bastard Stein stole my property and I'll be damned if this is the one that catches up with me.
Sir! You can't just burn down private property!
Where you from, son? This is *Malibu.* Houses burn down all the time.
Especially when they've had squatters in them.

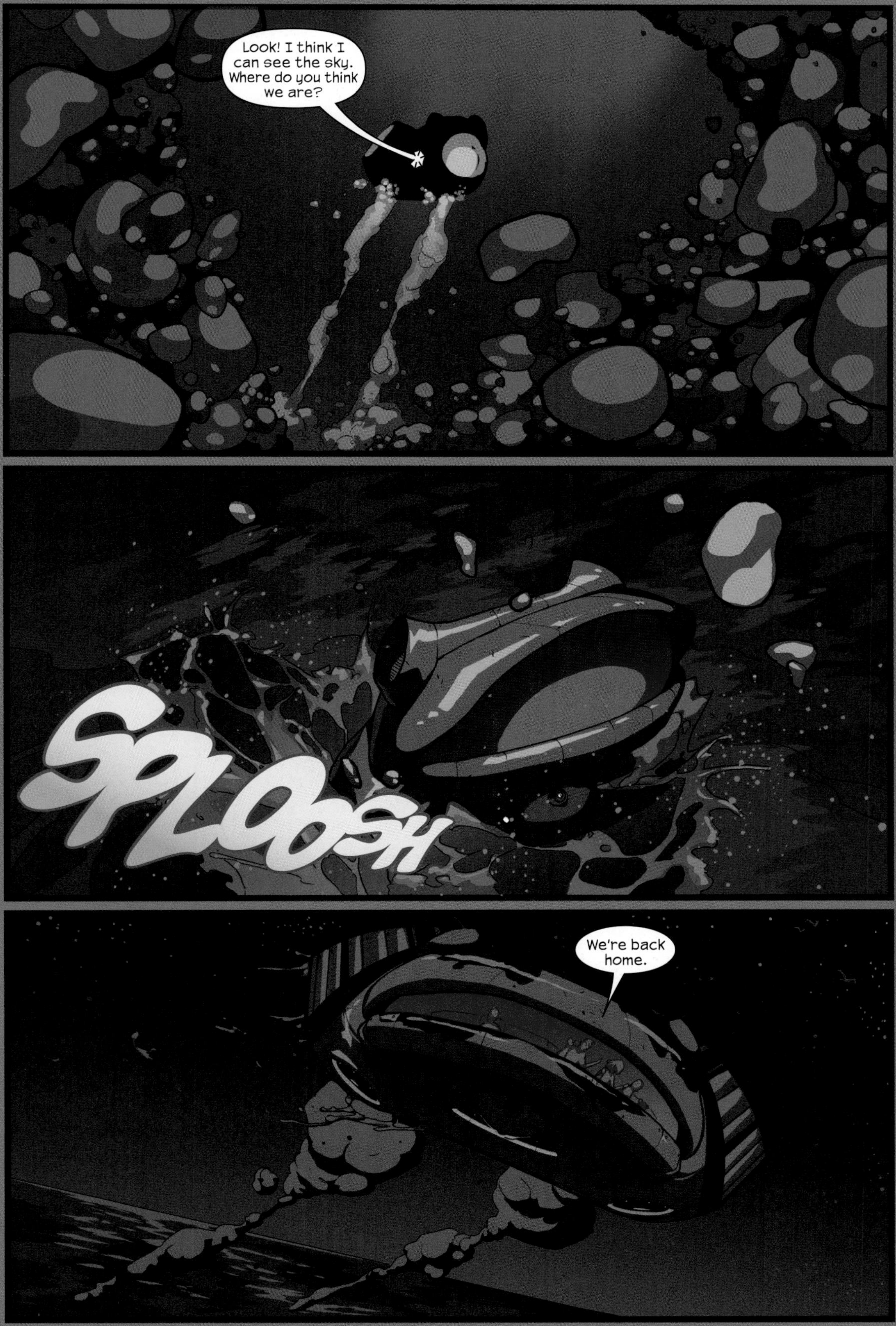
Look! I think I can see the sky. Where do you think we are?
SPLOOSH
We're back home.

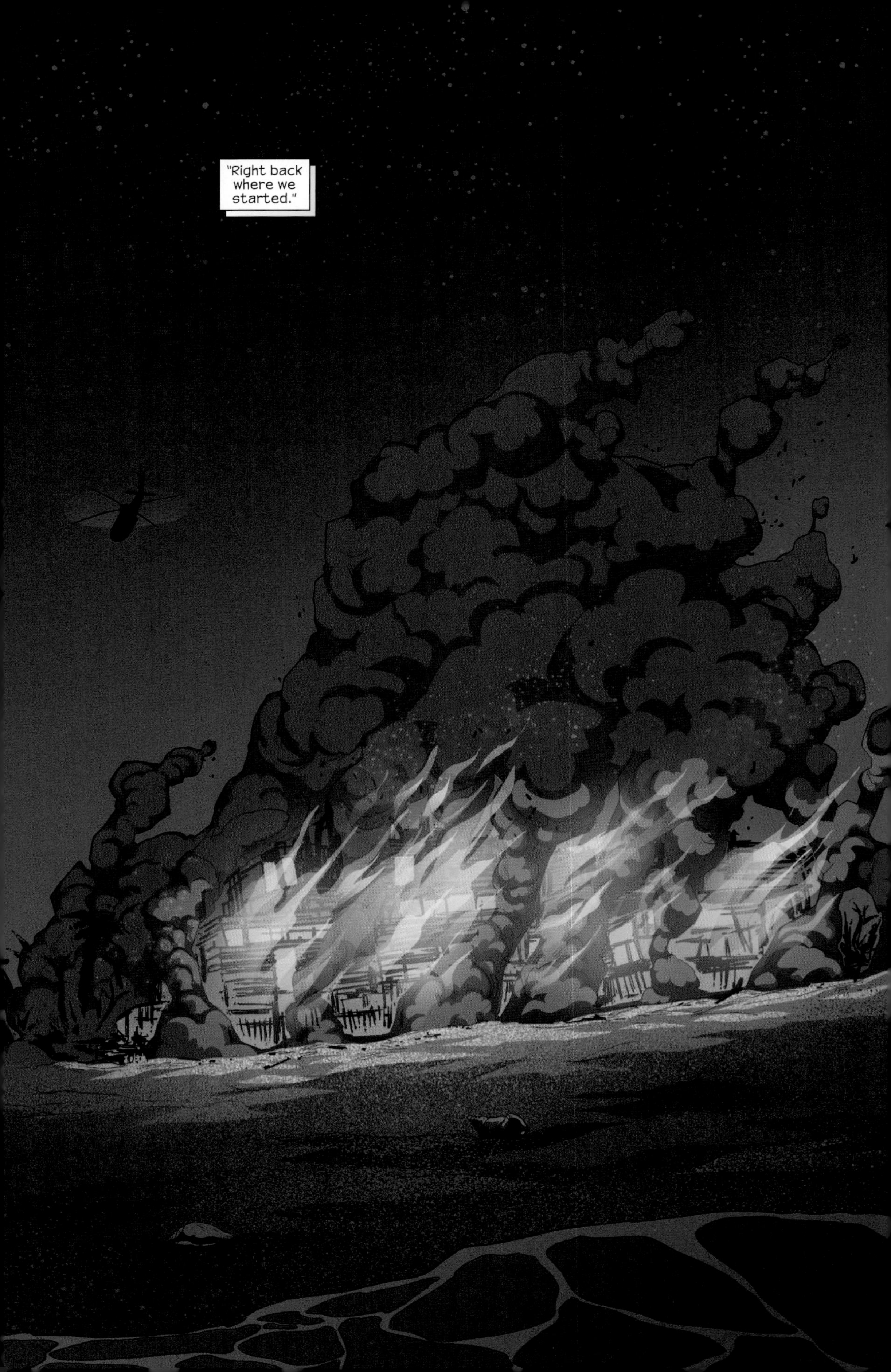
"Right back where we started."

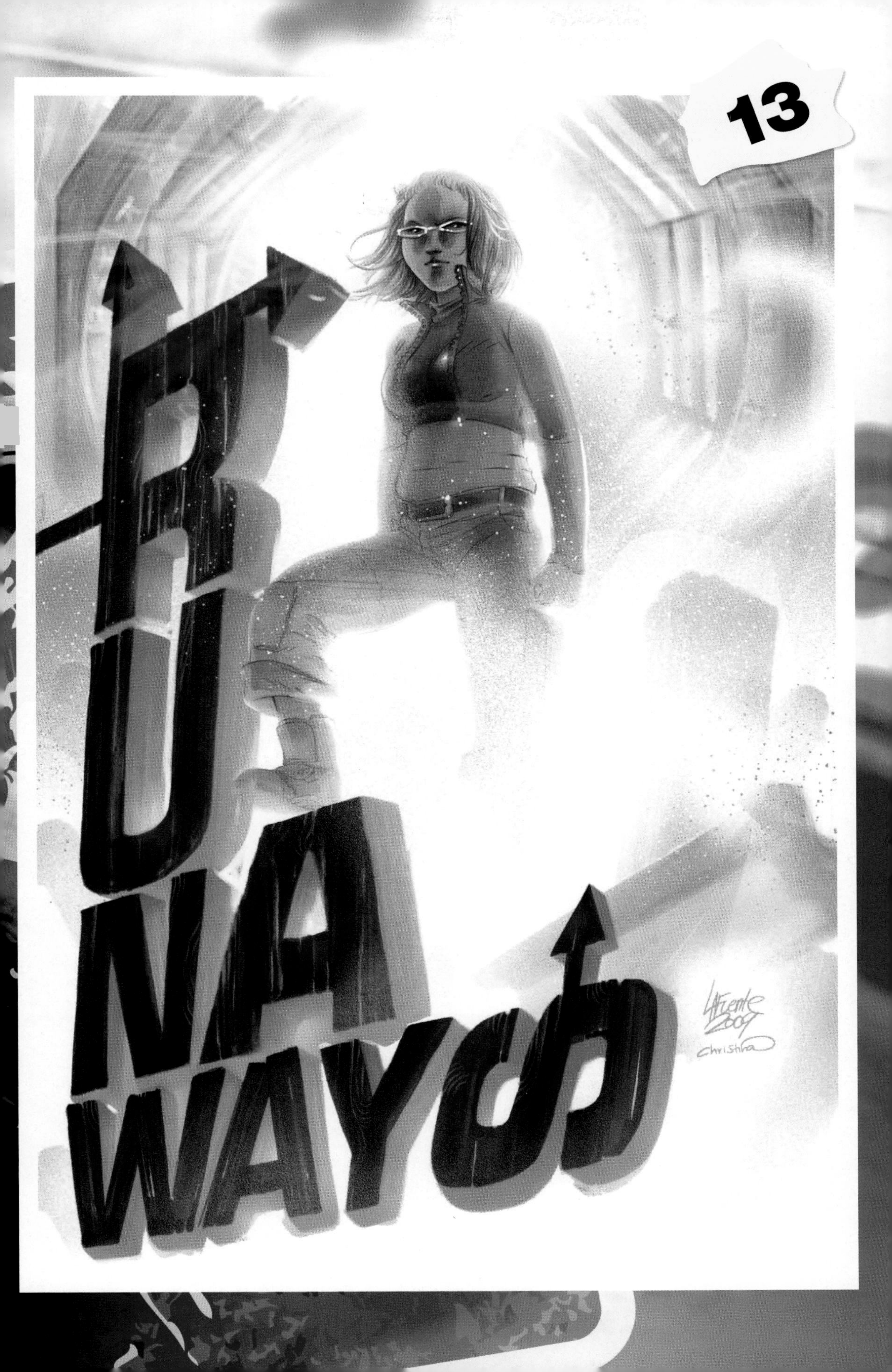
13
RUNAWAYS

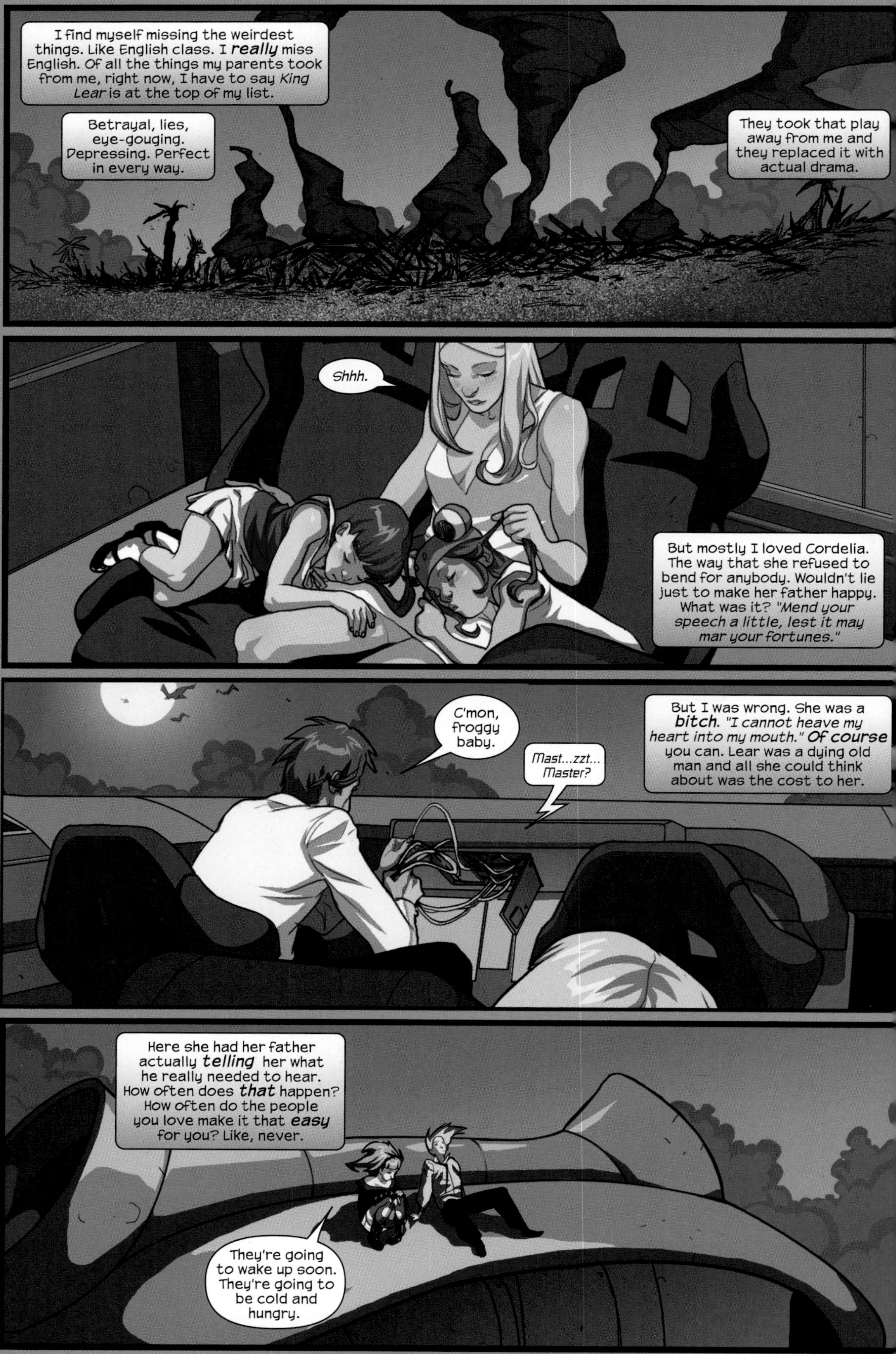

I find myself missing the weirdest things. Like English class. I *really* miss English. Of all the things my parents took from me, right now, I have to say *King Lear* is at the top of my list.
Betrayal, lies, eye-gouging. Depressing. Perfect in every way.
They took that play away from me and they replaced it with actual drama.
Shhh.
But mostly I loved Cordelia. The way that she refused to bend for anybody. Wouldn't lie just to make her father happy. What was it? *"Mend your speech a little, lest it may mar your fortunes."*
C'mon, froggy baby.
Mast...zzt... Master?
But I was wrong. She was a ***bitch***. *"I cannot heave my heart into my mouth."* ***Of course*** you can. Lear was a dying old man and all she could think about was the cost to her.
Here she had her father actually ***telling*** her what he really needed to hear. How often does ***that*** happen? How often do the people you love make it that ***easy*** for you? Like, never.
They're going to wake up soon. They're going to be cold and hungry.

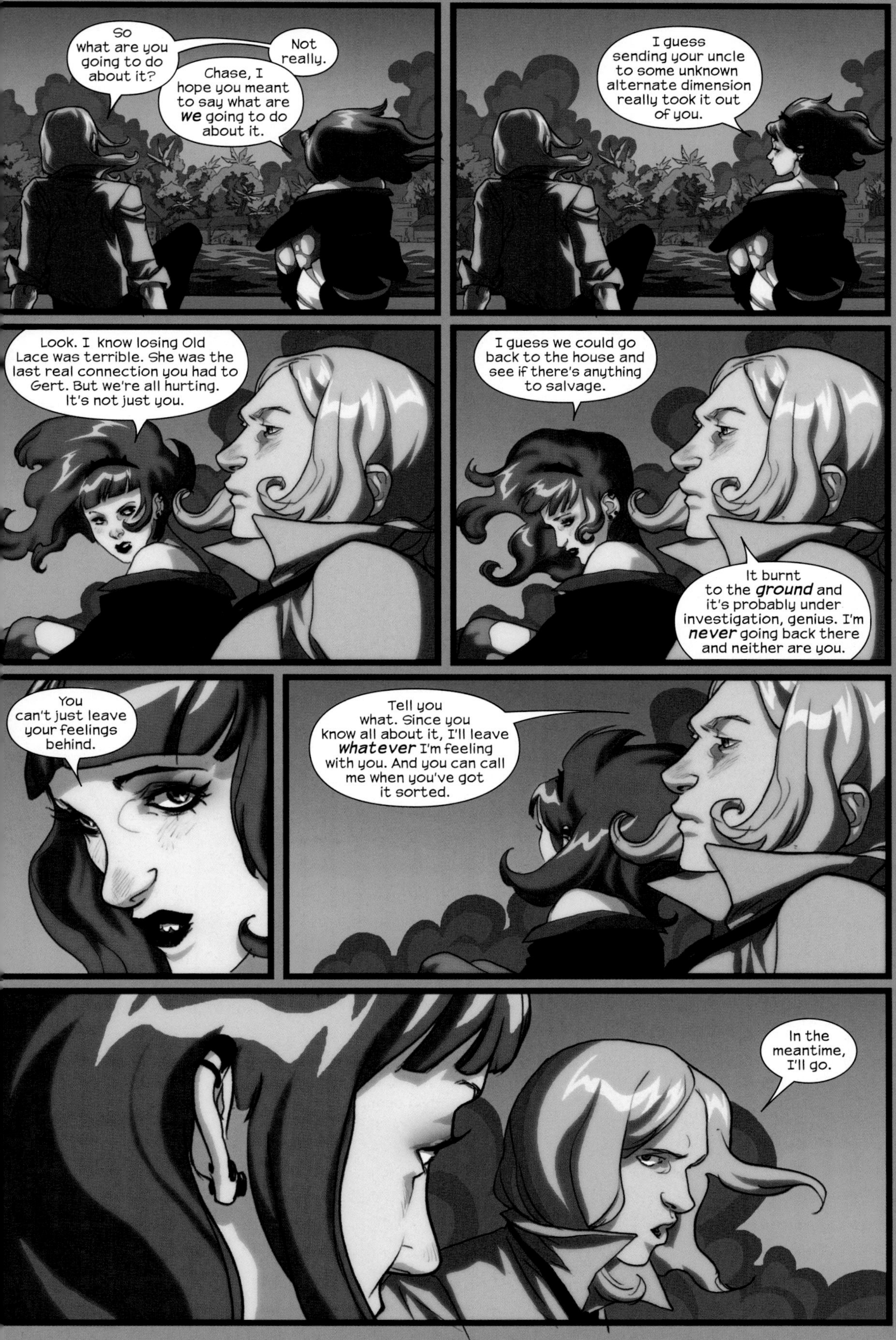

So what are you going to do about it?
Not really.
Chase, I hope you meant to say what are *we* going to do about it.
I guess sending your uncle to some unknown alternate dimension really took it out of you.
Look. I know losing Old Lace was terrible. She was the last real connection you had to Gert. But we're all hurting. It's not just you.
I guess we could go back to the house and see if there's anything to salvage.
It burnt to the *ground* and it's probably under investigation, genius. I'm *never* going back there and neither are you.
You can't just leave your feelings behind.
Tell you what. Since you know all about it, I'll leave *whatever* I'm feeling with you. And you can call me when you've got it sorted.
In the meantime, I'll go.

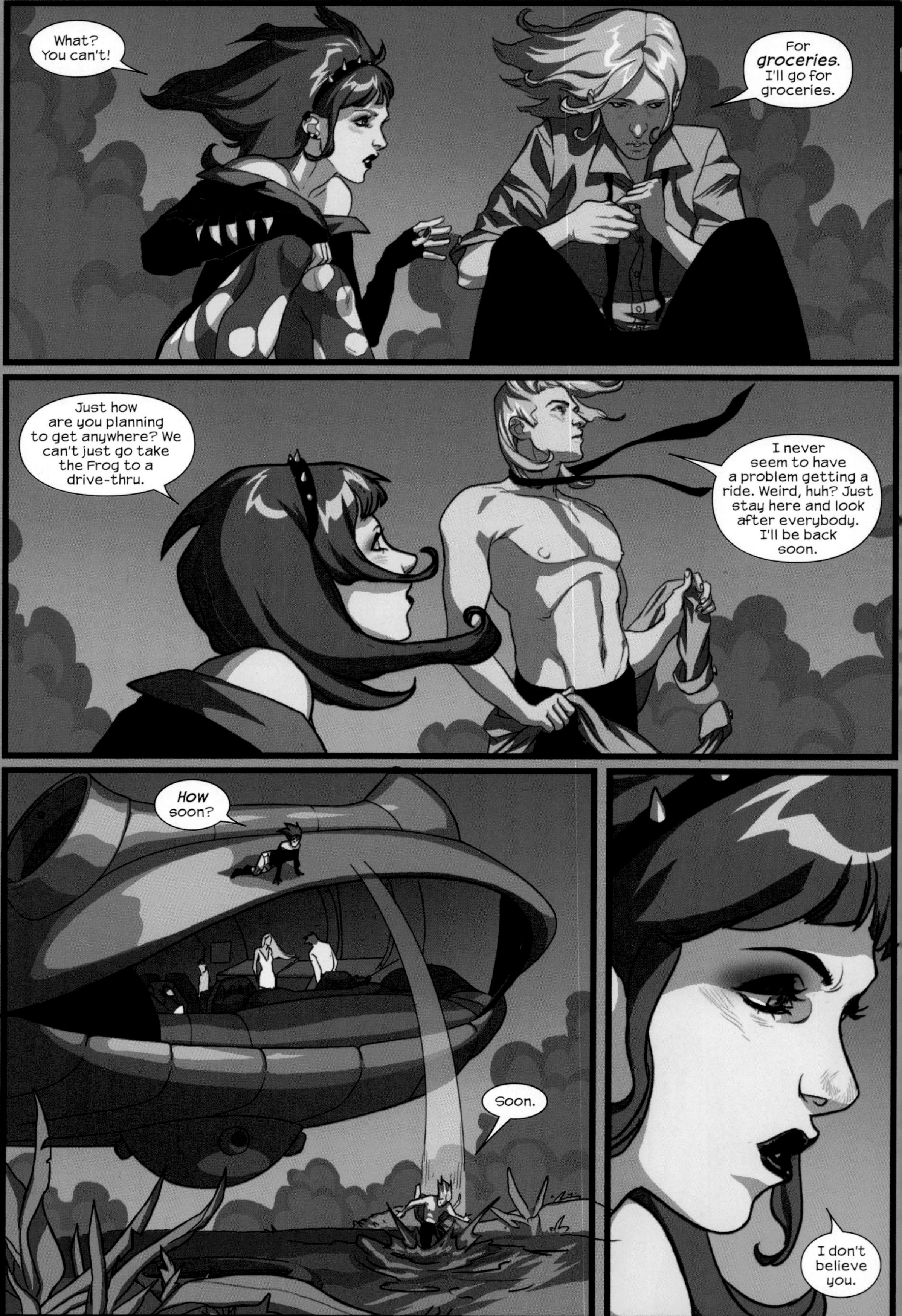
What? You can't!
For *groceries.* I'll go for groceries.
Just how are you planning to get anywhere? We can't just go take the Frog to a drive-thru.
I never seem to have a problem getting a ride. Weird, huh? Just stay here and look after everybody. I'll be back soon.
How soon?
Soon.
I don't believe you.

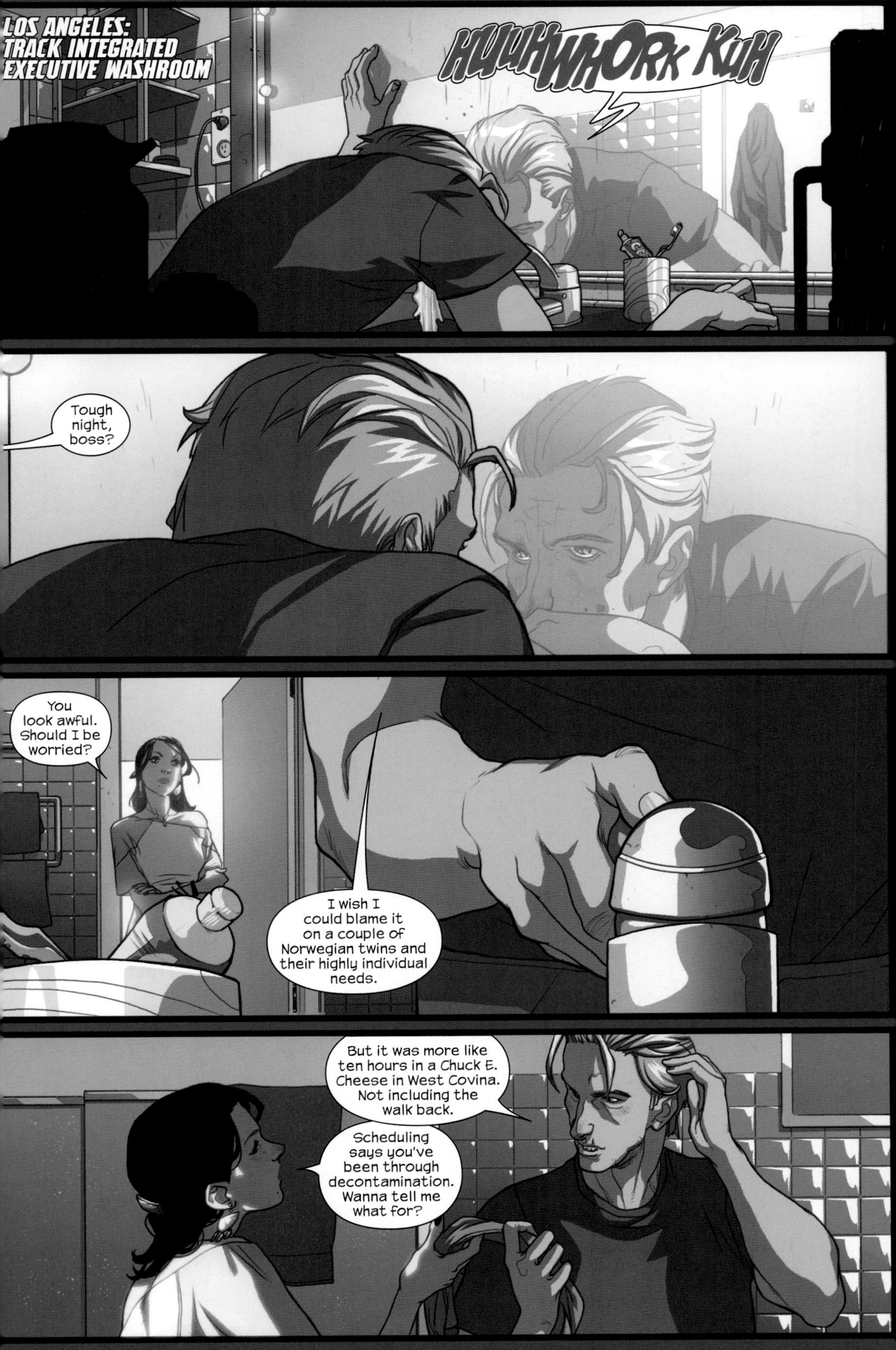
LOS ANGELES: TRACK INTEGRATED EXECUTIVE WASHROOM
HUUHWHORK KUH
Tough night, boss?
You look awful. Should I be worried?
I wish I could blame it on a couple of Norwegian twins and their highly individual needs.
But it was more like ten hours in a Chuck E. Cheese in West Covina. Not including the walk back.
Scheduling says you've been through decontamination. Wanna tell me what for?

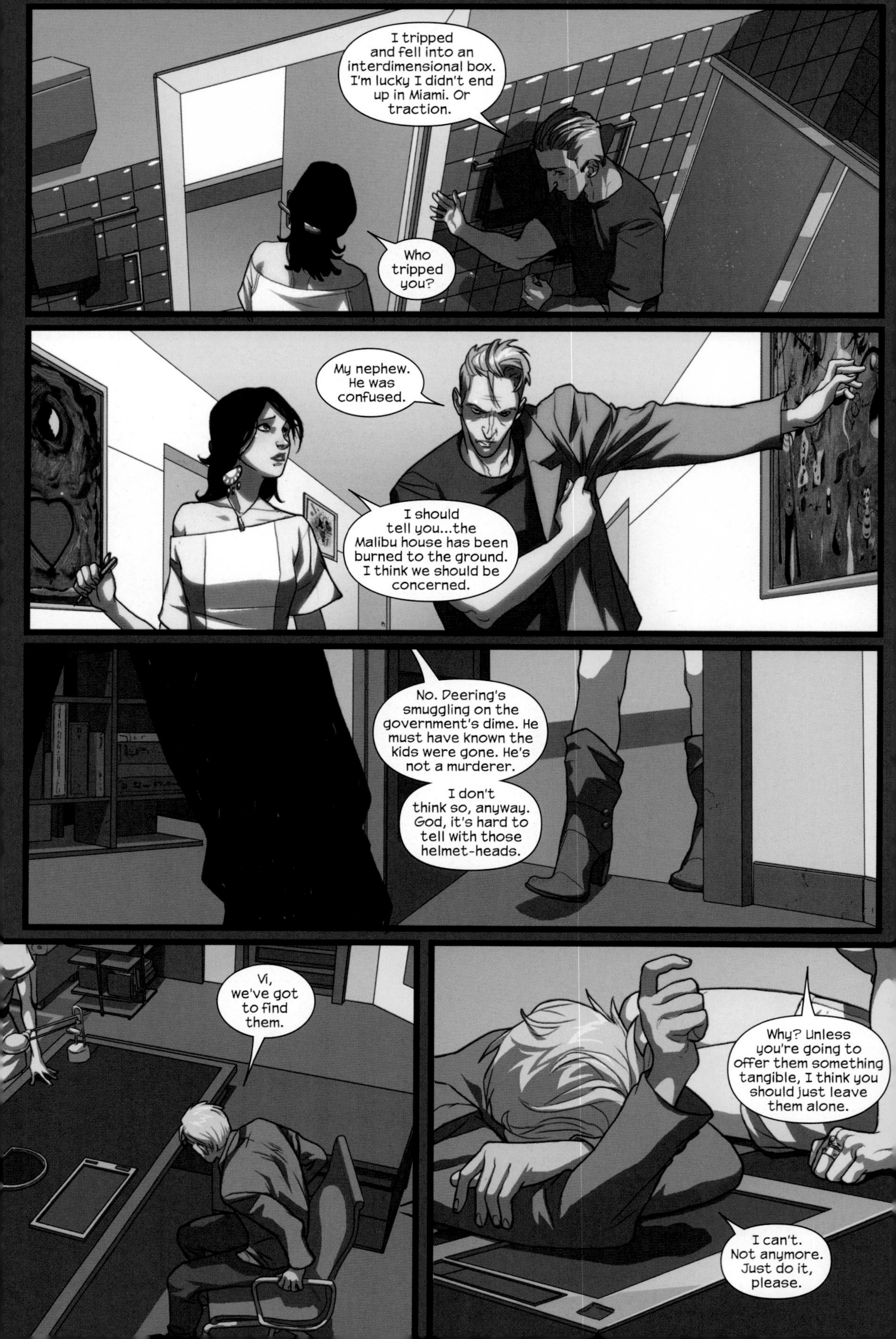
I tripped and fell into an interdimensional box. I'm lucky I didn't end up in Miami. Or traction.
Who tripped you?
My nephew. He was confused.
I should tell you...the Malibu house has been burned to the ground. I think we should be concerned.
No. Deering's smuggling on the government's dime. He must have known the kids were gone. He's not a murderer.
I don't think so, anyway. God, it's hard to tell with those helmet-heads.
Vi, we've got to find them.
Why? Unless you're going to offer them something tangible, I think you should just leave them alone.
I can't. Not anymore. Just do it, please.

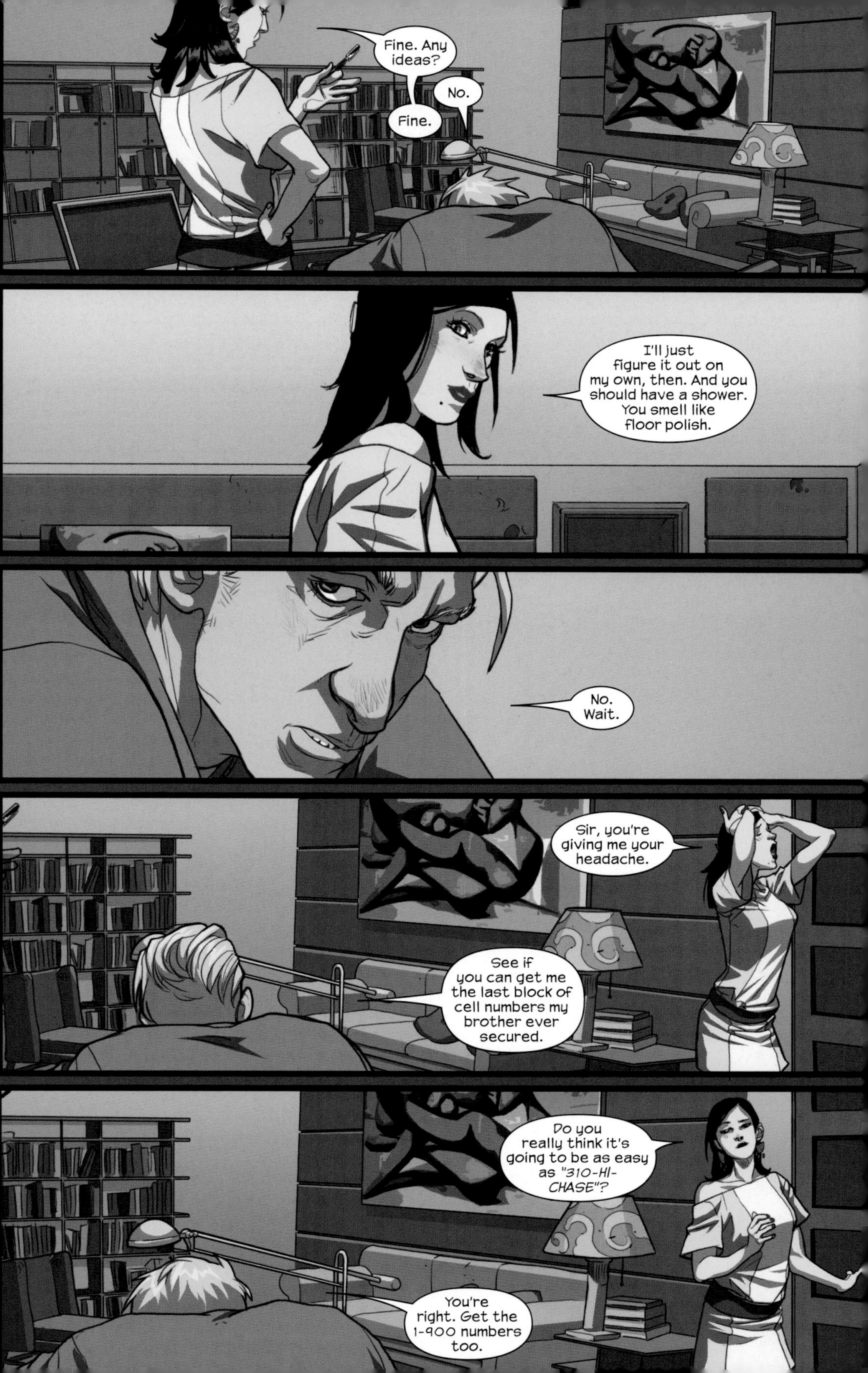
Fine. Any ideas?
Fine.
No.
I'll just figure it out on my own, then. And you should have a shower. You smell like floor polish.
No. Wait.
Sir, you're giving me your headache.
See if you can get me the last block of cell numbers my brother ever secured.
Do you really think it's going to be as easy as "310-HI-CHASE"?
You're right. Get the 1-900 numbers too.

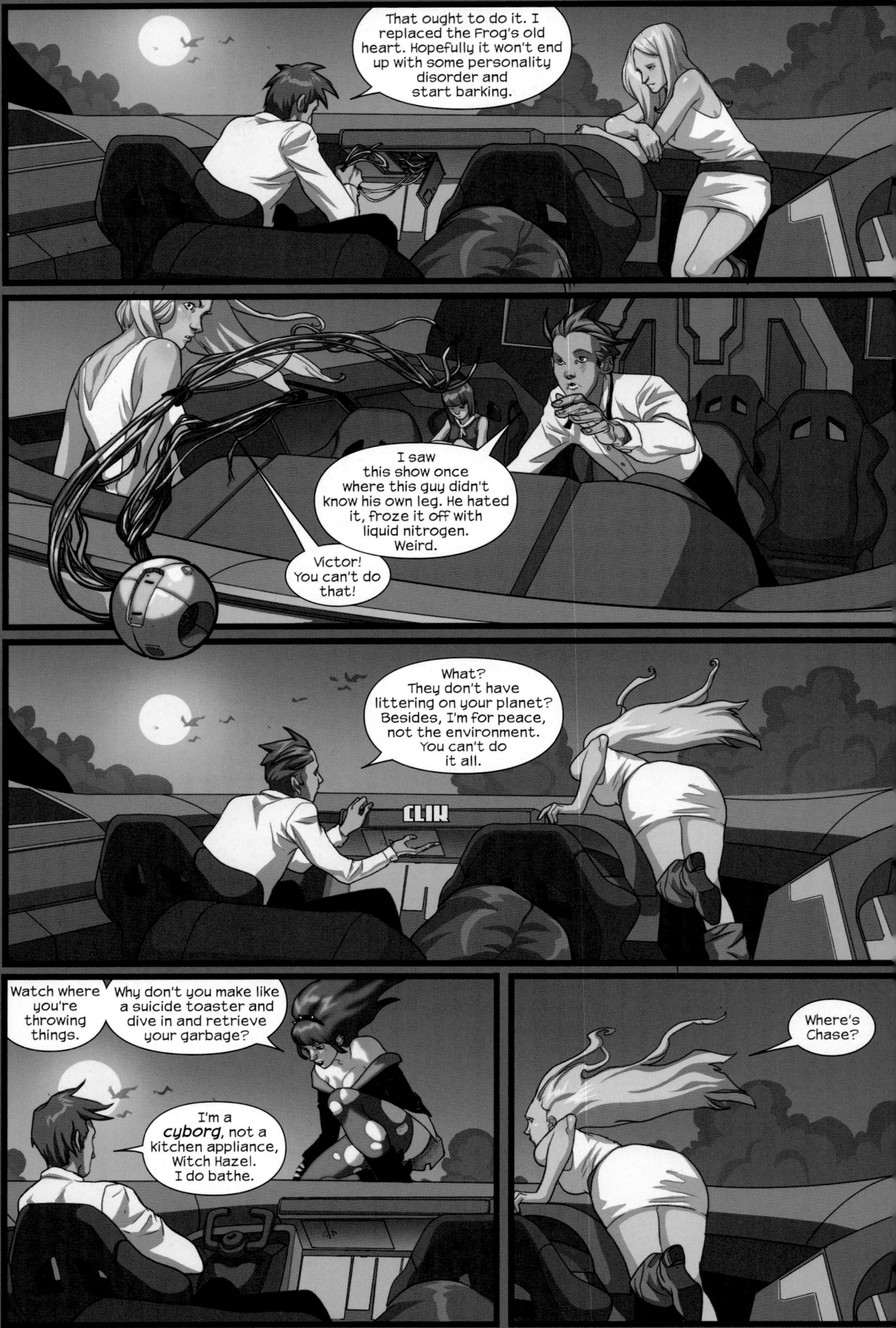
That ought to do it. I replaced the Frog's old heart. Hopefully it won't end up with some personality disorder and start barking.
I saw this show once where this guy didn't know his own leg. He hated it, froze it off with liquid nitrogen. Weird.
Victor! You can't do that!
What? They don't have littering on your planet? Besides, I'm for peace, not the environment. You can't do it all.
CLIK
Watch where you're throwing things.
Why don't you make like a suicide toaster and dive in and retrieve your garbage?
I'm a *cyborg*, not a kitchen appliance, Witch Hazel. I do bathe.
Where's Chase?

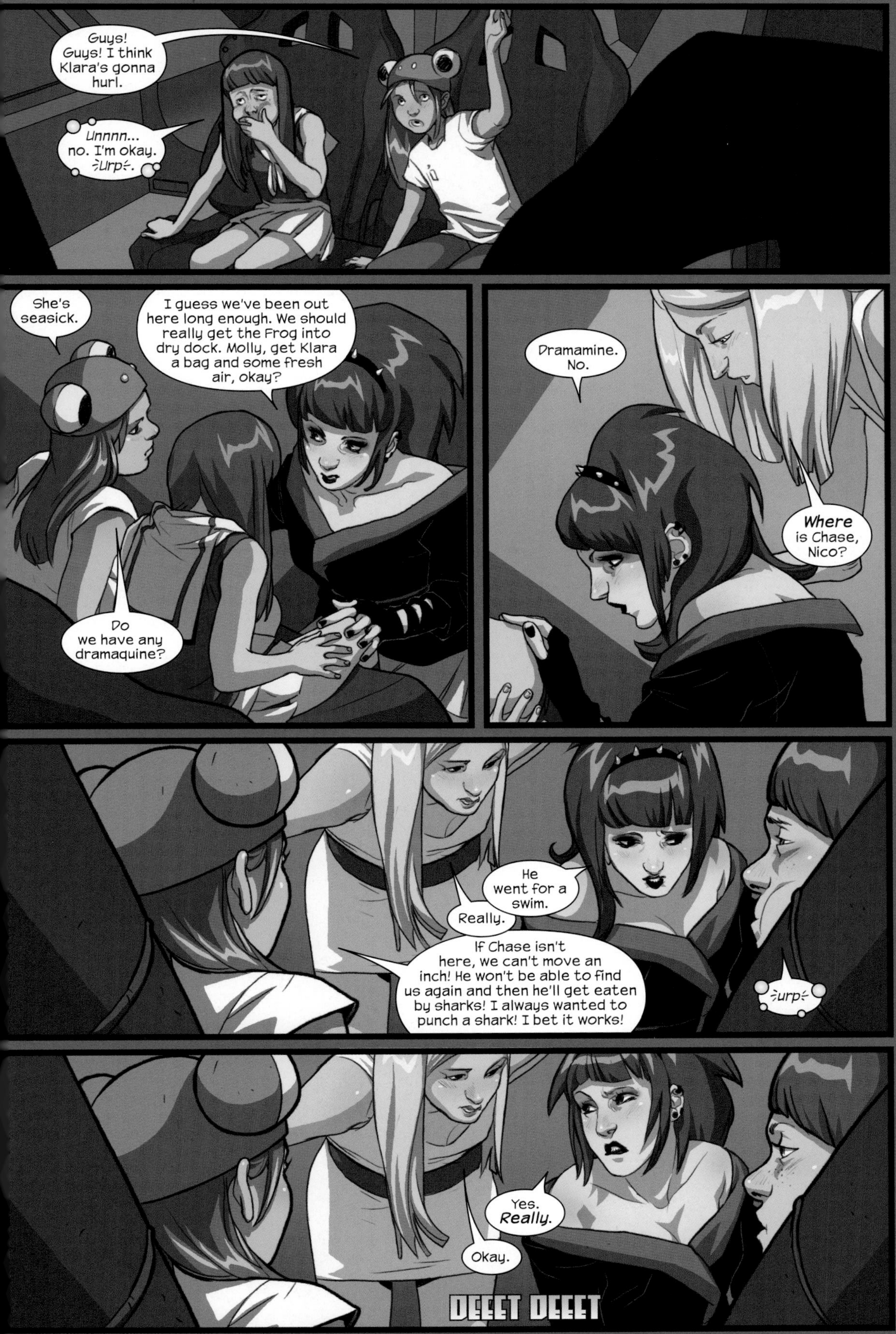

Guys! Guys! I think Klara's gonna hurl.
Unnnn... no. I'm okay. urp.
She's seasick.
I guess we've been out here long enough. We should really get the Frog into dry dock. Molly, get Klara a bag and some fresh air, okay?
Do we have any dramaquine?
Dramamine. No.
Where is Chase, Nico?
He went for a swim.
Really.
If Chase isn't here, we can't move an inch! He won't be able to find us again and then he'll get eaten by sharks! I always wanted to punch a shark! I bet it works!
urp
Yes. Really.
Okay.
DEEET DEEET

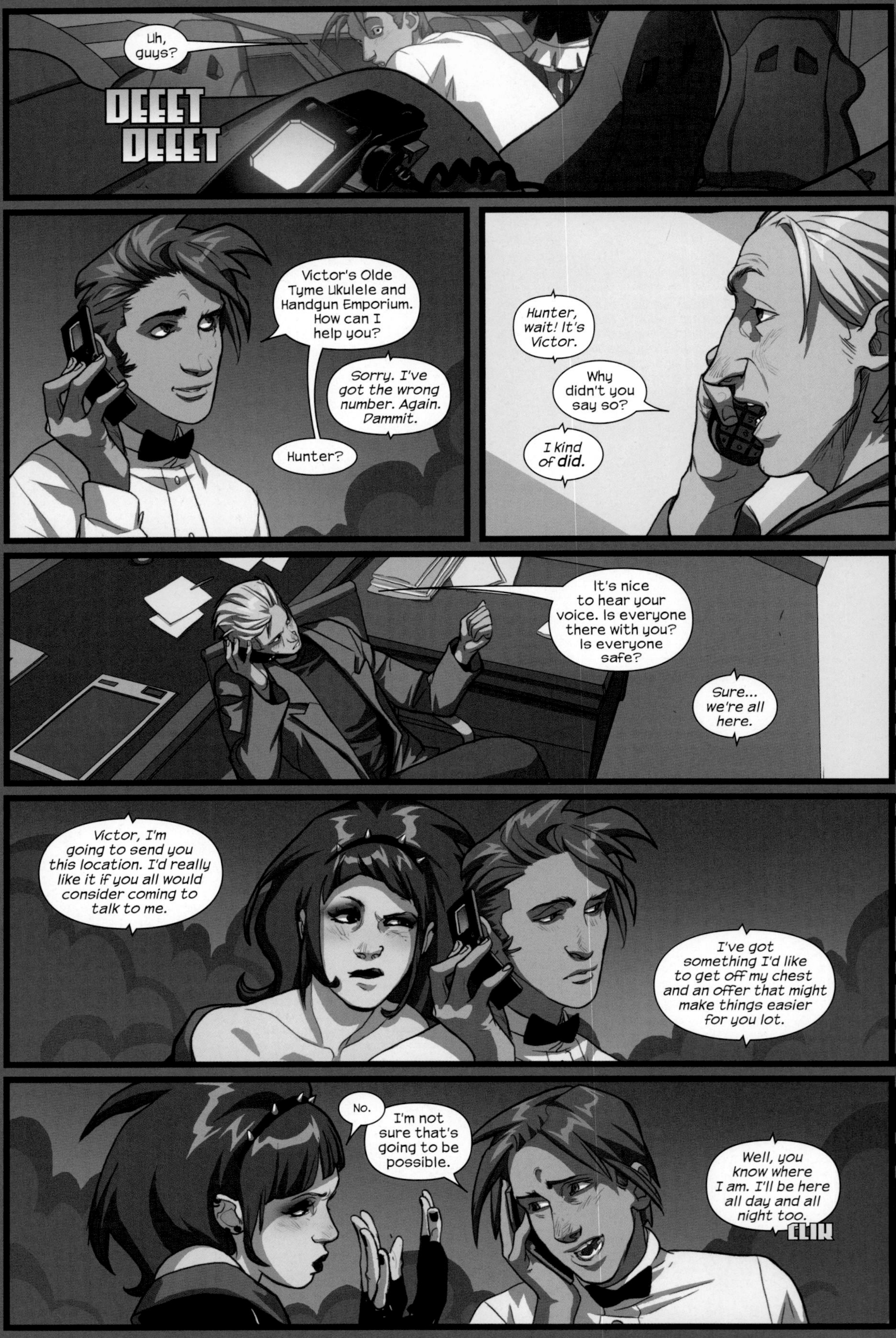
Uh, guys?
DEEEET DEEEET
Victor's Olde Tyme Ukulele and Handgun Emporium. How can I help you?
Sorry. I've got the wrong number. Again. Dammit.
Hunter?
Hunter, wait! It's Victor.
Why didn't you say so?
I kind of **did.**
It's nice to hear your voice. Is everyone there with you? Is everyone safe?
Sure... we're all here.
Victor, I'm going to send you this location. I'd really like it if you all would consider coming to talk to me.
I've got something I'd like to get off my chest and an offer that might make things easier for you lot.
No.
I'm not sure that's going to be possible.
Well, you know where I am. I'll be here all day and all night too.
CLIK

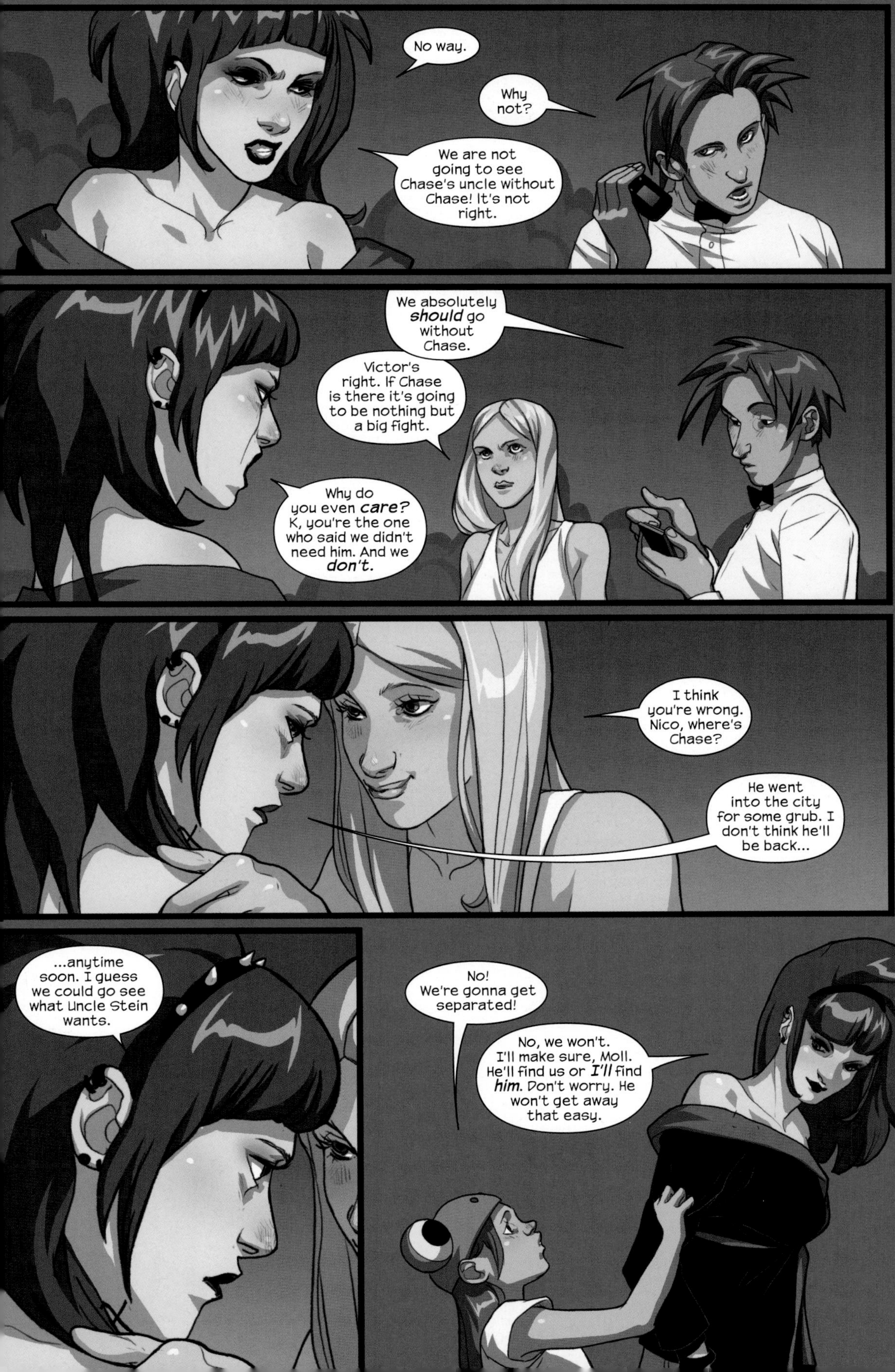
No way.
Why not?
We are not going to see Chase's uncle without Chase! It's not right.
We absolutely *should* go without Chase.
Victor's right. If Chase is there it's going to be nothing but a big fight.
Why do you even *care?* K, you're the one who said we didn't need him. And we *don't.*
I think you're wrong. Nico, where's Chase?
He went into the city for some grub. I don't think he'll be back...
...anytime soon. I guess we could go see what Uncle Stein wants.
No! We're gonna get separated!
No, we won't. I'll make sure, Moll. He'll find us or *I'll* find *him.* Don't worry. He won't get away that easy.

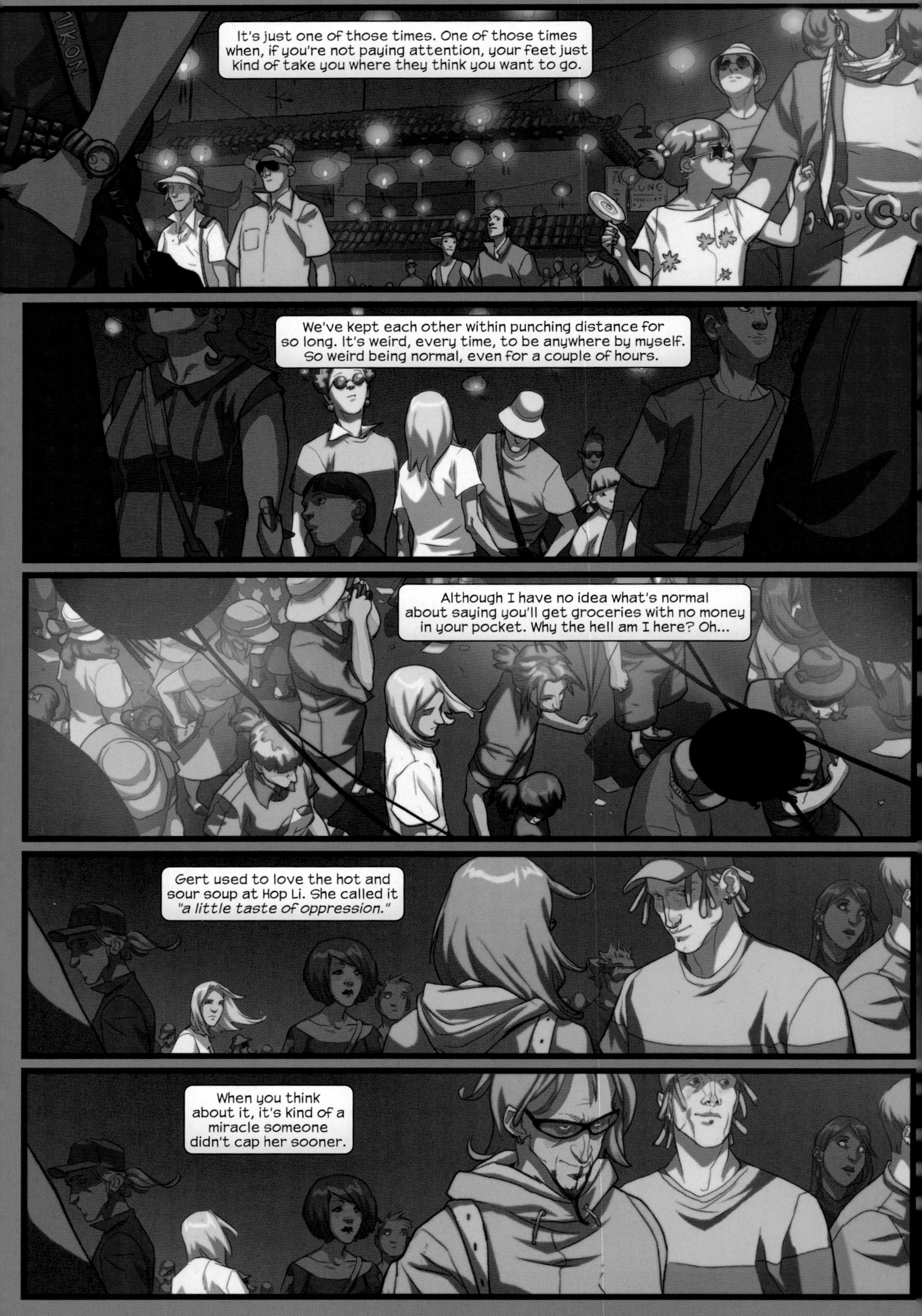
It's just one of those times. One of those times when, if you're not paying attention, your feet just kind of take you where they think you want to go.
We've kept each other within punching distance for so long. It's weird, every time, to be anywhere by myself. So weird being normal, even for a couple of hours.
Although I have no idea what's normal about saying you'll get groceries with no money in your pocket. Why the hell am I here? Oh...
Gert used to love the hot and sour soup at Hop Li. She called it *"a little taste of oppression."*
When you think about it, it's kind of a miracle someone didn't cap her sooner.

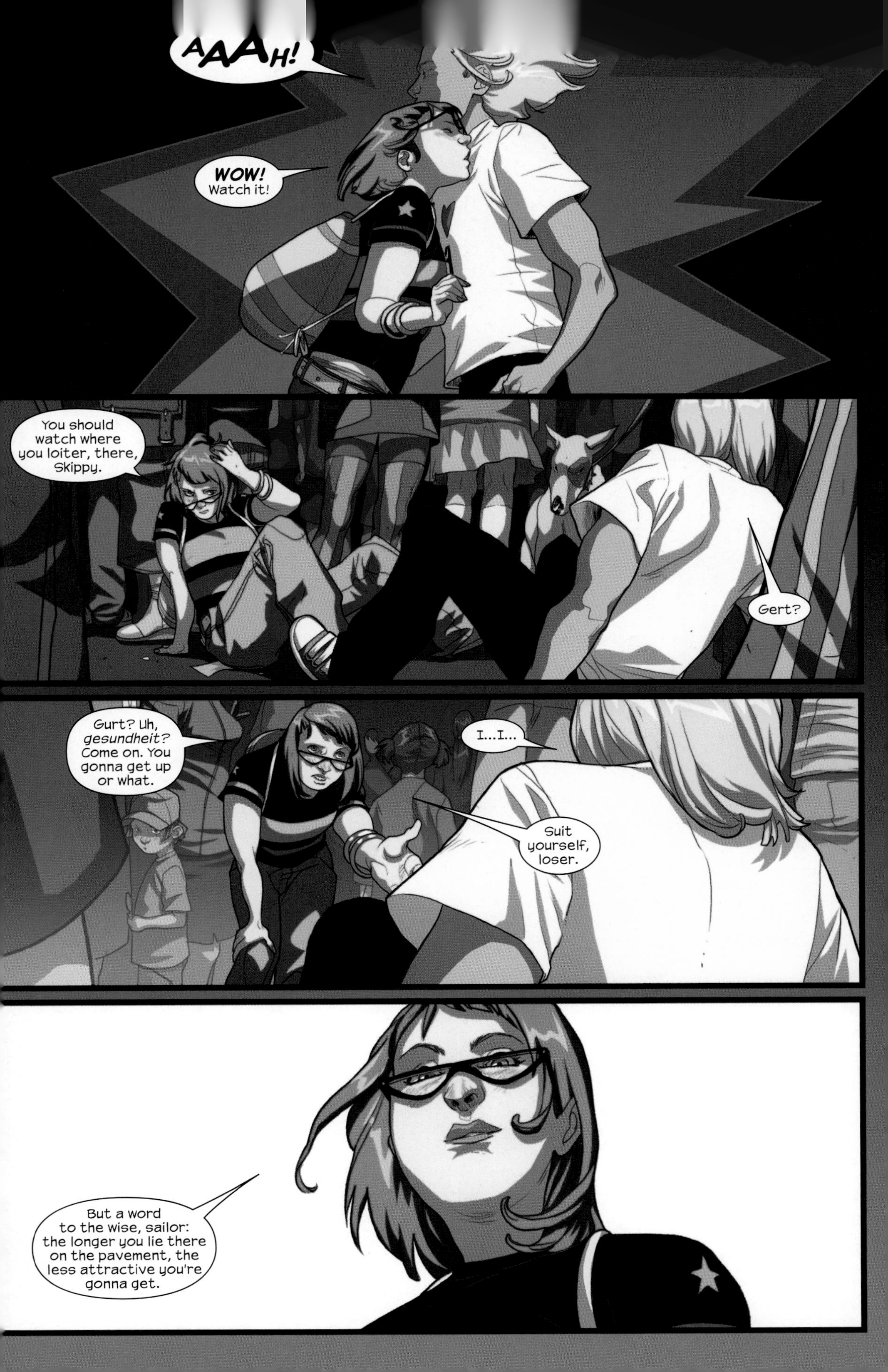
AAAH!
WOW! Watch it!
You should watch where you loiter, there, Skippy.
Gert?
Gurt? Uh, *gesundheit?* Come on. You gonna get up or what.
I...I...
Suit yourself, loser.
But a word to the wise, sailor: the longer you lie there on the pavement, the less attractive you're gonna get.

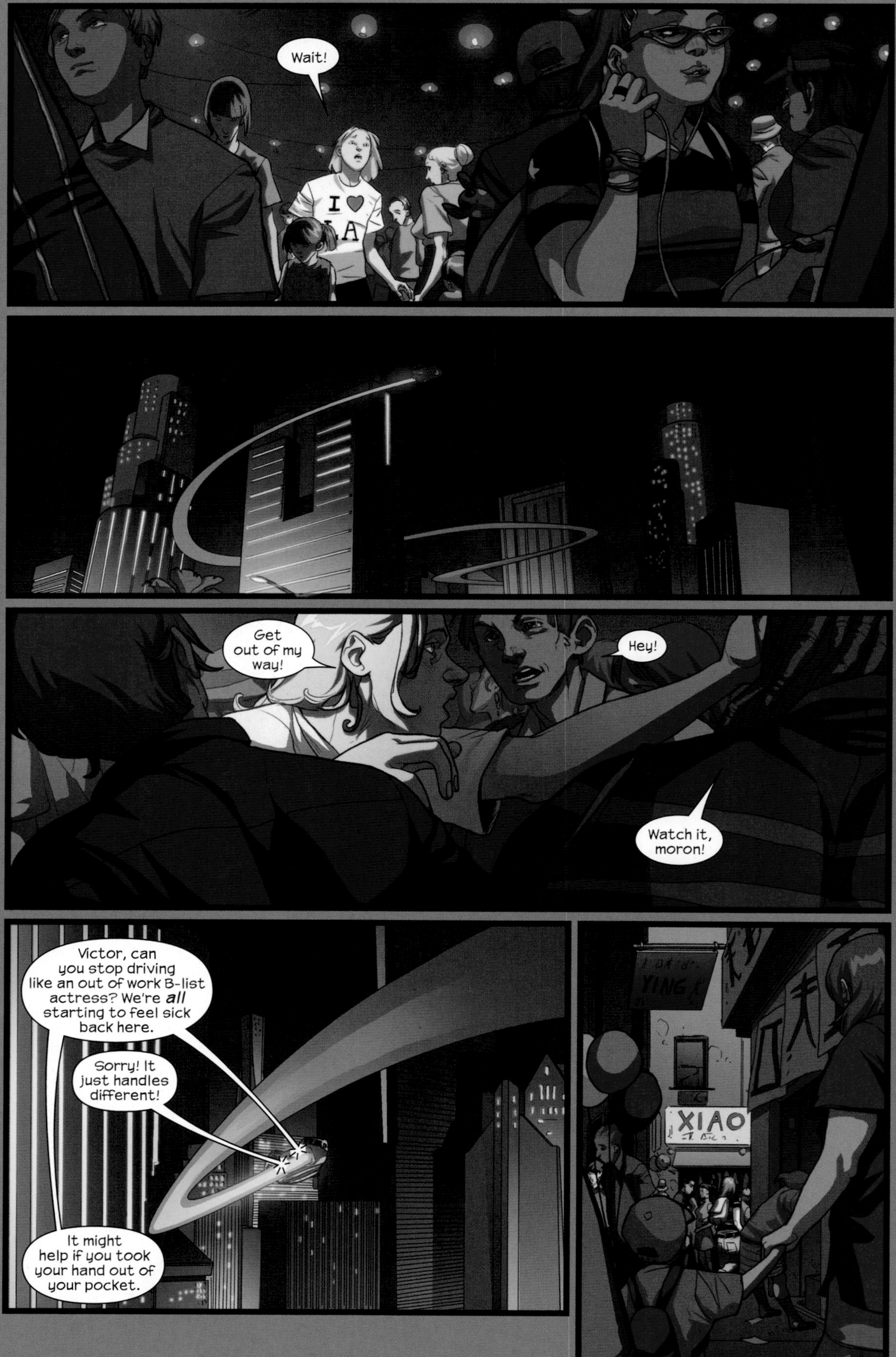
Wait!
Get out of my way!
Hey!
Watch it, moron!
Victor, can you stop driving like an out of work B-list actress? We're *all* starting to feel sick back here.
Sorry! It just handles different!
It might help if you took your hand out of your pocket.
YING
XIAO

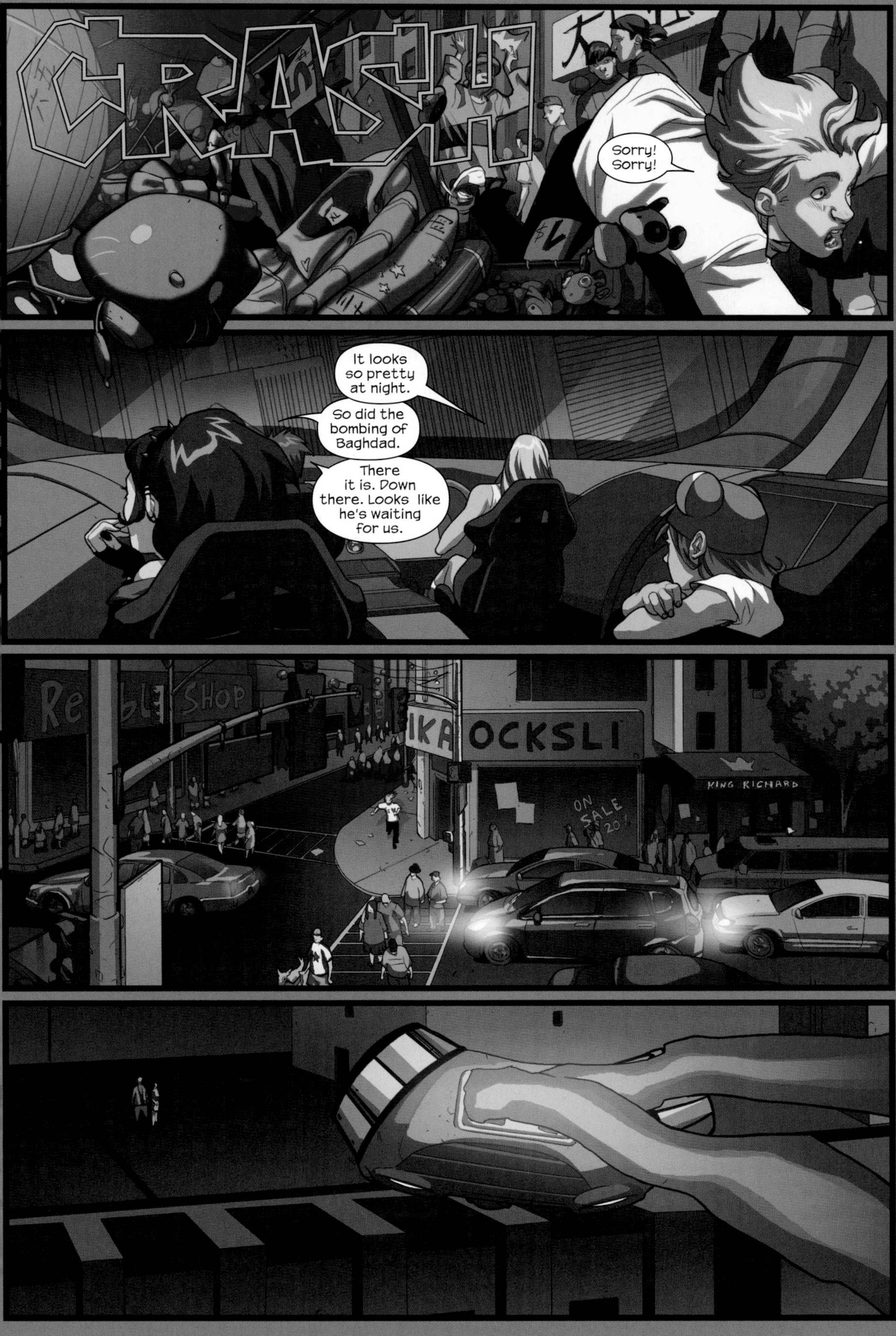
CRASH
Sorry! Sorry!
It looks so pretty at night.
So did the bombing of Baghdad.
There it is. Down there. Looks like he's waiting for us.
Re ble SHOP
IKA
OCKSLI
KING RICHARD
ON SALE 20%

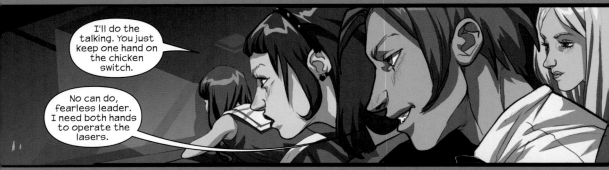

I'll do the talking. You just keep one hand on the chicken switch.

No can do, fearless leader. I need both hands to operate the lasers.

HEY! WAIT! WAIT, PLEASE! TURN AROUND!

Your lip is bleeding.

I *know*.

Is that really necessary?

The Staff of One refers to a magical object, not the Runaways operational headcount. I'd like it to stay that way.

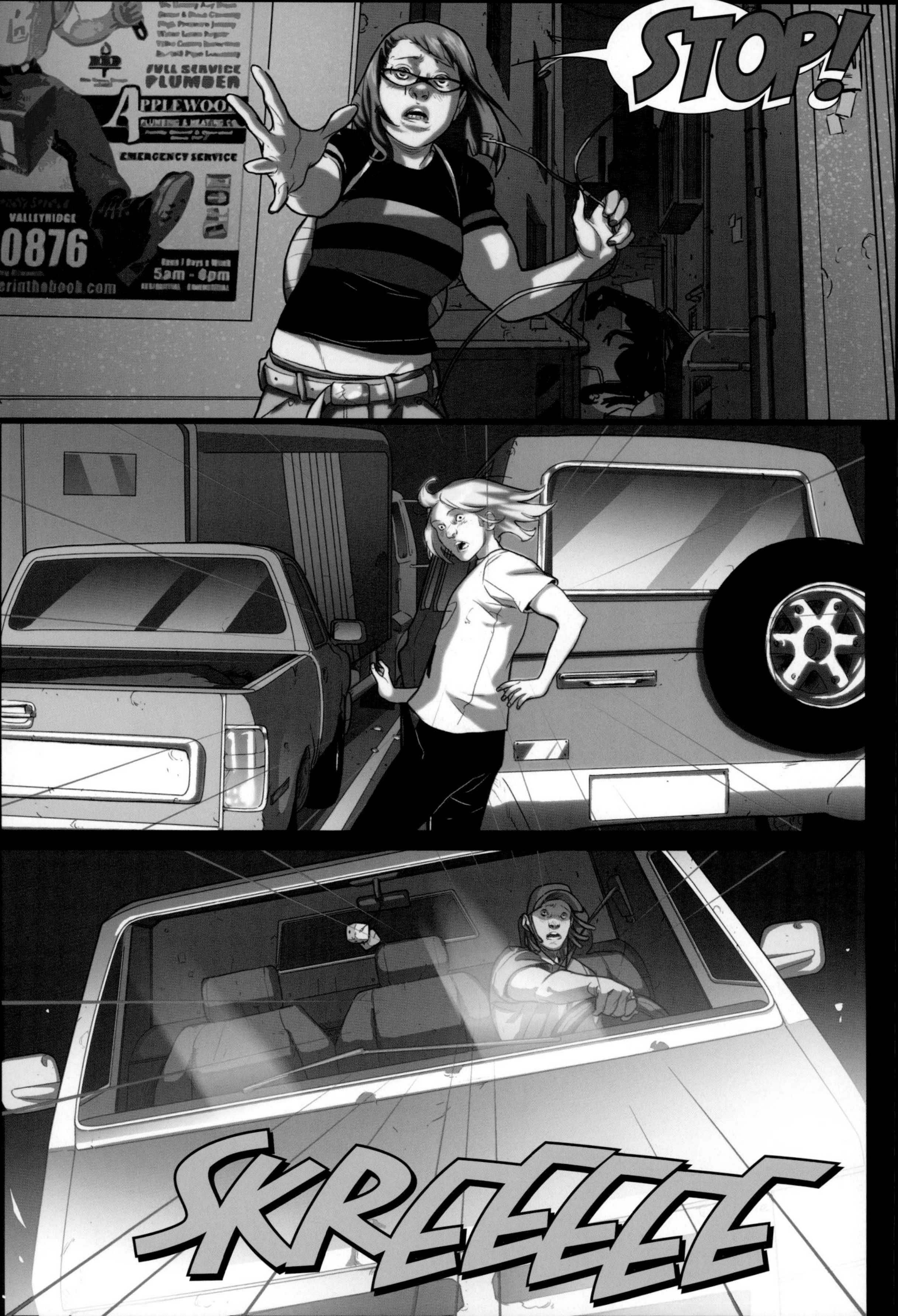
FULL SERVICE
PLUMBER
APPLEWOOD
PLUMBING & HEATING CO.
EMERGENCY SERVICE
VALLEYRIDGE
0876
5am - 6pm
STOP!
SKREEEEE

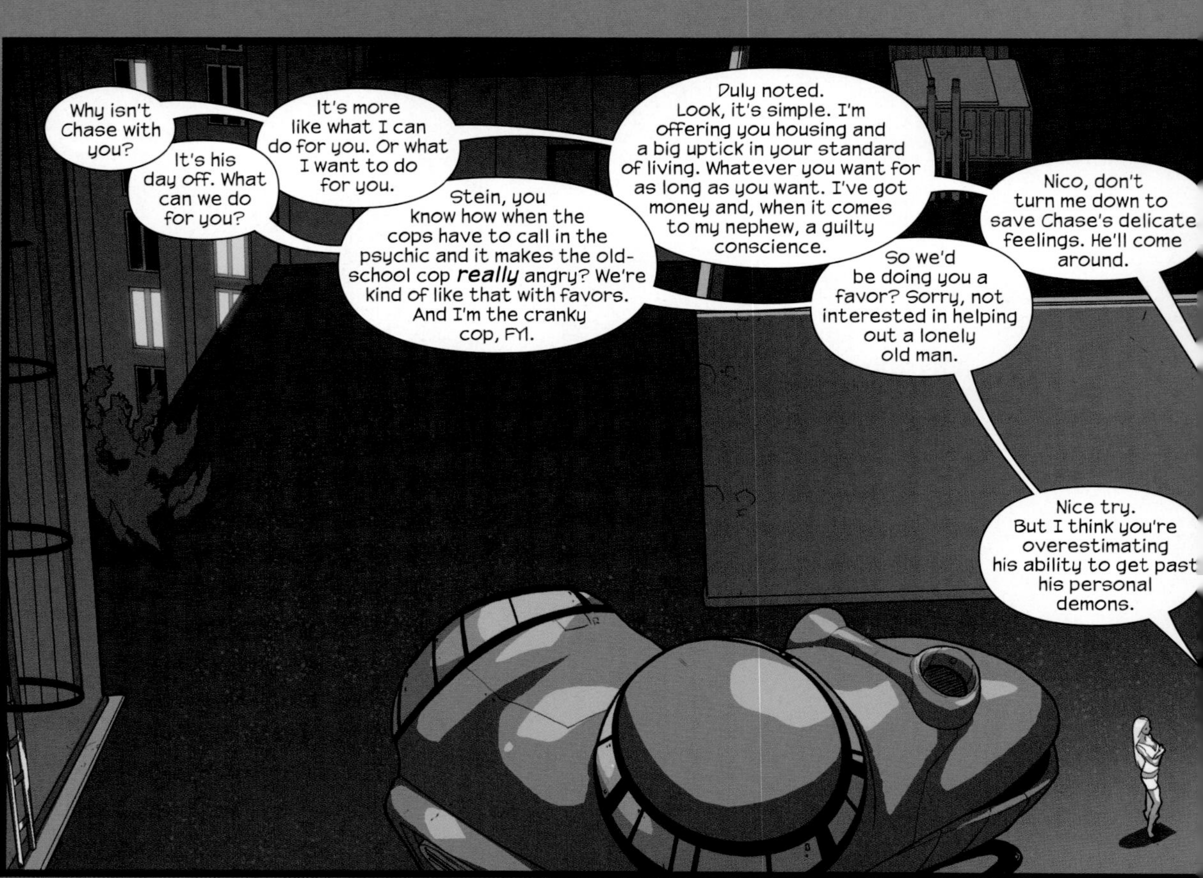
Why isn't Chase with you?
It's his day off. What can we do for you?
It's more like what I can do for you. Or what I want to do for you.
Stein, you know how when the cops have to call in the psychic and it makes the old-school cop *really* angry? We're kind of like that with favors. And I'm the cranky cop, FYI.
Duly noted. Look, it's simple. I'm offering you housing and a big uptick in your standard of living. Whatever you want for as long as you want. I've got money and, when it comes to my nephew, a guilty conscience.
So we'd be doing you a favor? Sorry, not interested in helping out a lonely old man.
Nico, don't turn me down to save Chase's delicate feelings. He'll come around.
Nice try. But I think you're overestimating his ability to get past his personal demons.

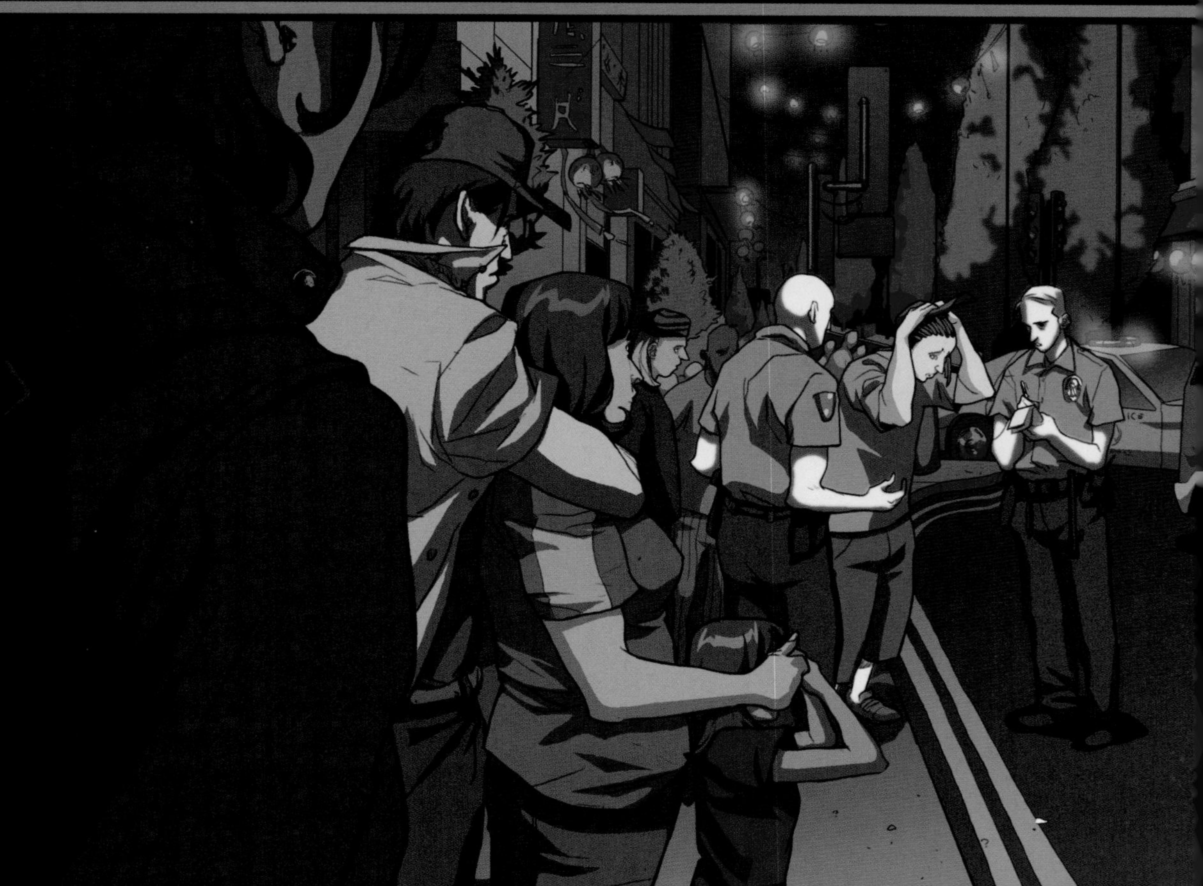

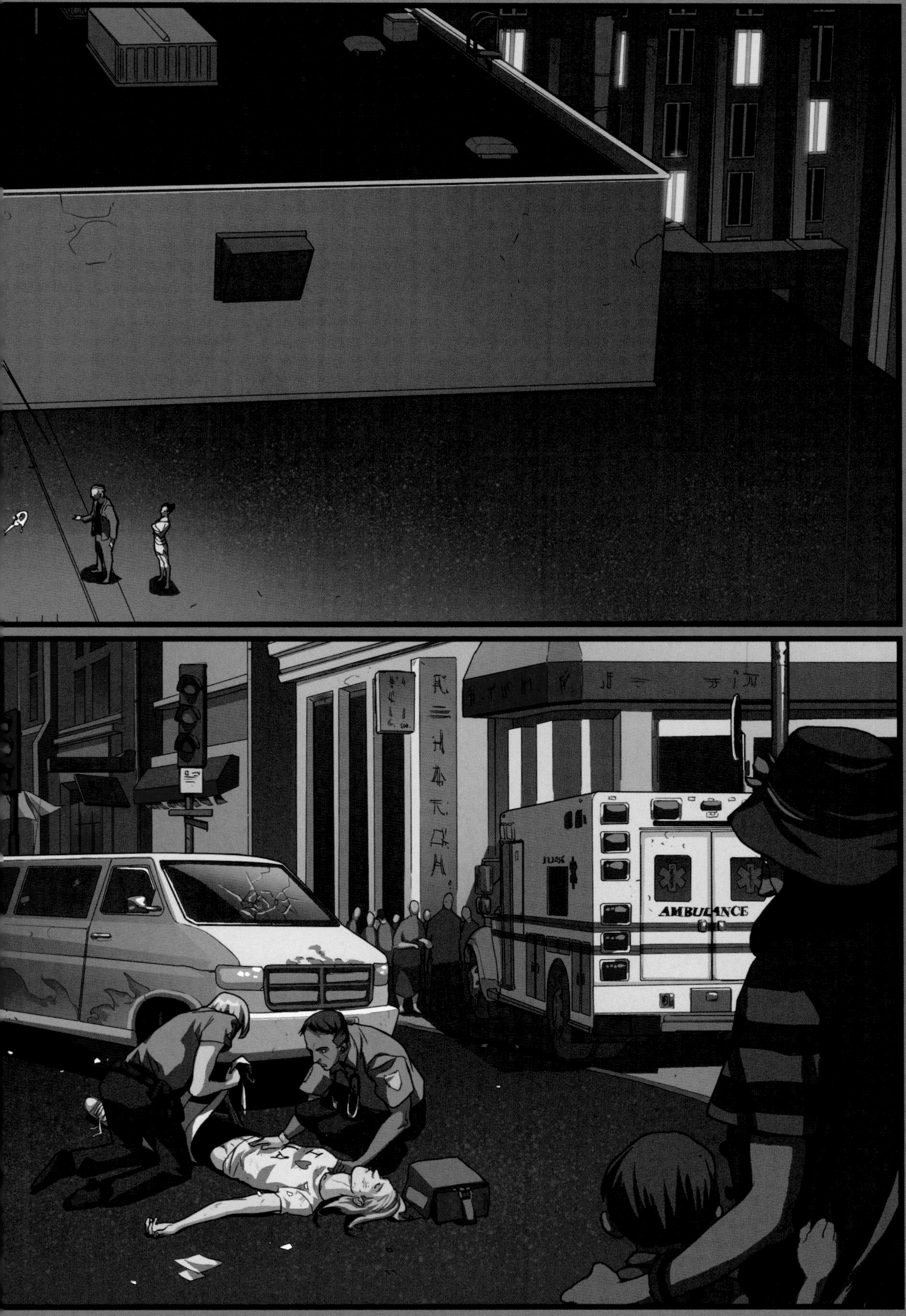
AMBULANCE

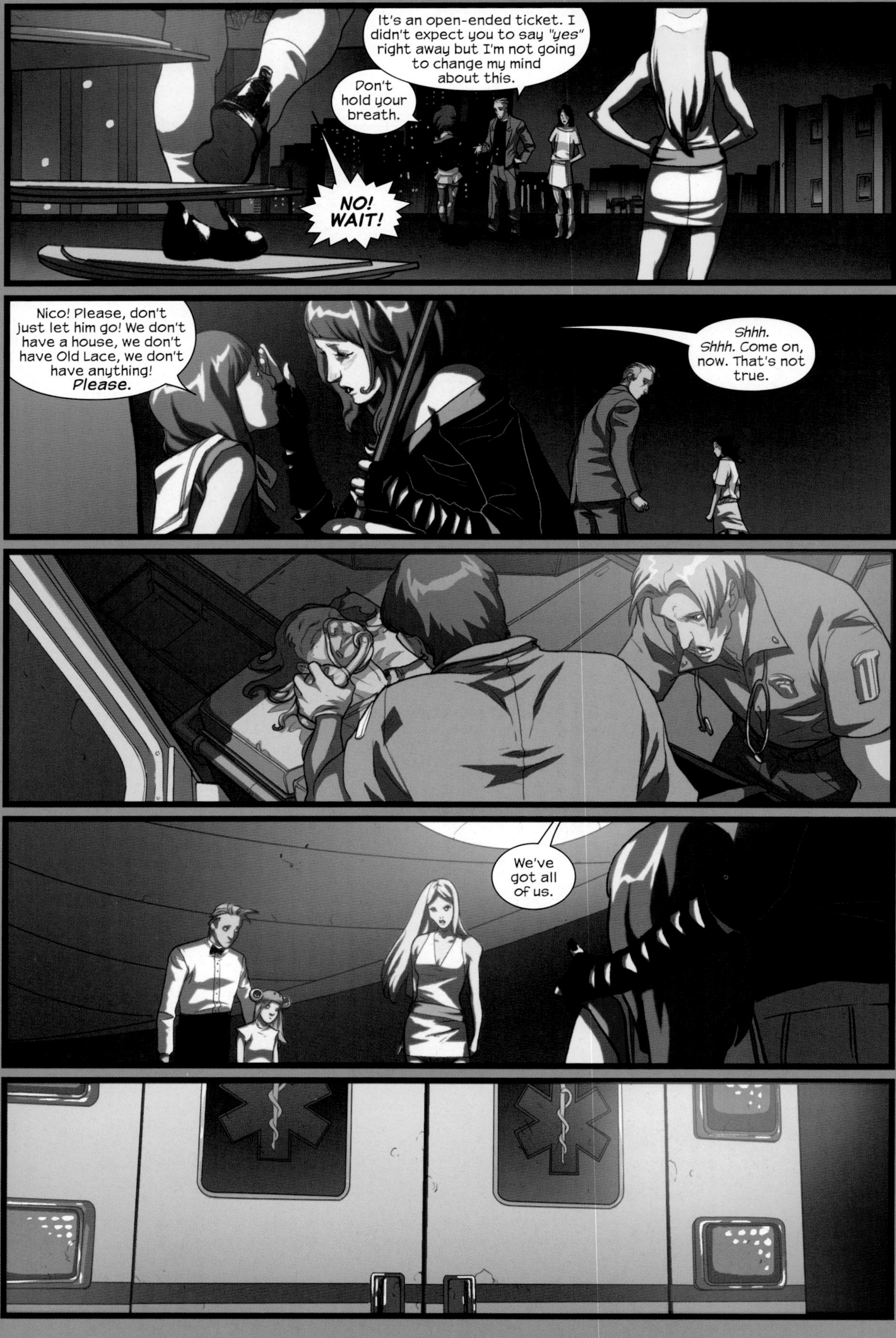
It's an open-ended ticket. I didn't expect you to say "yes" right away but I'm not going to change my mind about this.
Don't hold your breath.
NO! WAIT!
Nico! Please, don't just let him go! We don't have a house, we don't have Old Lace, we don't have anything! Please.
Shhh. Shhh. Come on, now. That's not true.
We've got all of us.

And we've got all of this.

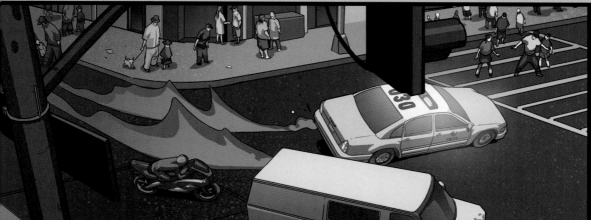

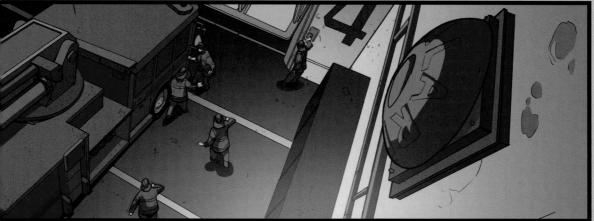

EMERGENC
ROOM

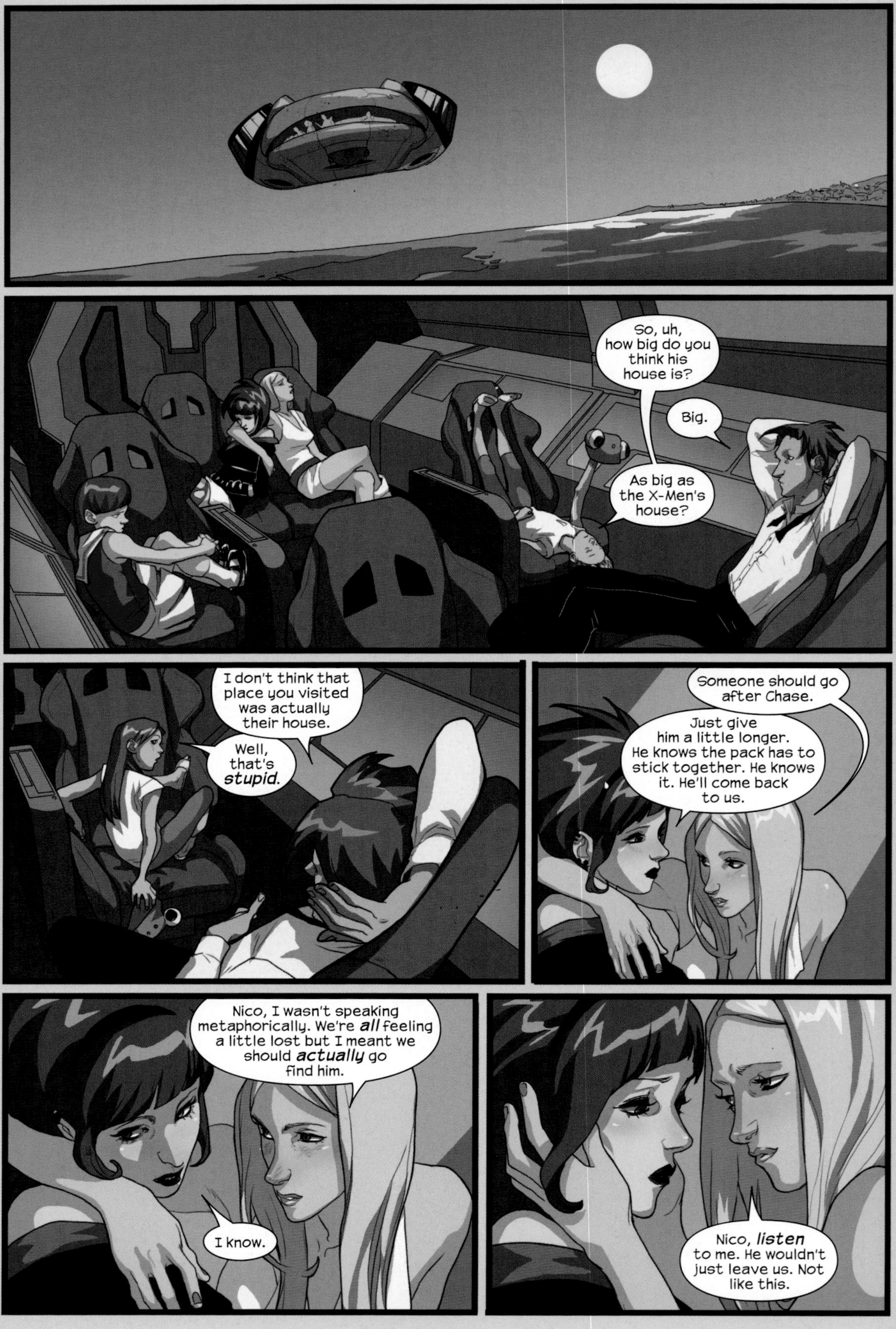
So, uh, how big do you think his house is?
Big.
As big as the X-Men's house?
I don't think that place you visited was actually their house.
Well, that's *stupid*.
Someone should go after Chase.
Just give him a little longer. He knows the pack has to stick together. He knows it. He'll come back to us.
Nico, I wasn't speaking metaphorically. We're *all* feeling a little lost but I meant we should *actually* go find him.
I know.
Nico, *listen* to me. He wouldn't just leave us. Not like this.

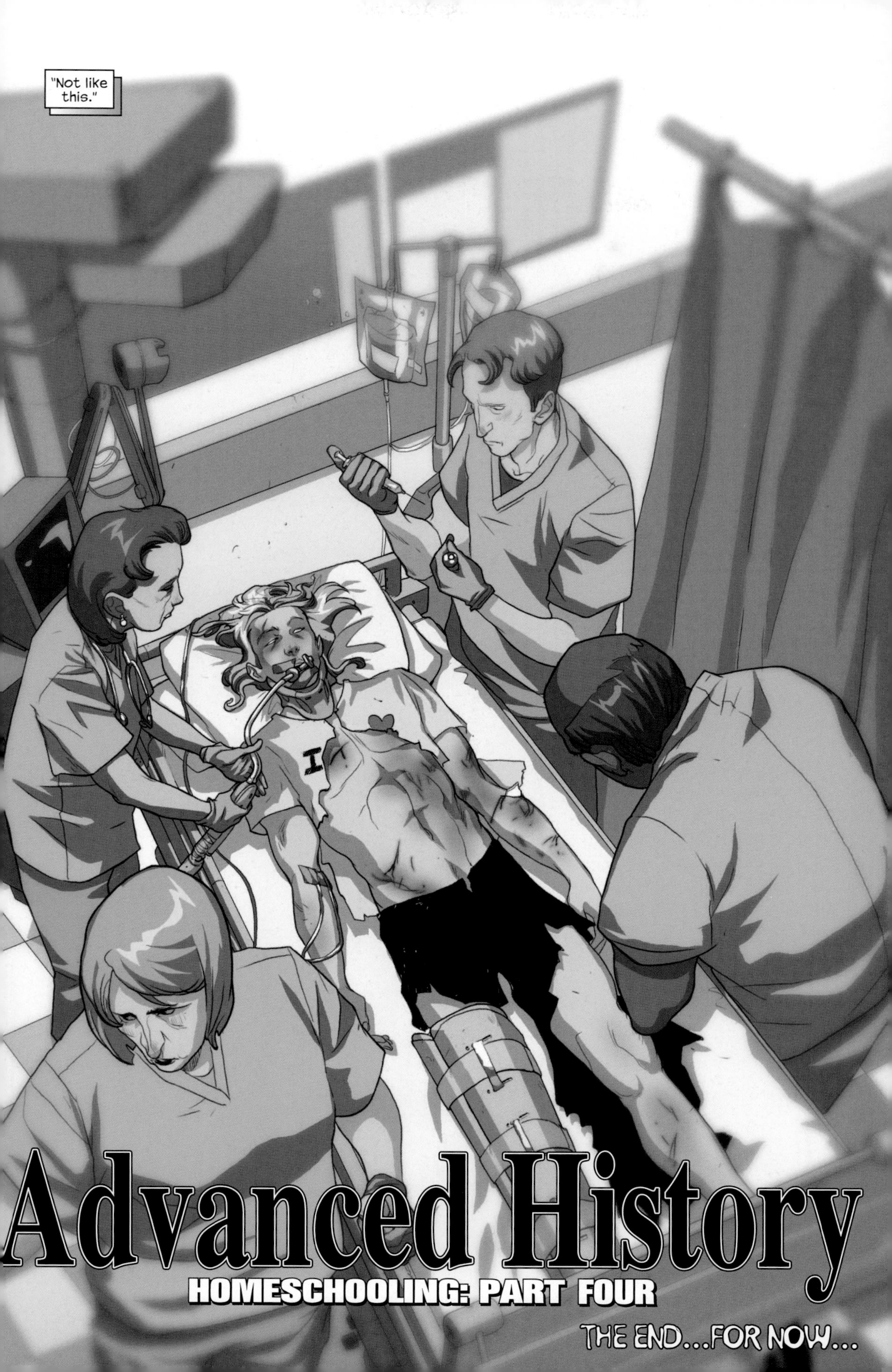
"Not like this."
Advanced History
HOMESCHOOLING: PART FOUR
THE END...FOR NOW...

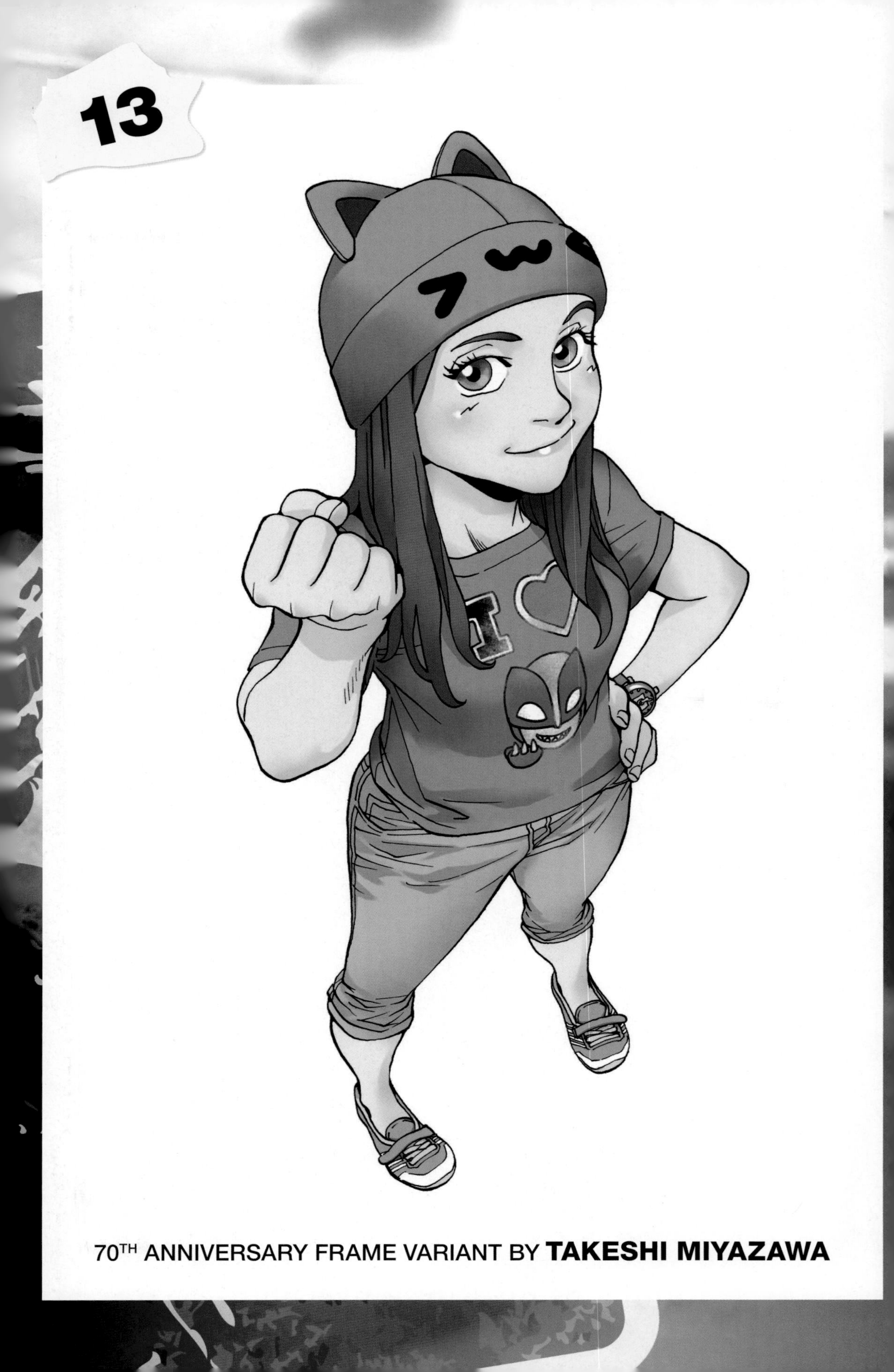
13
I

70TH ANNIVERSARY FRAME VARIANT BY **TAKESHI MIYAZAWA**

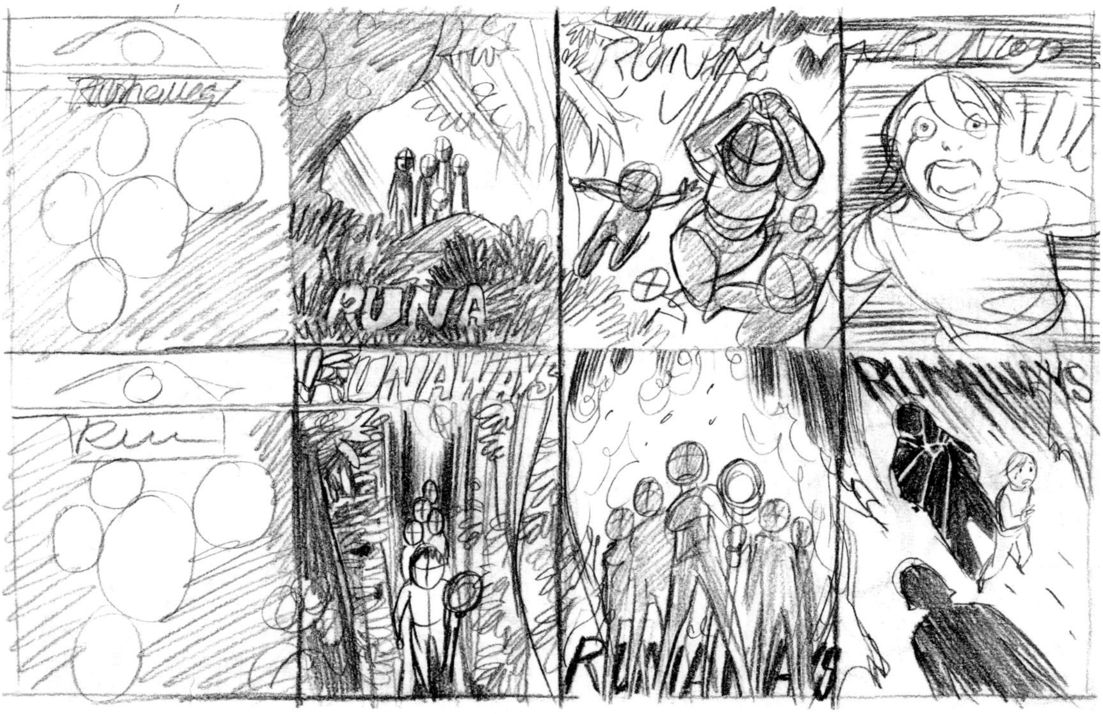
RUNA
RUNAWAYS

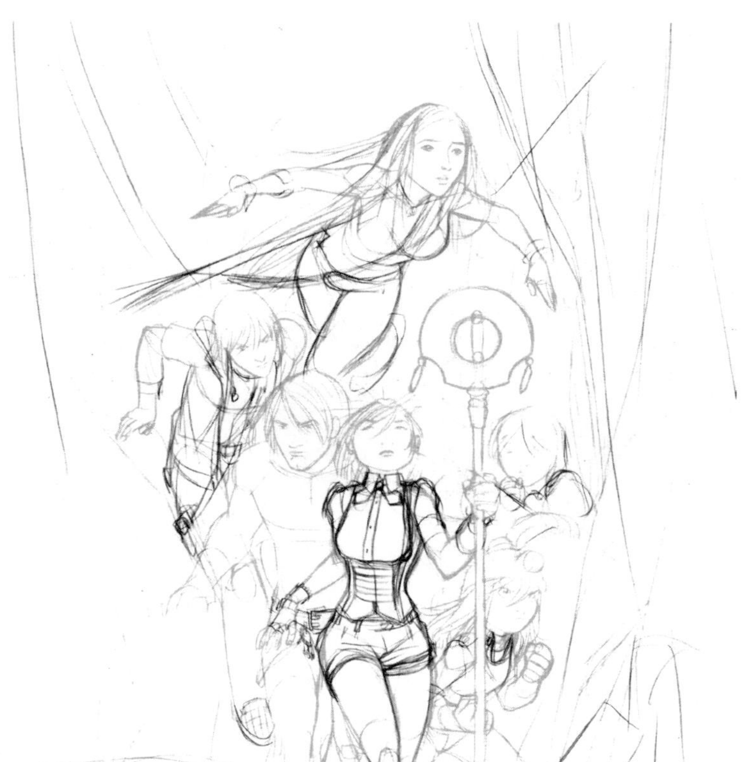

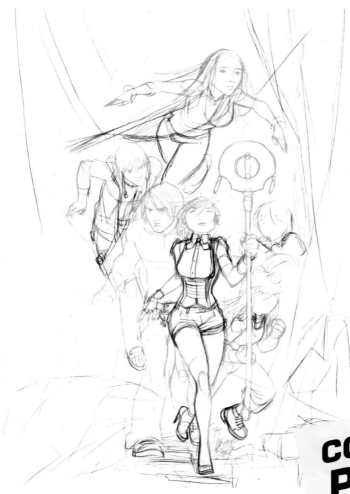

COVER #11-14 PROCESS
BY DAVID LAFUENTE

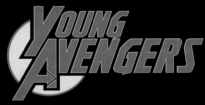

YOUNG AVENGERS

Assembled by Iron Lad (a teenaged version of the time-traveling conqueror known as Kang) Patriot, Hawkeye, Wiccan, Hulkling, Stature, Speed and the Vision are the Young Avengers, following in the footsteps of Earth's mightiest heroes!

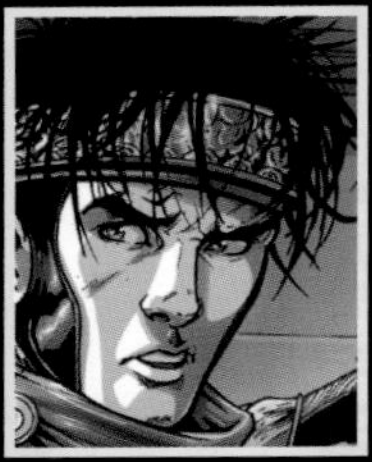
WICCAN

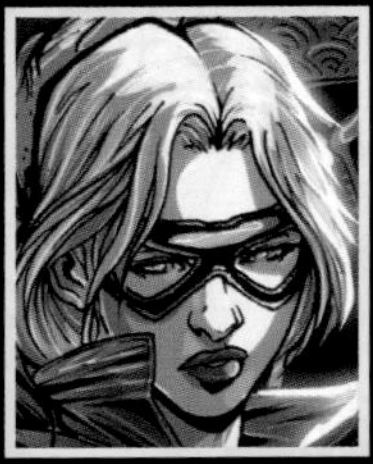
HAWKEYE

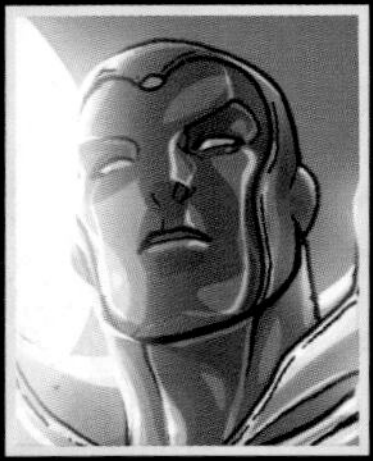
VISION

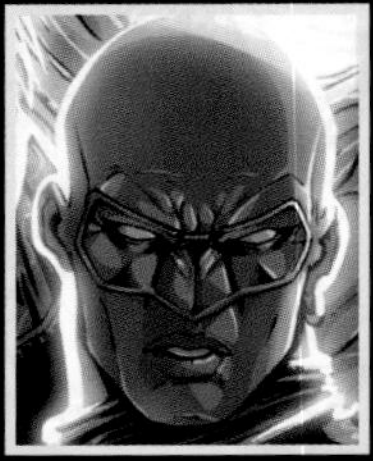
PATRIOT

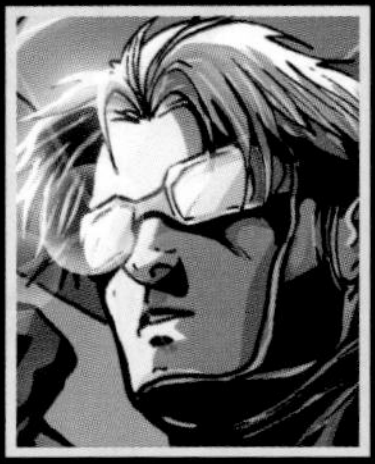
SPEED

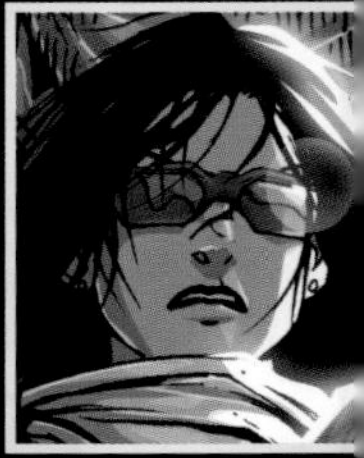
STATURE

RUNAWAYS

At some point in their lives, all kids think their parents are evil. For Molly Hayes and her friends, this is especially true, as they discover their parents are in fact a group of super-powered crime bosses called "The Pride". Using technology and resources stolen from their parents, the teens break The Pride's criminal hold on Los Angeles. But they've been on the run ever since.

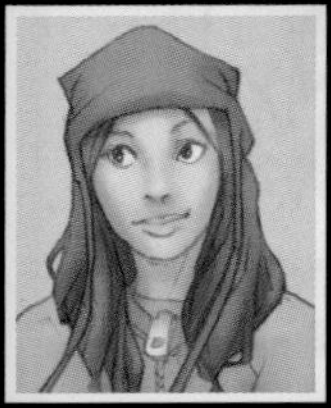
MOLLY HAYES

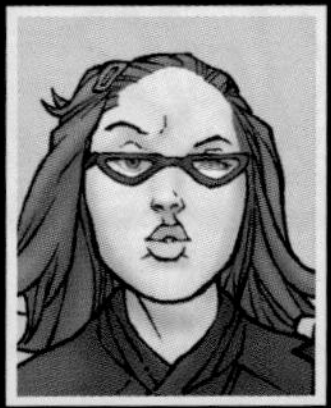
GERT STEIN

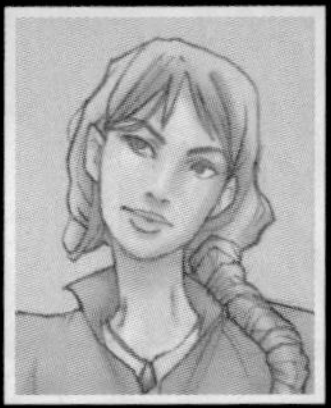
KAROLINA DEAN

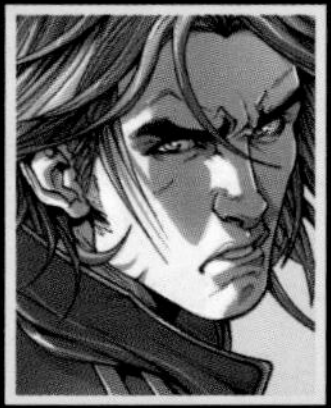
VICTOR MANCHA

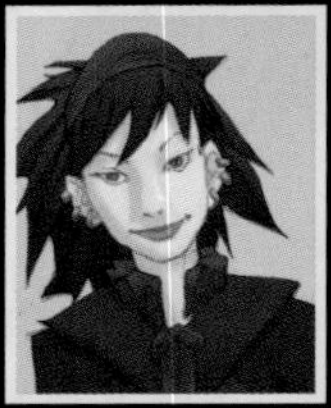
NICO MINORU

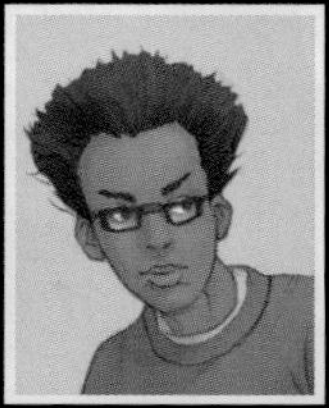
ALEX WILDER

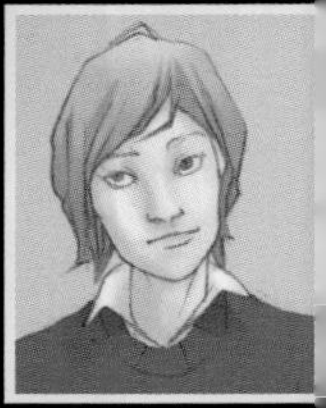
CHASE STEIN

These two teams of super-powered teens have crossed paths before in troubled times, but what if fate proposed a different path for the fledgling heroes? What if their destinities were intertwined in ways they could never be prepared for? What if... the Runaways became the Young Avengers?!

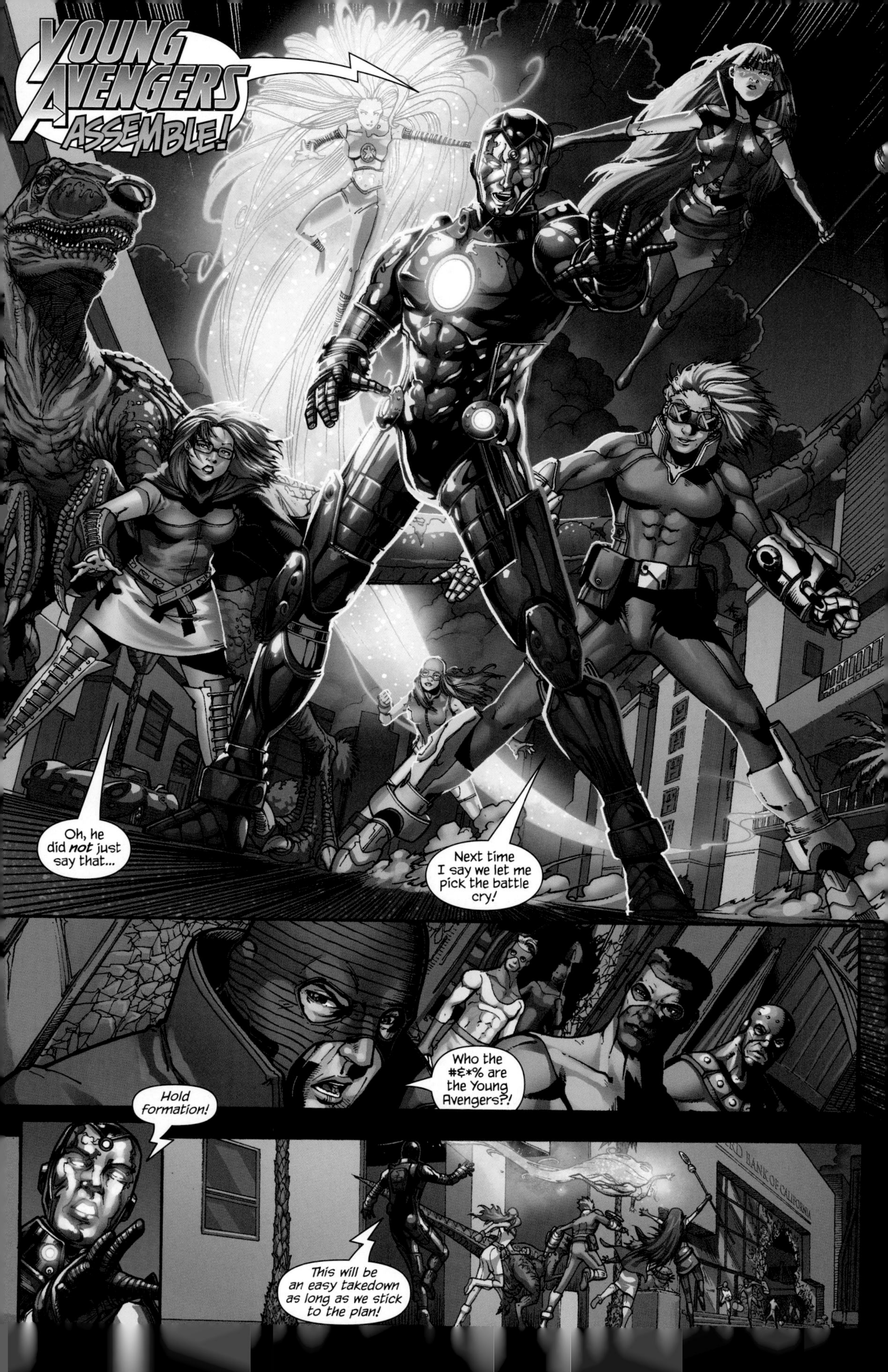
YOUNG AVENGERS ASSEMBLE!
Oh, he did *not* just say that...
Next time I say we let me pick the battle cry!
Who the #£*% are the Young Avengers?!
Hold formation!
This will be an easy takedown as long as we stick to the plan!

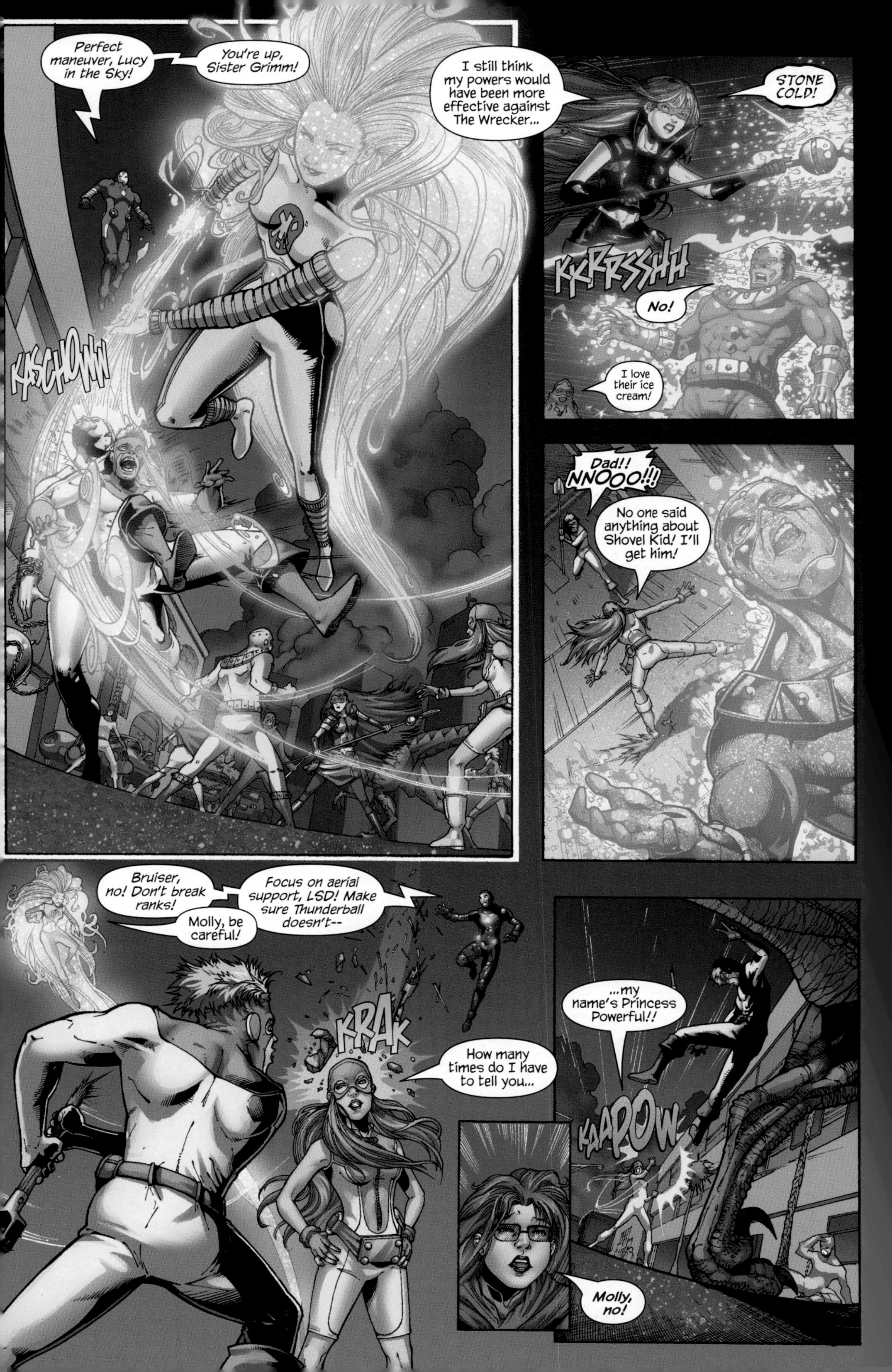

Perfect maneuver, Lucy in the Sky!
You're up, Sister Grimm!
KASCHOWW
I still think my powers would have been more effective against The Wrecker...
STONE COLD!
KKRRSSHH
No!
I love their ice cream!
Dad!! NNOOO!!!
No one said anything about Shovel Kid! I'll get him!
Bruiser, no! Don't break ranks!
Focus on aerial support, LSD! Make sure Thunderball doesn't--
Molly, be careful!
KRAK
How many times do I have to tell you...
...my name's Princess Powerful!!
KAAPOW
Molly, no!

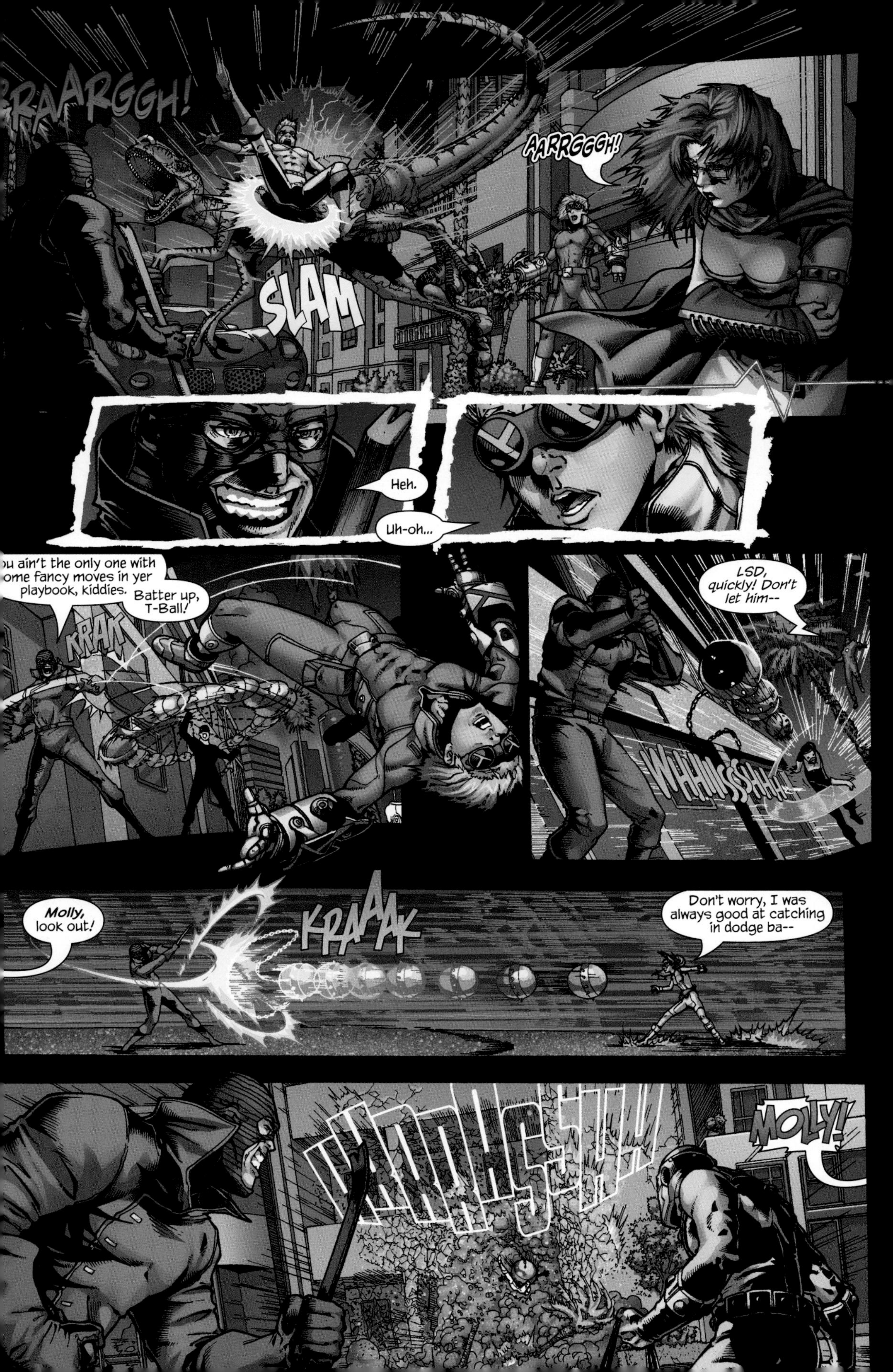
BRAARGGH!
SLAM
AARRGGGH!
Heh.
Uh-oh...
ou ain't the only one with
ome fancy moves in yer
playbook, kiddies.
Batter up, T-Ball!
KRAK
LSD, quickly! Don't let him--
WHHHSSHHH
Molly, look out!
KRAAAK
Don't worry, I was always good at catching in dodge ba--
MOLLY!

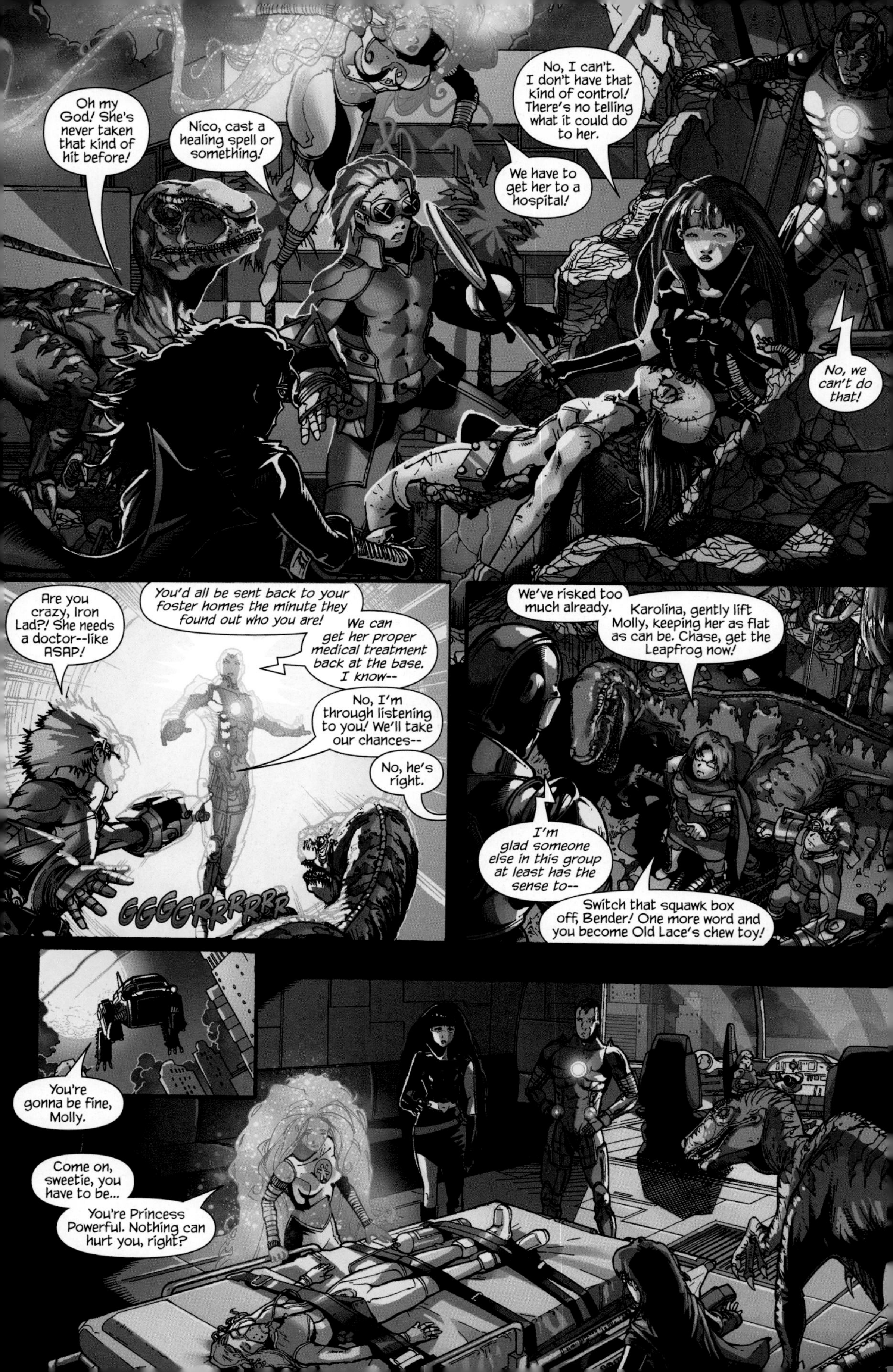
Oh my God! She's never taken that kind of hit before!
Nico, cast a healing spell or something!
No, I can't. I don't have that kind of control! There's no telling what it could do to her.
We have to get her to a hospital!
No, we can't do that!
Are you crazy, Iron Lad?! She needs a doctor--like ASAP!
You'd all be sent back to your foster homes the minute they found out who you are!
We can get her proper medical treatment back at the base. I know--
No, I'm through listening to you! We'll take our chances--
No, he's right.
GGGGRRRRRR
We've risked too much already.
Karolina, gently lift Molly, keeping her as flat as can be. Chase, get the Leapfrog now!
I'm glad someone else in this group at least has the sense to--
Switch that squawk box off, Bender! One more word and you become Old Lace's chew toy!
You're gonna be fine, Molly.
Come on, sweetie, you have to be...
You're Princess Powerful. Nothing can hurt you, right?

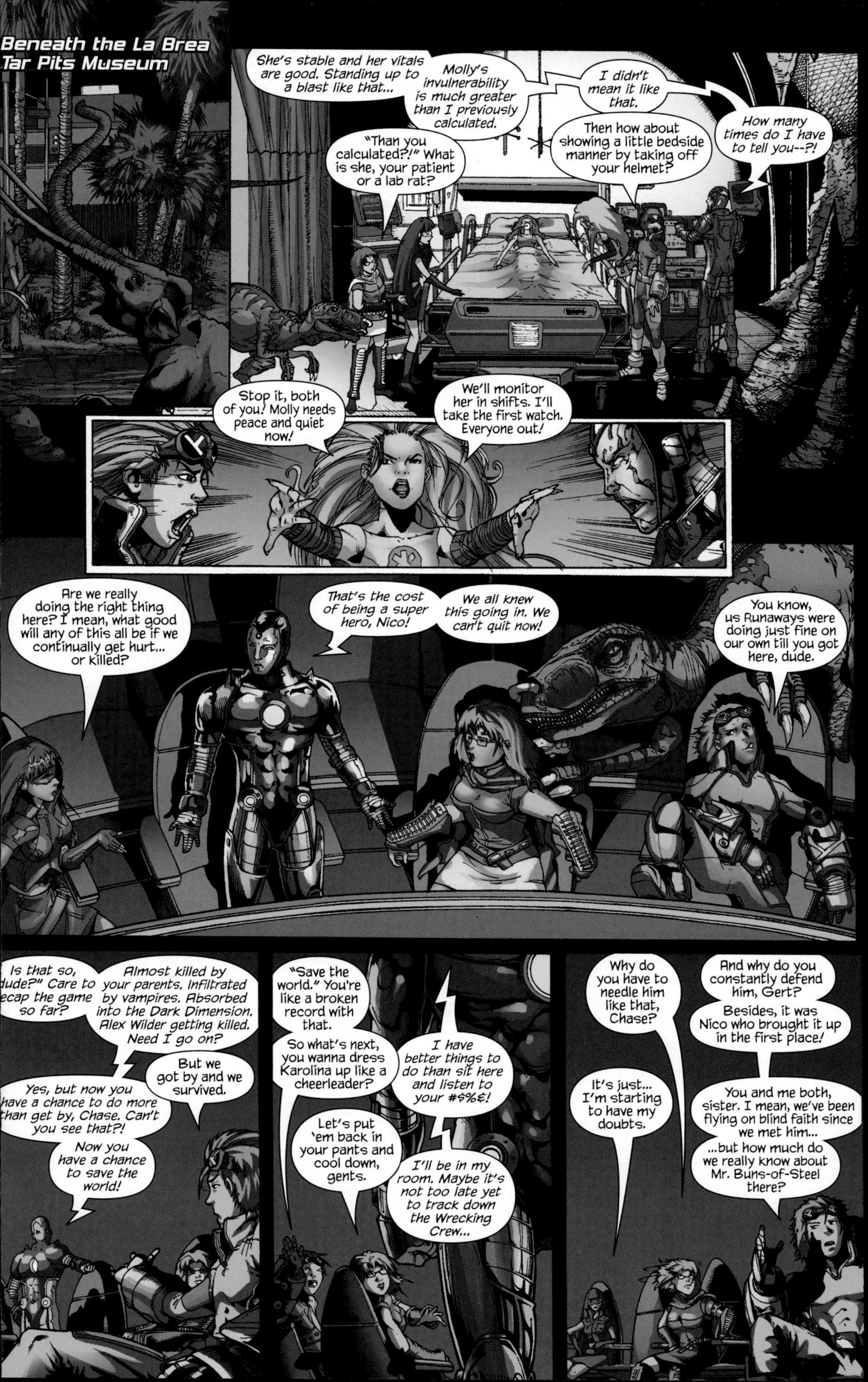
Beneath the La Brea Tar Pits Museum
She's stable and her vitals are good. Standing up to a blast like that...
Molly's invulnerability is much greater than I previously calculated.
"Than you calculated?!" What is she, your patient or a lab rat?
I didn't mean it like that.
Then how about showing a little bedside manner by taking off your helmet?
How many times do I have to tell you--?!
Stop it, both of you! Molly needs peace and quiet now!
We'll monitor her in shifts. I'll take the first watch. Everyone out!
Are we really doing the right thing here? I mean, what good will any of this all be if we continually get hurt... or killed?
That's the cost of being a super hero, Nico!
We all knew this going in. We can't quit now!
You know, us Runaways were doing just fine on our own till you got here, dude.
Is that so, dude?" Care to recap the game so far?
Almost killed by your parents. Infiltrated by vampires. Absorbed into the Dark Dimension. Alex Wilder getting killed. Need I go on?
But we got by and we survived.
Yes, but now you have a chance to do more than get by, Chase. Can't you see that?!
Now you have a chance to save the world!
"Save the world." You're like a broken record with that.
So what's next, you wanna dress Karolina up like a cheerleader?
I have better things to do than sit here and listen to your #$%&!
Let's put 'em back in your pants and cool down, gents.
I'll be in my room. Maybe it's not too late yet to track down the Wrecking Crew...
Why do you have to needle him like that, Chase?
It's just... I'm starting to have my doubts.
And why do you constantly defend him, Gert?
Besides, it was Nico who brought it up in the first place!
You and me both, sister. I mean, we've been flying on blind faith since we met him...
...but how much do we really know about Mr. Buns-of-Steel there?

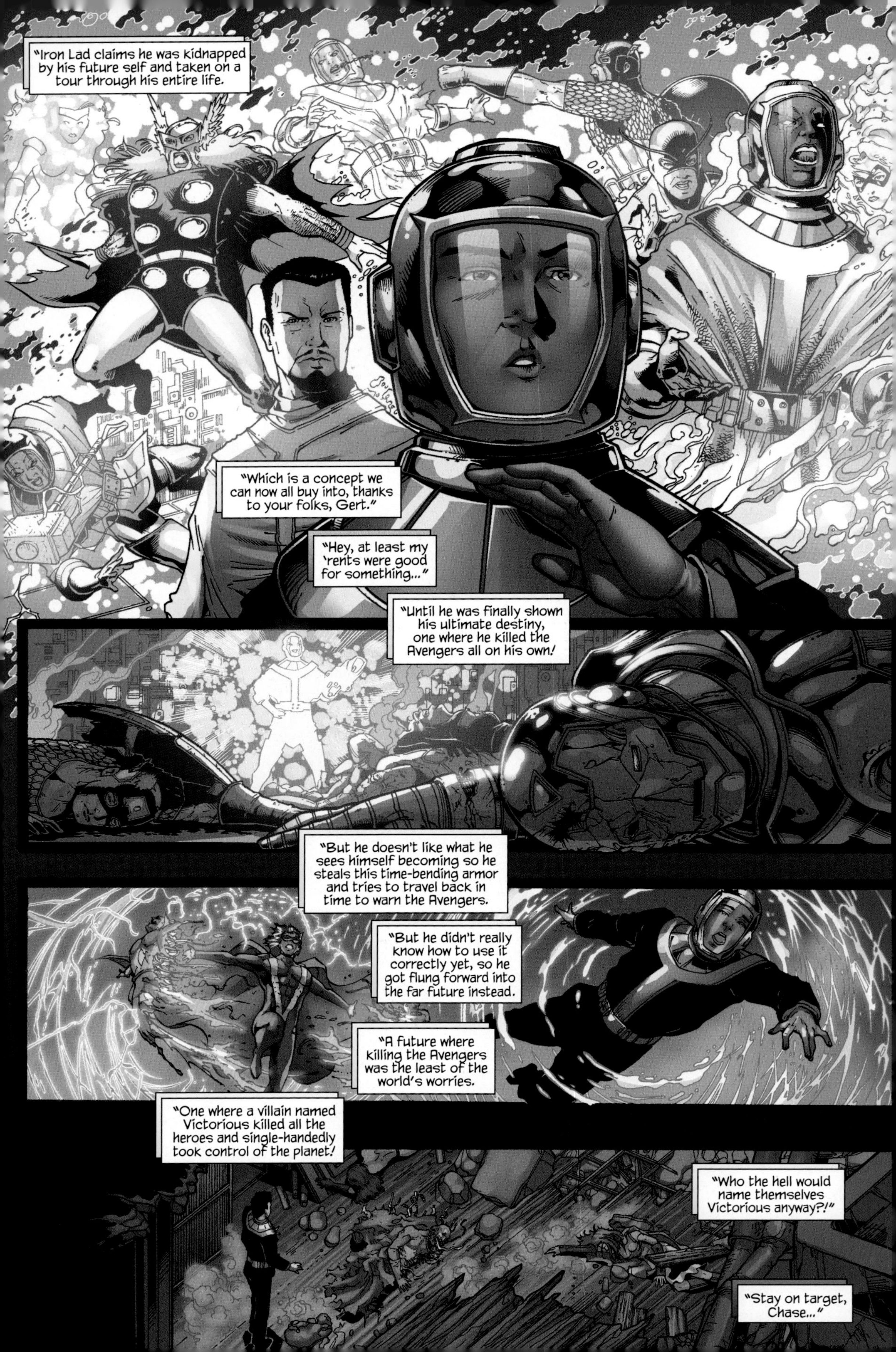
"Iron Lad claims he was kidnapped by his future self and taken on a tour through his entire life.
"Which is a concept we can now all buy into, thanks to your folks, Gert."
"Hey, at least my 'rents were good for something..."
"Until he was finally shown his ultimate destiny, one where he killed the Avengers all on his own!
"But he doesn't like what he sees himself becoming so he steals this time-bending armor and tries to travel back in time to warn the Avengers.
"But he didn't really know how to use it correctly yet, so he got flung forward into the far future instead.
"A future where killing the Avengers was the least of the world's worries.
"One where a villain named Victorious killed all the heroes and single-handedly took control of the planet!
"Who the hell would name themselves Victorious anyway?!"
"Stay on target, Chase..."

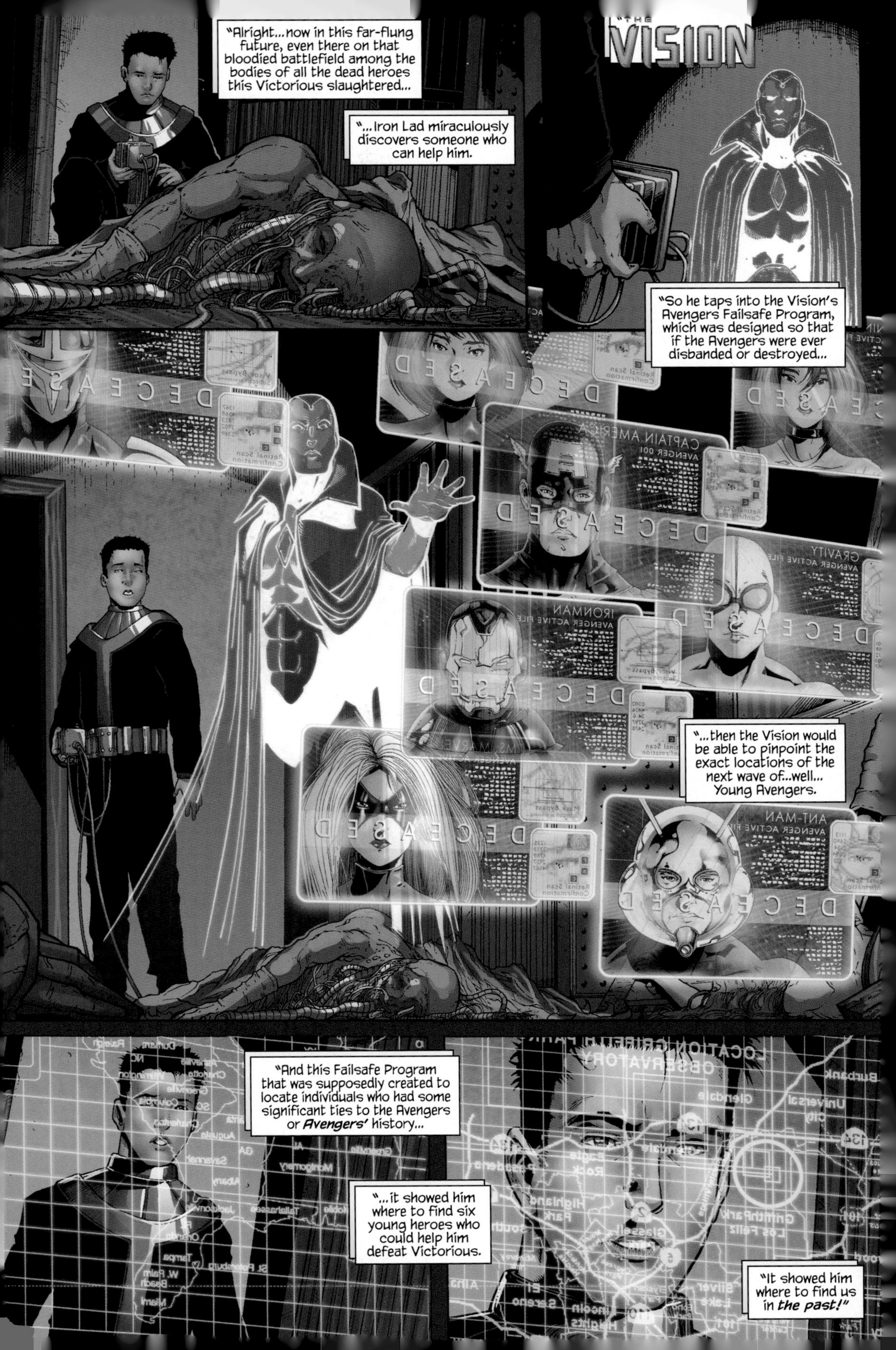
"Alright...now in this far-flung future, even there on that bloodied battlefield among the bodies of all the dead heroes this Victorious slaughtered...
"...Iron Lad miraculously discovers someone who can help him.
THE VISION
"So he taps into the Vision's Avengers Failsafe Program, which was designed so that if the Avengers were ever disbanded or destroyed...
"...then the Vision would be able to pinpoint the exact locations of the next wave of...well... Young Avengers.
"And this Failsafe Program that was supposedly created to locate individuals who had some significant ties to the Avengers or *Avengers'* history...
"...it showed him where to find six young heroes who could help him defeat Victorious.
"It showed him where to find us in *the past!*"

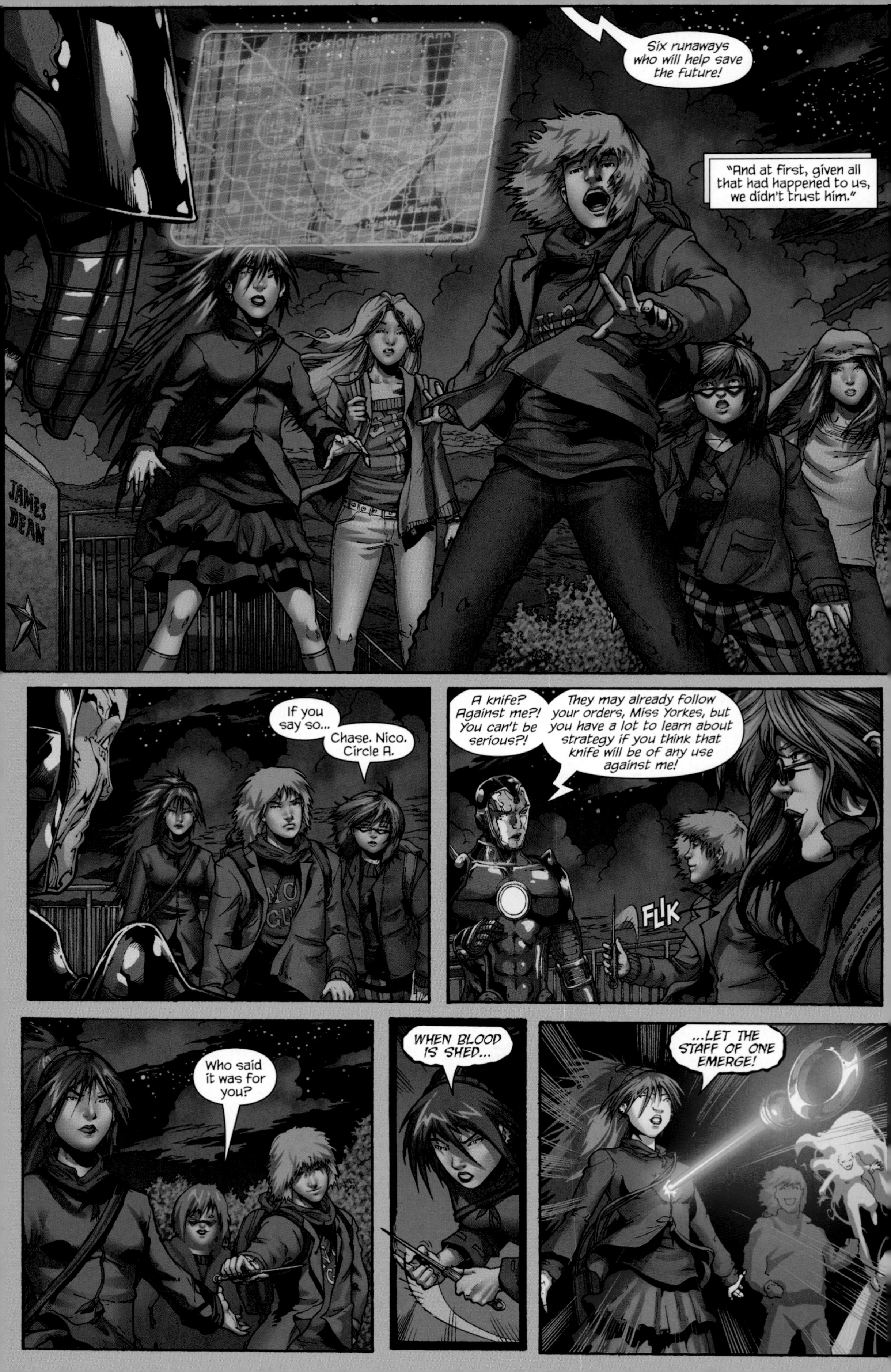

Six runaways who will help save the future!
"And at first, given all that had happened to us, we didn't trust him."
JAMES DEAN
If you say so...
Chase. Nico. Circle A.
A knife? Against me?! You can't be serious?!
They may already follow your orders, Miss Yorkes, but you have a lot to learn about strategy if you think that knife will be of any use against me!
FLIK
Who said it was for you?
WHEN BLOOD IS SHED...
...LET THE STAFF OF ONE EMERGE!

POPSICLE.

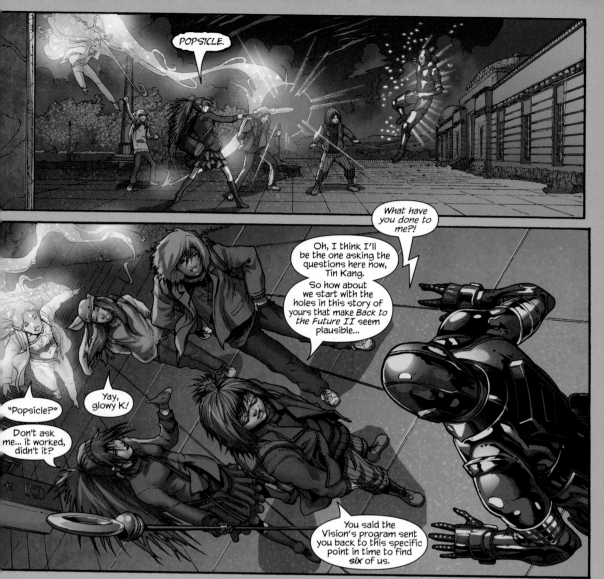

What have you done to me?!

Oh, I think I'll be the one asking the questions here now, Tin Kang.

So how about we start with the holes in this story of yours that make *Back to the Future II* seem plausible...

"Popsicle?"

Don't ask me... it worked, didn't it?

Yay, glowy K!

You said the Vision's program sent you back to this specific point in time to find *six* of us.

So I guess you can't count or were expecting Alex Wilder to still be with us.

Which, either way, means you're seriously mistaken.

I'm well aware of the fact that Alex Wilder is dead.

Whoever said I was looking for only humans?

If you'd have let me finish, I could've simply told you that the sixth hero is...

...Old Lace!

Your missing pet dinosaur, Gertrude.

First off, she's a velociraptor.

Secondly, if you're trying to play me by using her name to get--

Why would I do that? It's in my best interests to reunite you all as quickly as possible.

You know where they took her? You can take me to her?

If it will help convince you that I'm telling the truth... gladly.

Then let's get you unfrozen so you can lead on, McDuff!

Interesting choice of words, Macbeth's last...

And I'll make sure you speak *yours* if you're lying to me!

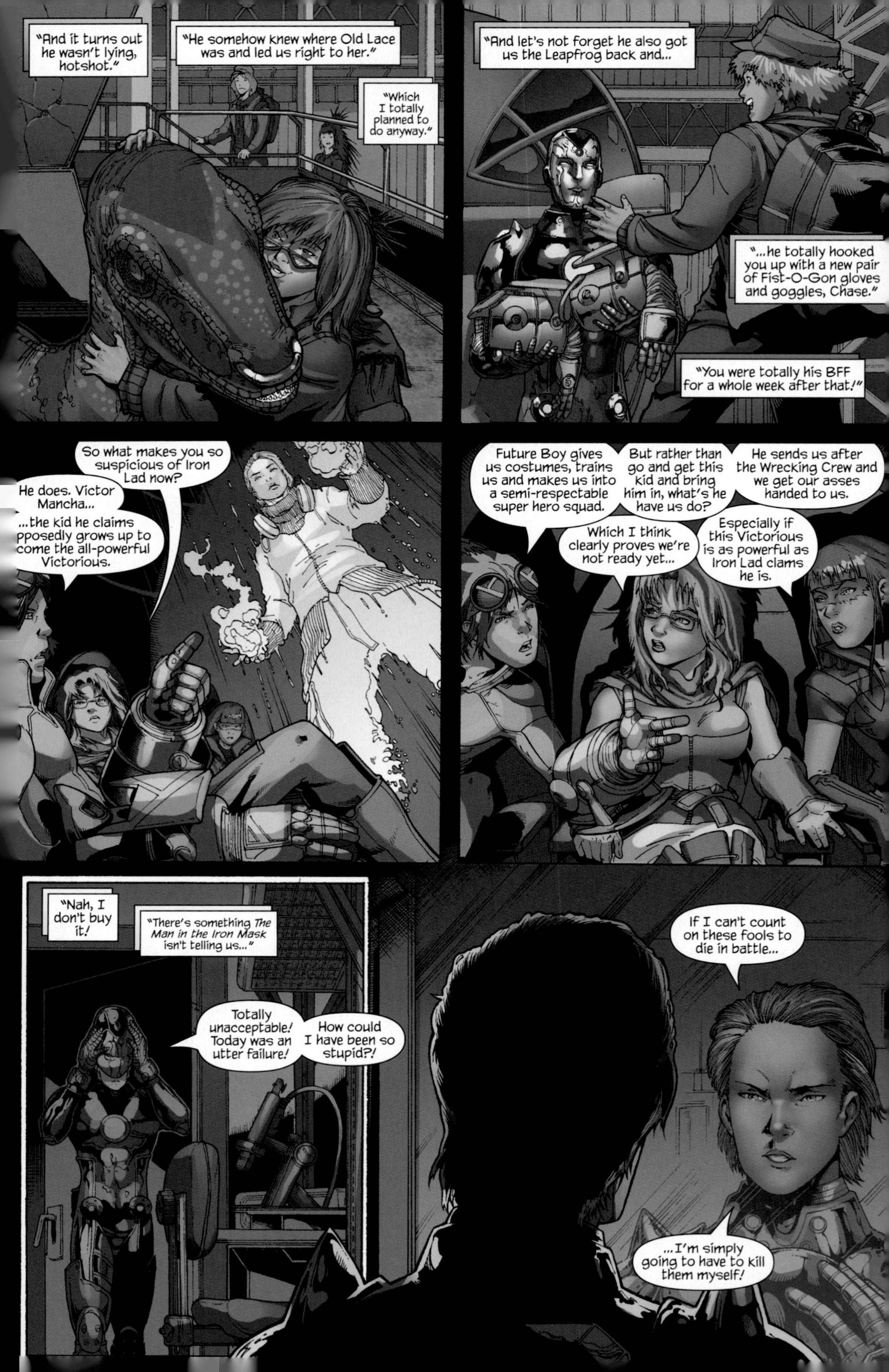

"And it turns out he wasn't lying, hotshot."
"He somehow knew where Old Lace was and led us right to her."
"Which I totally planned to do anyway."
"And let's not forget he also got us the Leapfrog back and...
"...he totally hooked you up with a new pair of Fist-O-Gon gloves and goggles, Chase."
"You were totally his BFF for a whole week after that!"
So what makes you so suspicious of Iron Lad now?
He does. Victor Mancha...
...the kid he claims pposedly grows up to come the all-powerful Victorious.
Future Boy gives us costumes, trains us and makes us into a semi-respectable super hero squad.
But rather than go and get this kid and bring him in, what's he have us do?
He sends us after the Wrecking Crew and we get our asses handed to us.
Which I think clearly proves we're not ready yet...
Especially if this Victorious is as powerful as Iron Lad clams he is.
"Nah, I don't buy it!
"There's something *The Man in the Iron Mask* isn't telling us..."
Totally unacceptable! Today was an utter failure!
How could I have been so stupid?!
If I can't count on these fools to die in battle...
...I'm simply going to have to kill them myself!

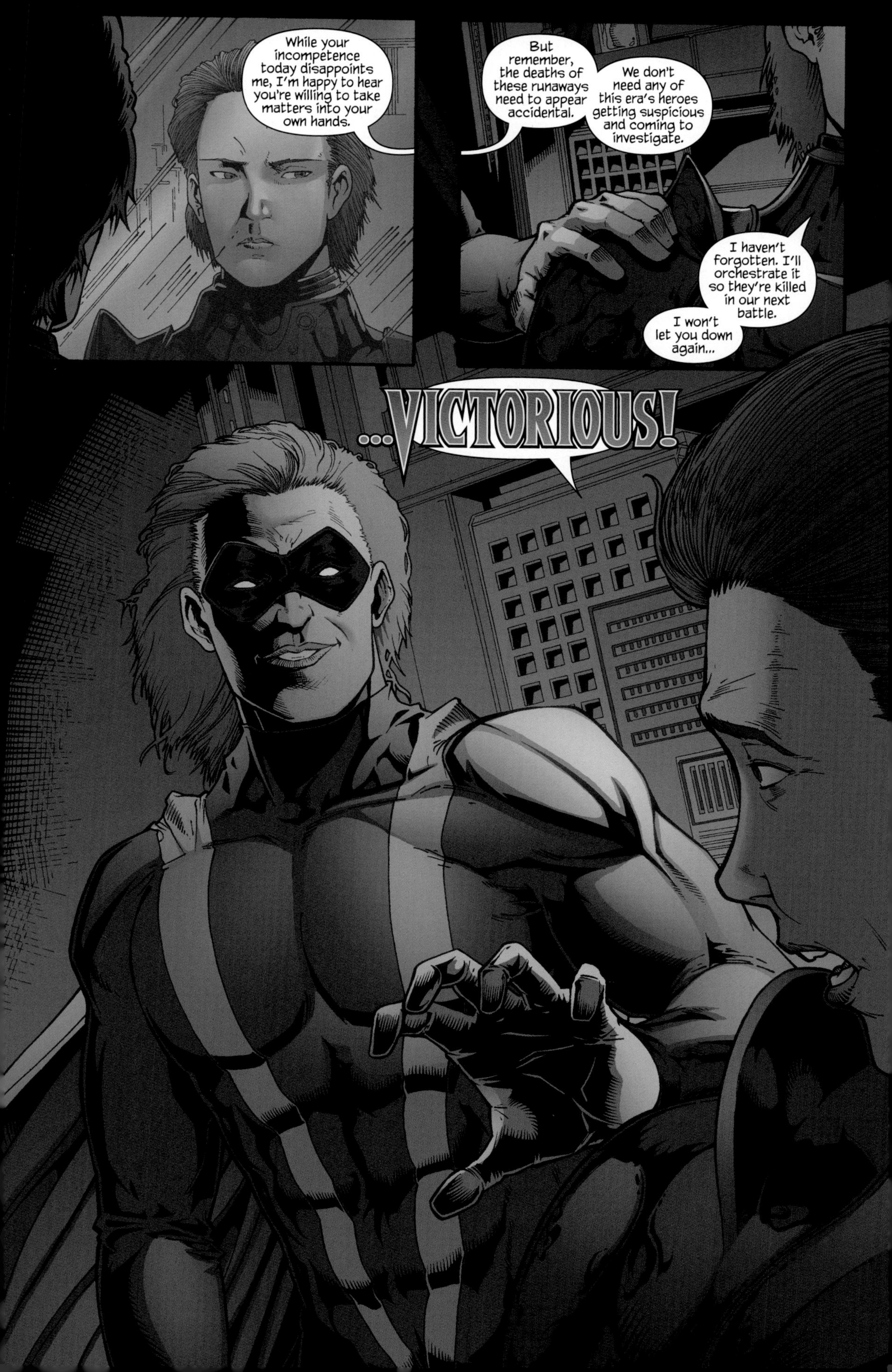
While your incompetence today disappoints me, I'm happy to hear you're willing to take matters into your own hands.
But remember, the deaths of these runaways need to appear accidental.
We don't need any of this era's heroes getting suspicious and coming to investigate.
I haven't forgotten. I'll orchestrate it so they're killed in our next battle.
I won't let you down again...
...VICTORIOUS!

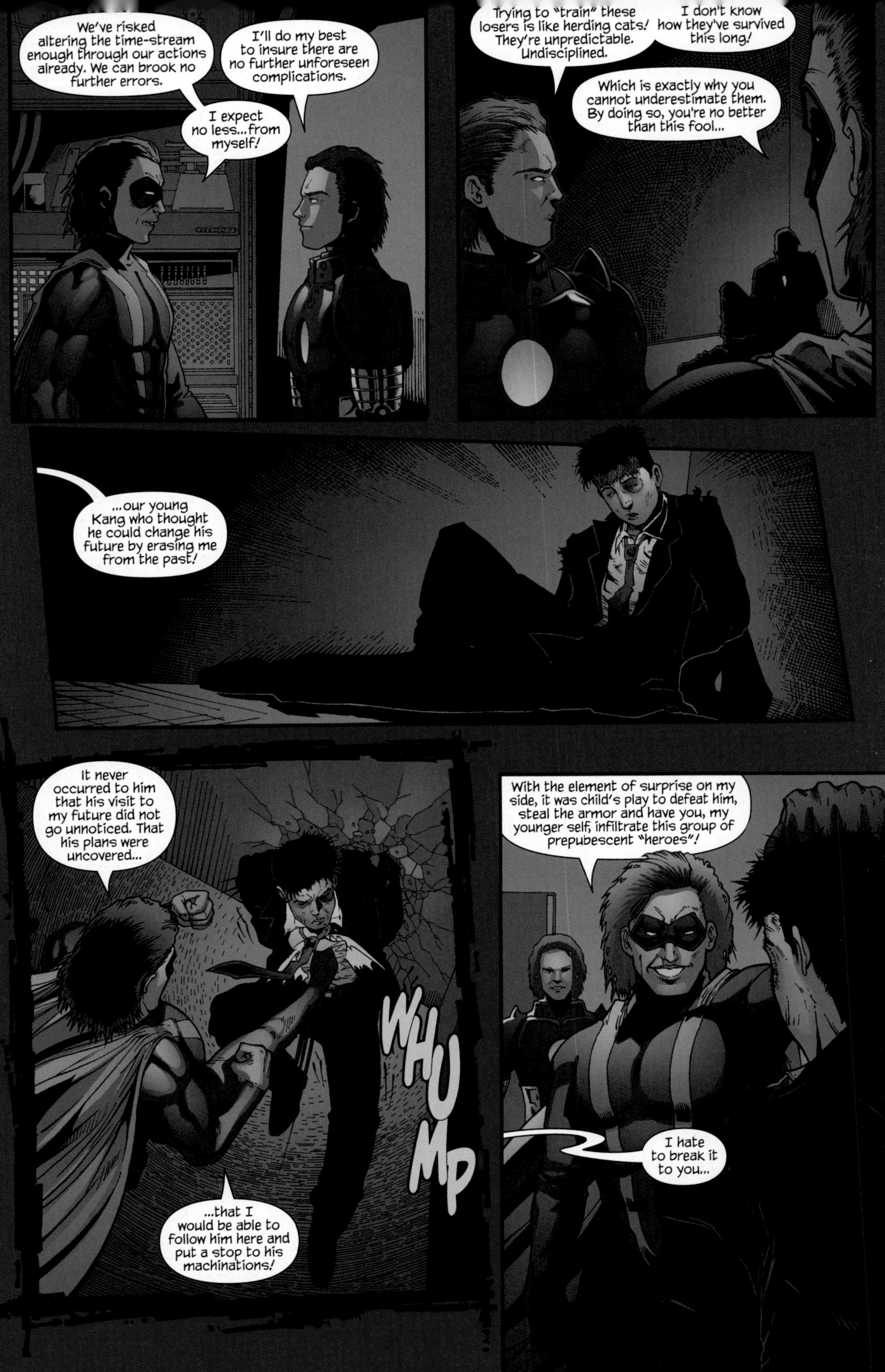
We've risked altering the time-stream enough through our actions already. We can brook no further errors.
I'll do my best to insure there are no further unforeseen complications.
I expect no less...from myself!
Trying to "train" these losers is like herding cats! They're unpredictable. Undisciplined.
I don't know how they've survived this long!
Which is exactly why you cannot underestimate them. By doing so, you're no better than this fool...
...our young Kang who thought he could change his future by erasing me from the past!
It never occurred to him that his visit to my future did not go unnoticed. That his plans were uncovered...
WHUMP
...that I would be able to follow him here and put a stop to his machinations!
With the element of surprise on my side, it was child's play to defeat him, steal the armor and have you, my younger self, infiltrate this group of prepubescent "heroes"!
I hate to break it to you...

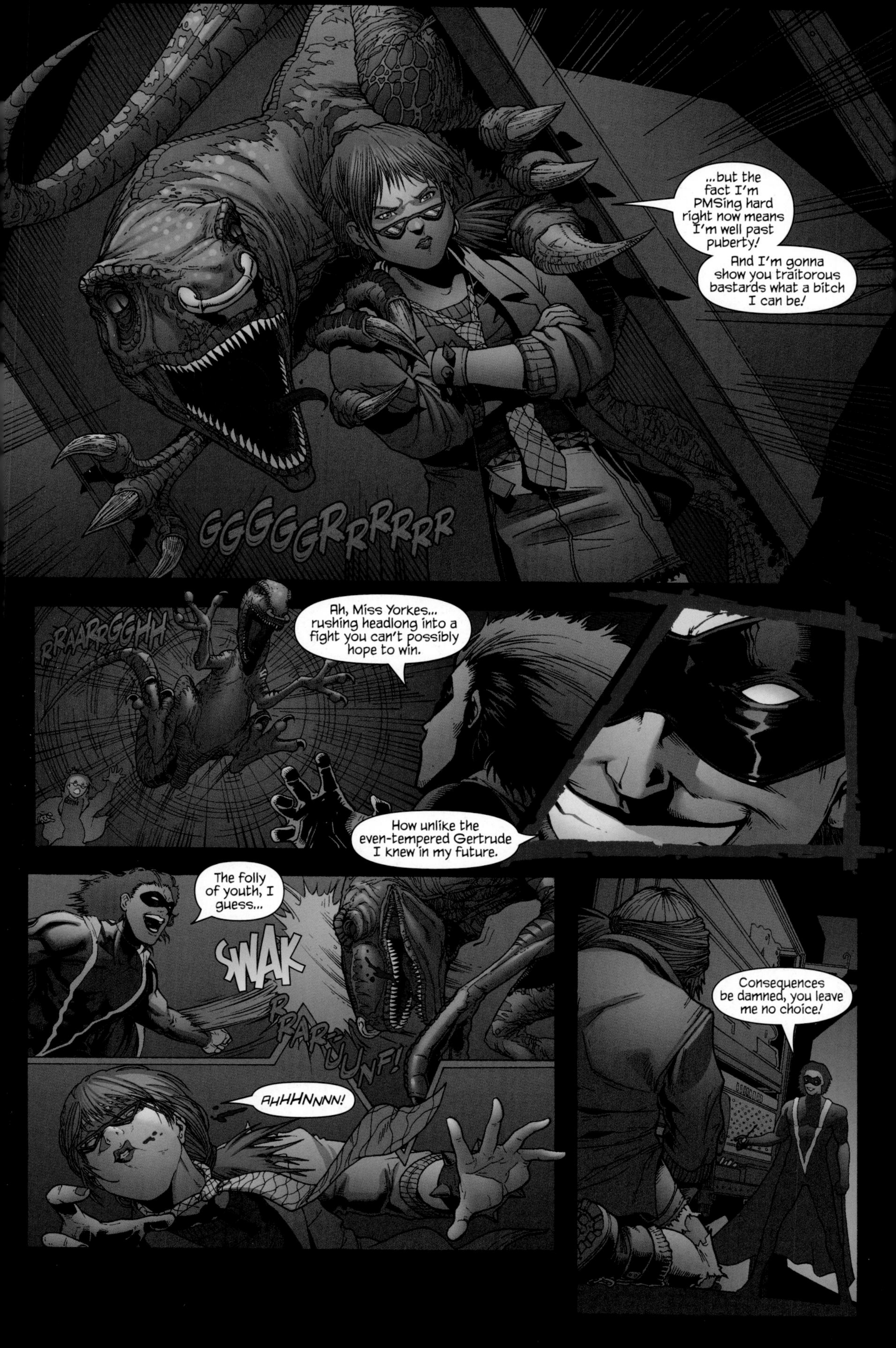

...but the fact I'm PMSing hard right now means I'm well past puberty!
And I'm gonna show you traitorous bastards what a bitch I can be!
GGGGGRRRRRR
RRAARRGGHH
Ah, Miss Yorkes... rushing headlong into a fight you can't possibly hope to win.
How unlike the even-tempered Gertrude I knew in my future.
The folly of youth, I guess...
SWAK
RRAR-UUNF!
AHHHNNNN!
Consequences be damned, you leave me no choice!

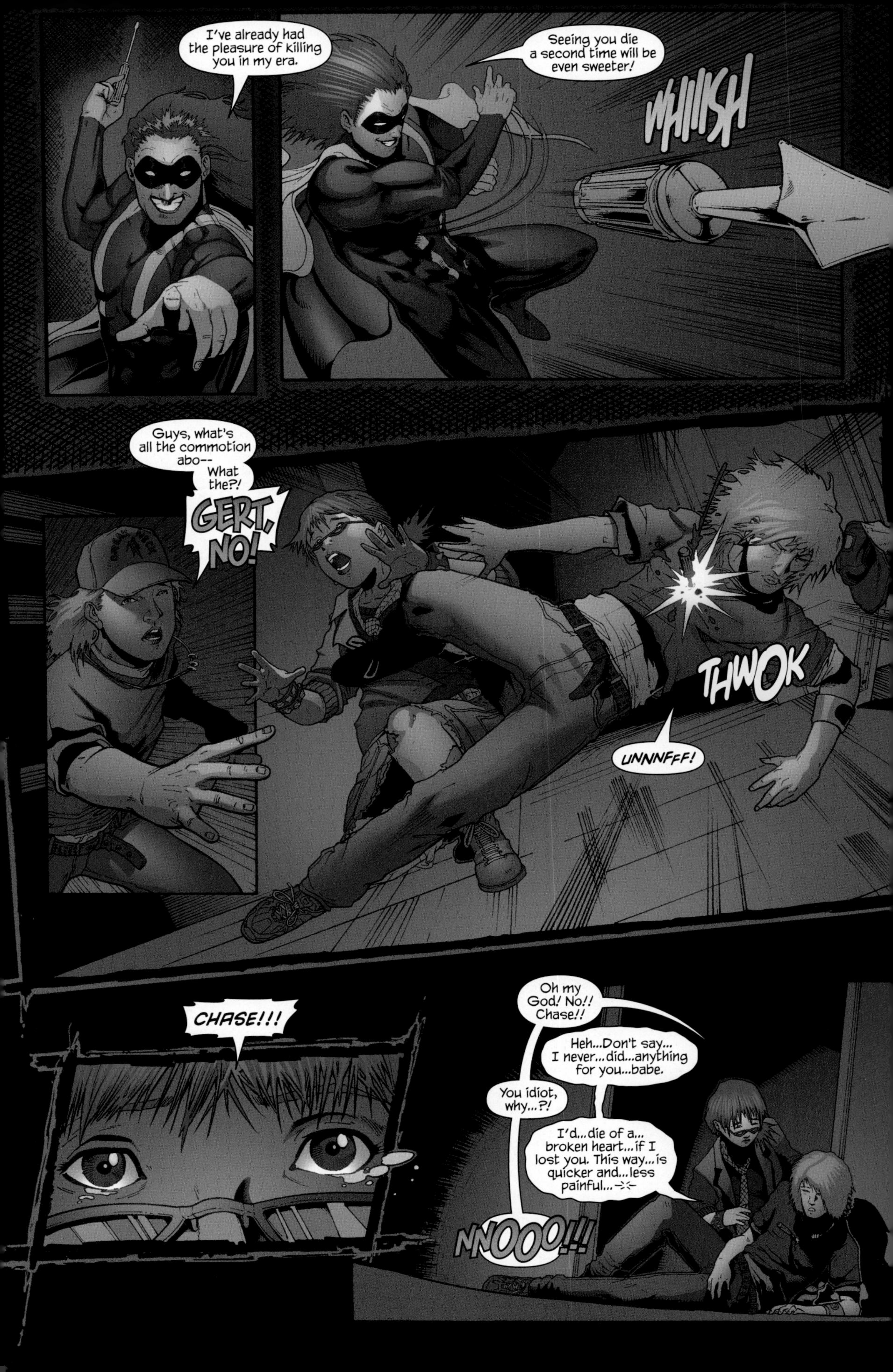
I've already had the pleasure of killing you in my era.
Seeing you die a second time will be even sweeter!
WHIIISH
Guys, what's all the commotion abo-- What the?!
GERT, NO!
THWOK
UNNNFFF!
CHASE!!!
Oh my God! No!! Chase!!
Heh...Don't say... I never...did...anything for you...babe.
You idiot, why...?!
I'd...die of a... broken heart...if I lost you. This way...is quicker and...less painful...
NNOOO!!!

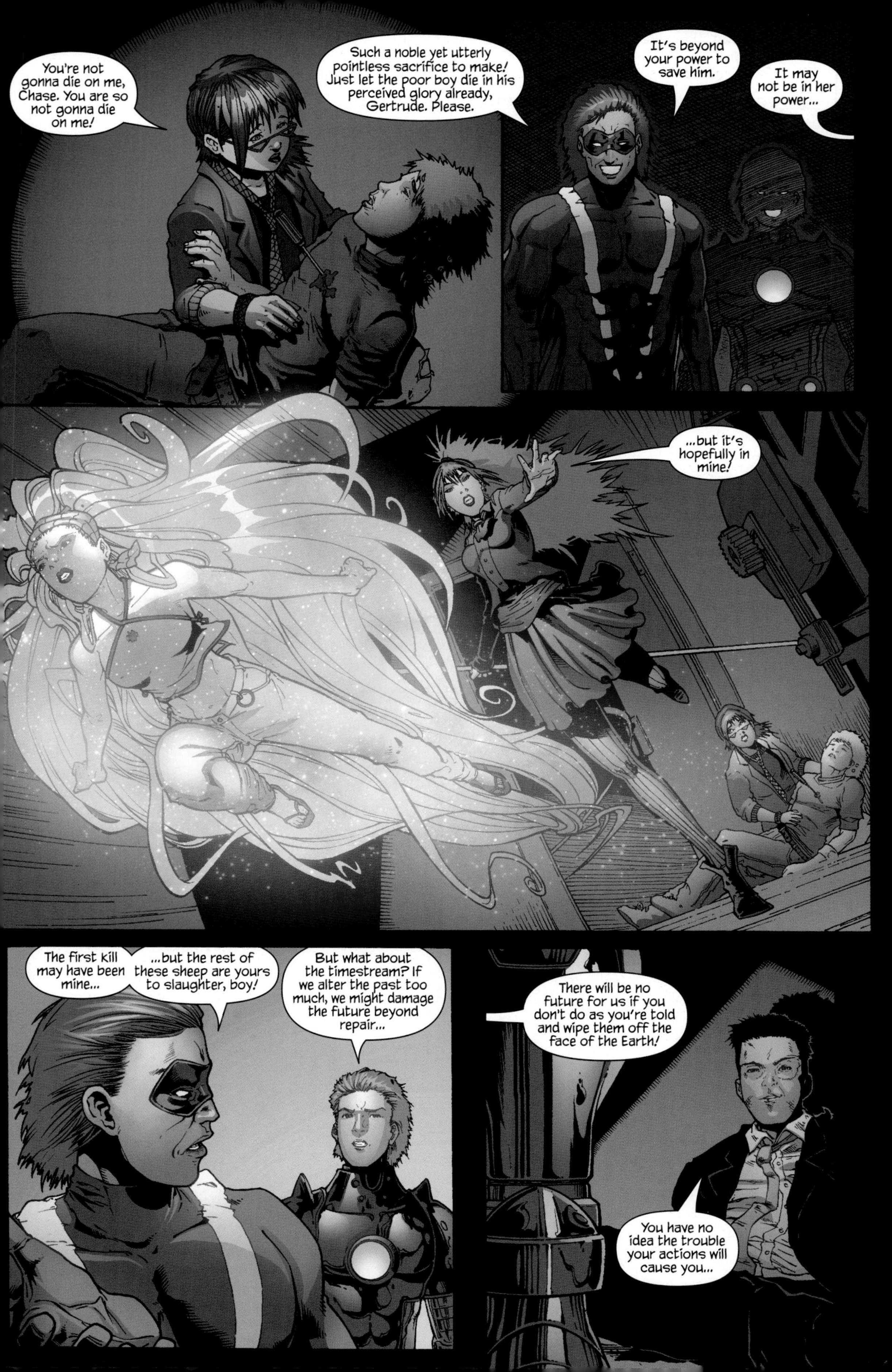
You're not gonna die on me, Chase. You are so not gonna die on me!
Such a noble yet utterly pointless sacrifice to make! Just let the poor boy die in his perceived glory already, Gertrude. Please.
It's beyond your power to save him.
It may not be in her power...
...but it's hopefully in mine!
The first kill may have been mine...
...but the rest of these sheep are yours to slaughter, boy!
But what about the timestream? If we alter the past too much, we might damage the future beyond repair...
There will be no future for us if you don't do as you're told and wipe them off the face of the Earth!
You have no idea the trouble your actions will cause you...

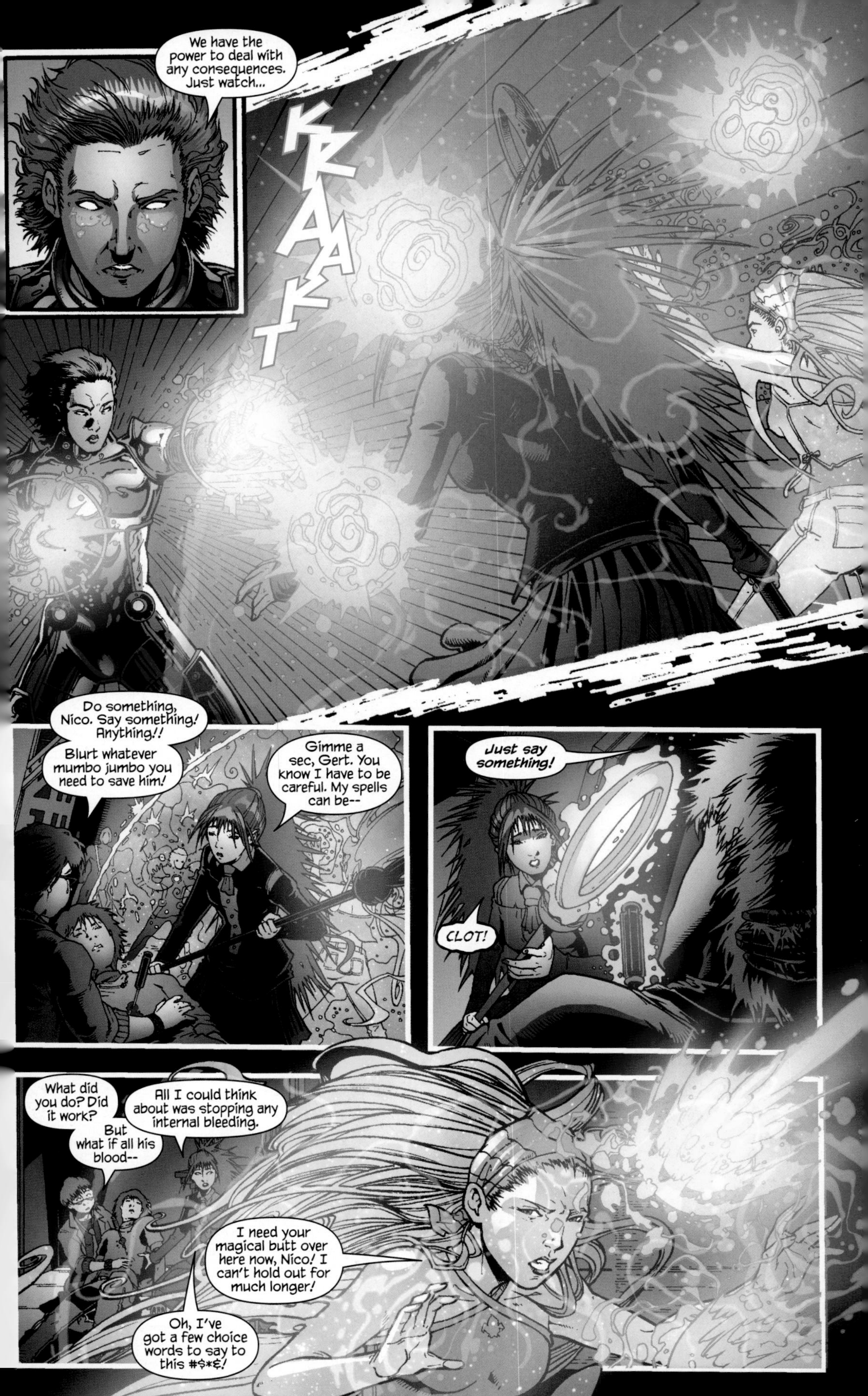
We have the power to deal with any consequences. Just watch...
KRAAKT
Do something, Nico. Say something! Anything!!
Blurt whatever mumbo jumbo you need to save him!
Gimme a sec, Gert. You know I have to be careful. My spells can be--
Just say something!
CLOT!
What did you do? Did it work?
All I could think about was stopping any internal bleeding.
But what if all his blood--
I need your magical butt over here now, Nico! I can't hold out for much longer!
Oh, I've got a few choice words to say to this #$*&!

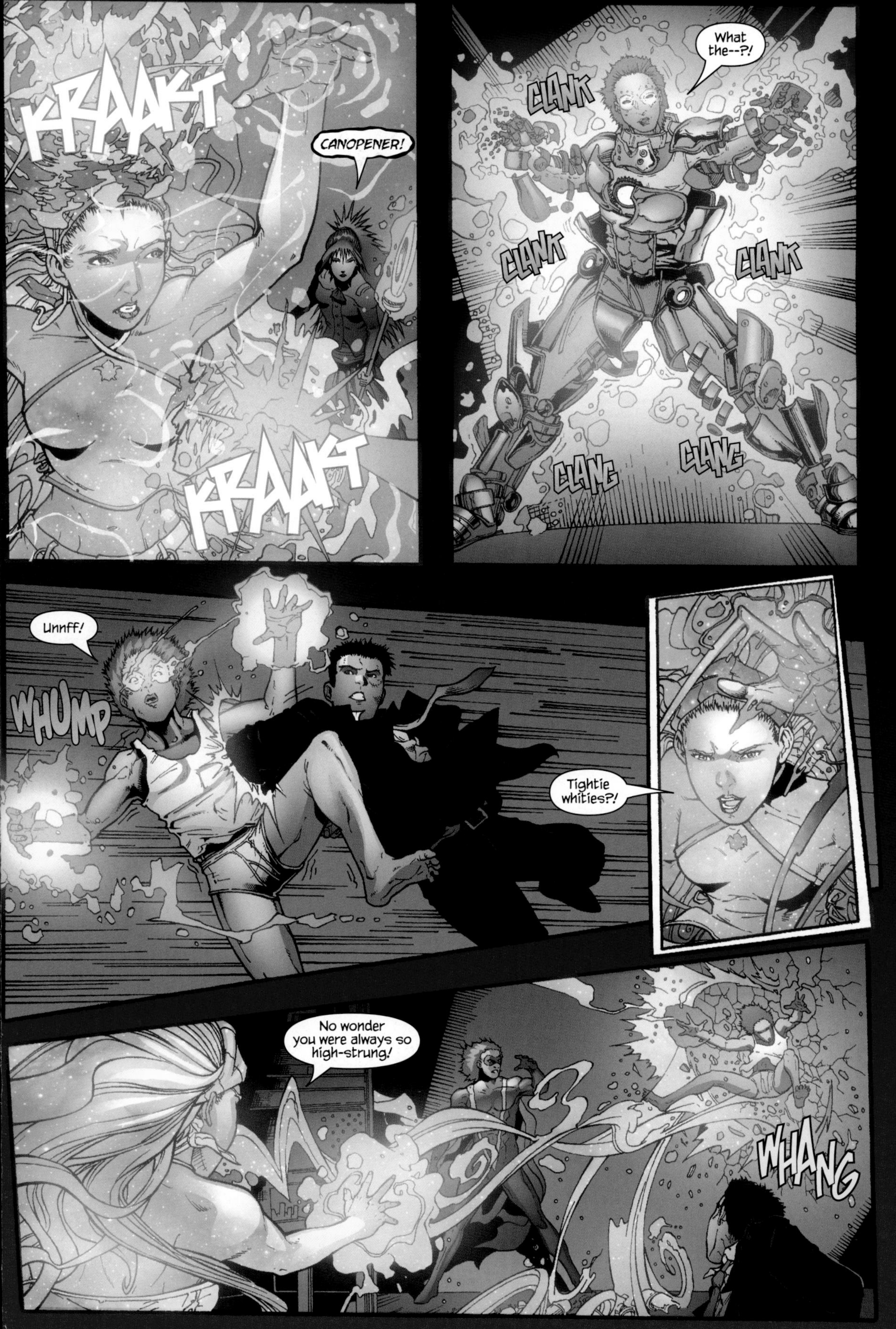
KRAAKT
CANOPENER!
KRAAKT
What the--?!
CLANK
CLANK
CLANK
CLANG
CLANG
Unnff!
WHUMP
Tightie whities?!
No wonder you were always so high-strung!
WHANG

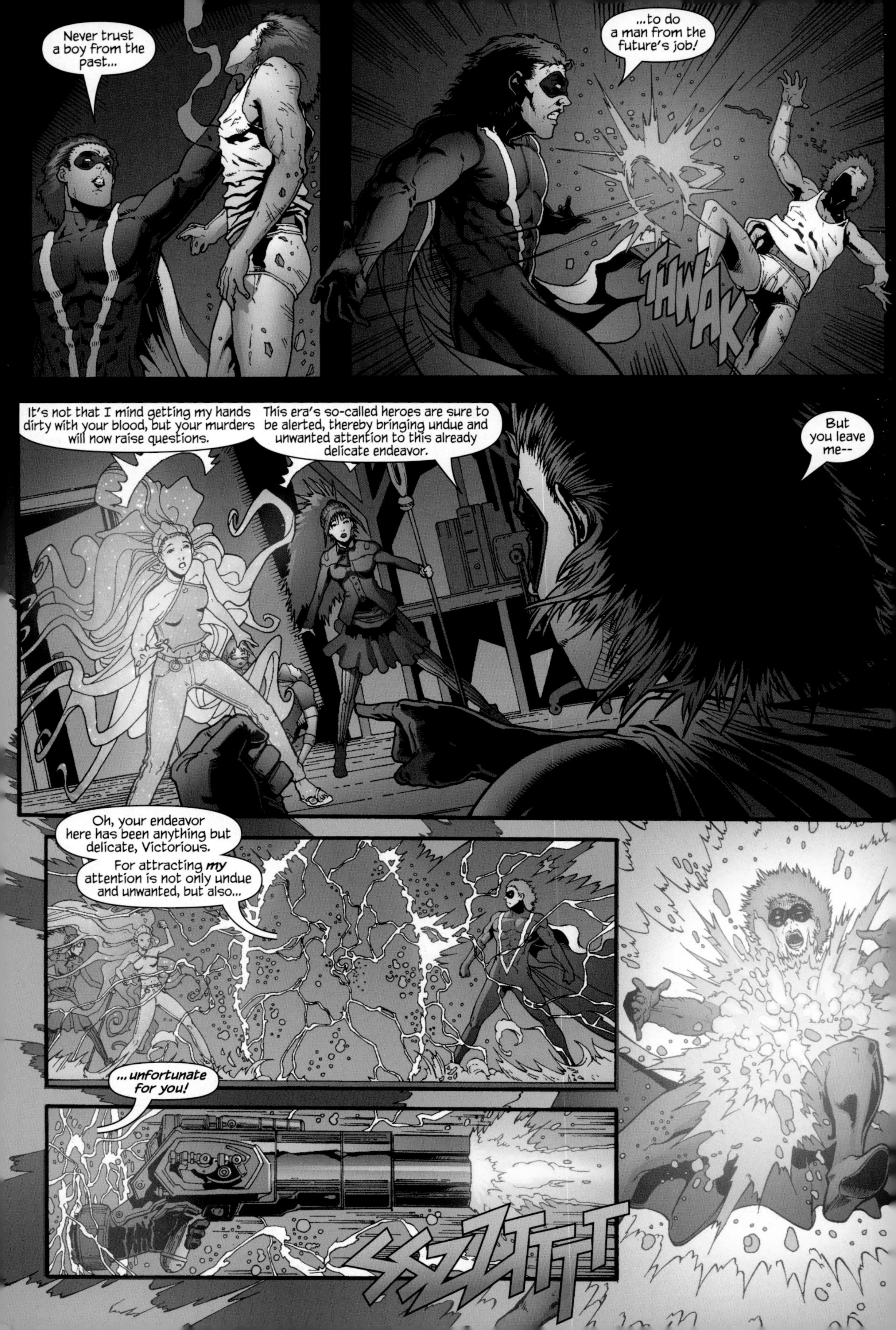
Never trust a boy from the past...
...to do a man from the future's job!
THWAK
It's not that I mind getting my hands dirty with your blood, but your murders will now raise questions.
This era's so-called heroes are sure to be alerted, thereby bringing undue and unwanted attention to this already delicate endeavor.
But you leave me--
Oh, your endeavor here has been anything but delicate, Victorious.
For attracting *my* attention is not only undue and unwanted, but also...
...unfortunate for you!
SSZZTTTT

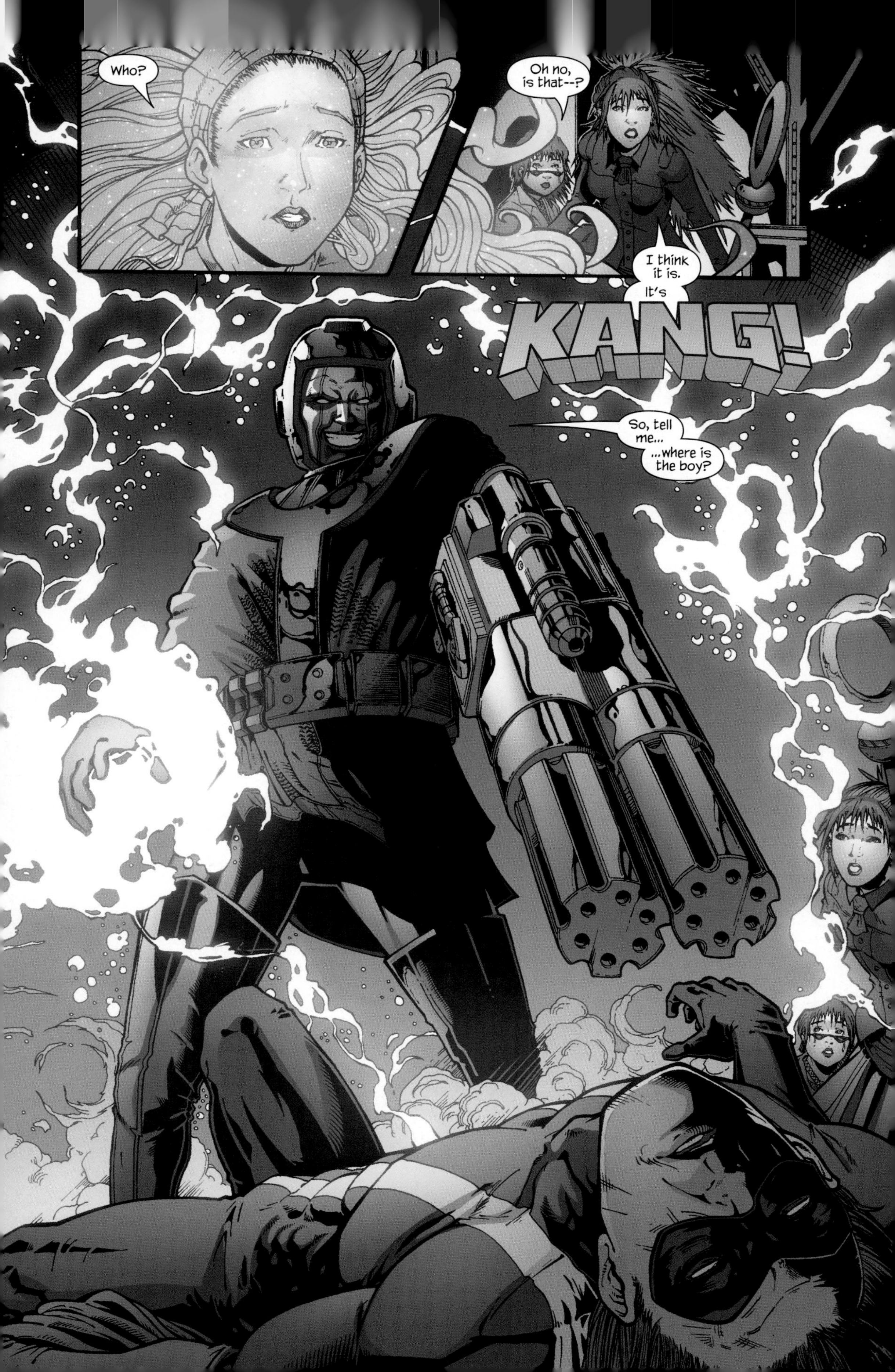
Who?
Oh no, is that--?
I think it is.
It's
KANG!
So, tell me...
...where is the boy?

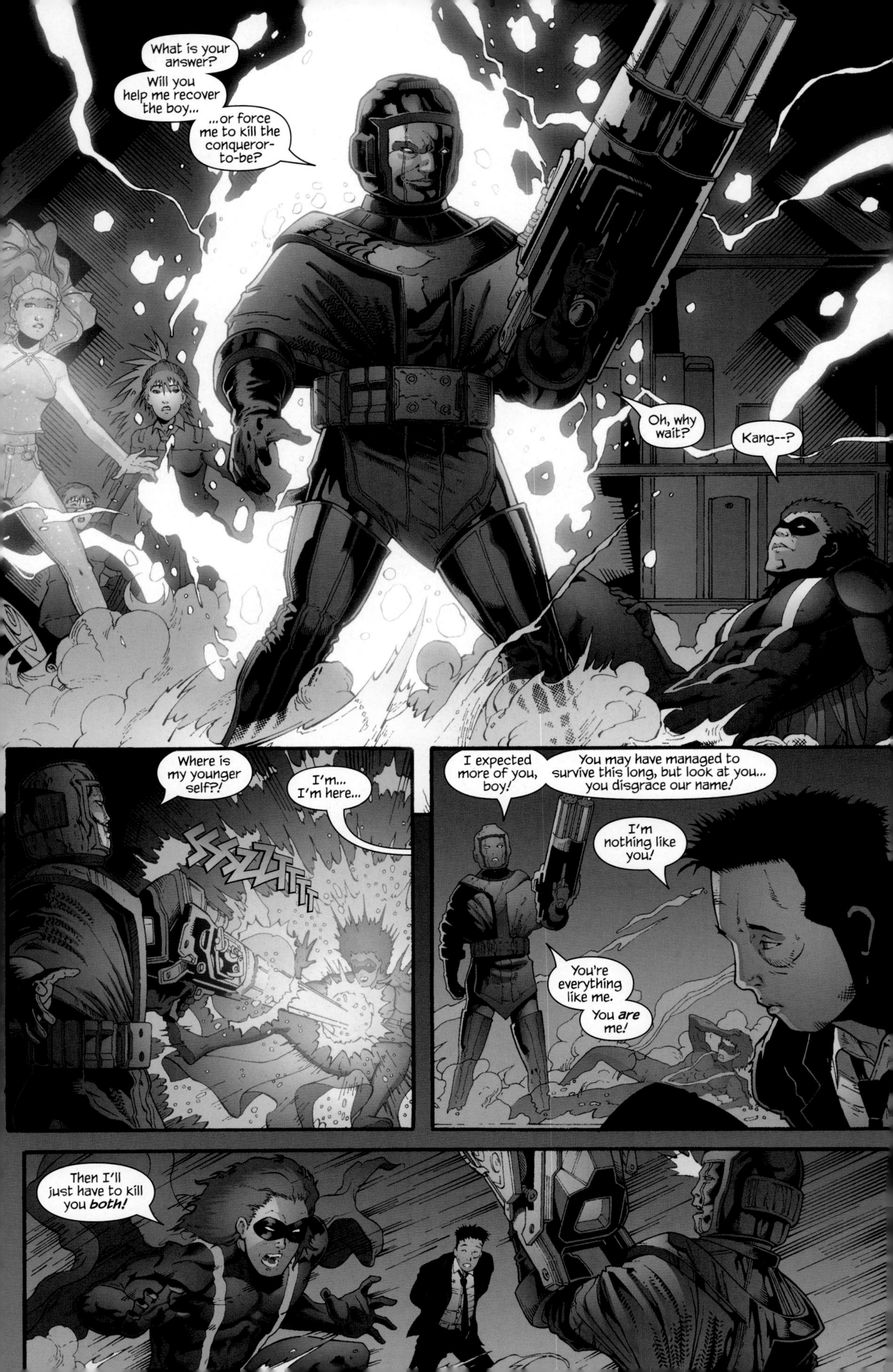
What is your answer?
Will you help me recover the boy...
...or force me to kill the conqueror-to-be?
Oh, why wait?
Kang--?
Where is my younger self?!
SSSZZZTTTT
I'm... I'm here...
I expected more of you, boy!
You may have managed to survive this long, but look at you... you disgrace our name!
I'm nothing like you!
You're everything like me.
You *are* me!
Then I'll just have to kill you ***both!***

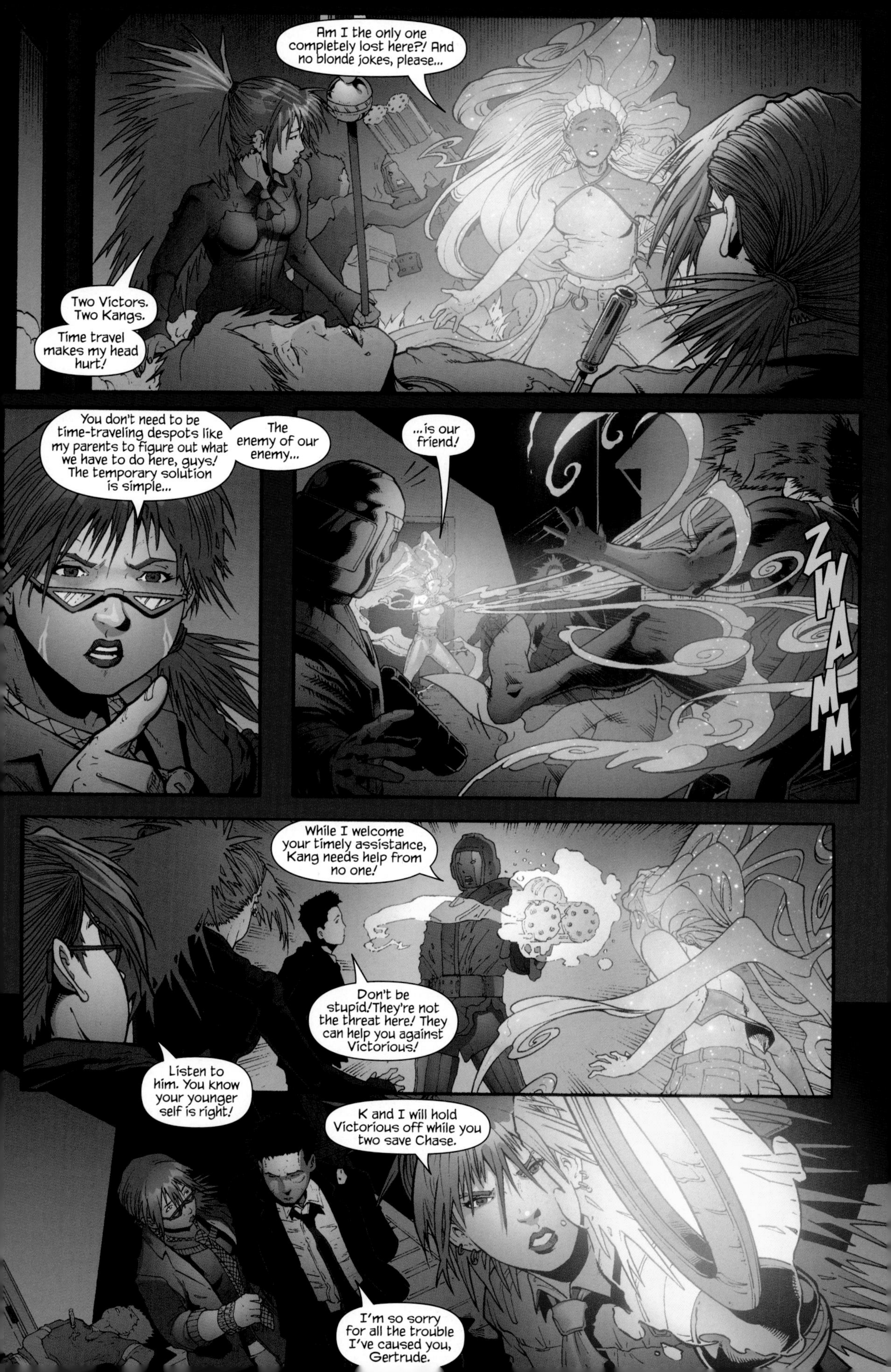
Am I the only one completely lost here?! And no blonde jokes, please...
Two Victors. Two Kangs.
Time travel makes my head hurt!
You don't need to be time-traveling despots like my parents to figure out what we have to do here, guys! The temporary solution is simple...
The enemy of our enemy...
...is our friend!
ZWAMM
While I welcome your timely assistance, Kang needs help from no one!
Don't be stupid! They're not the threat here! They can help you against Victorious!
Listen to him. You know your younger self is right!
K and I will hold Victorious off while you two save Chase.
I'm so sorry for all the trouble I've caused you, Gertrude.

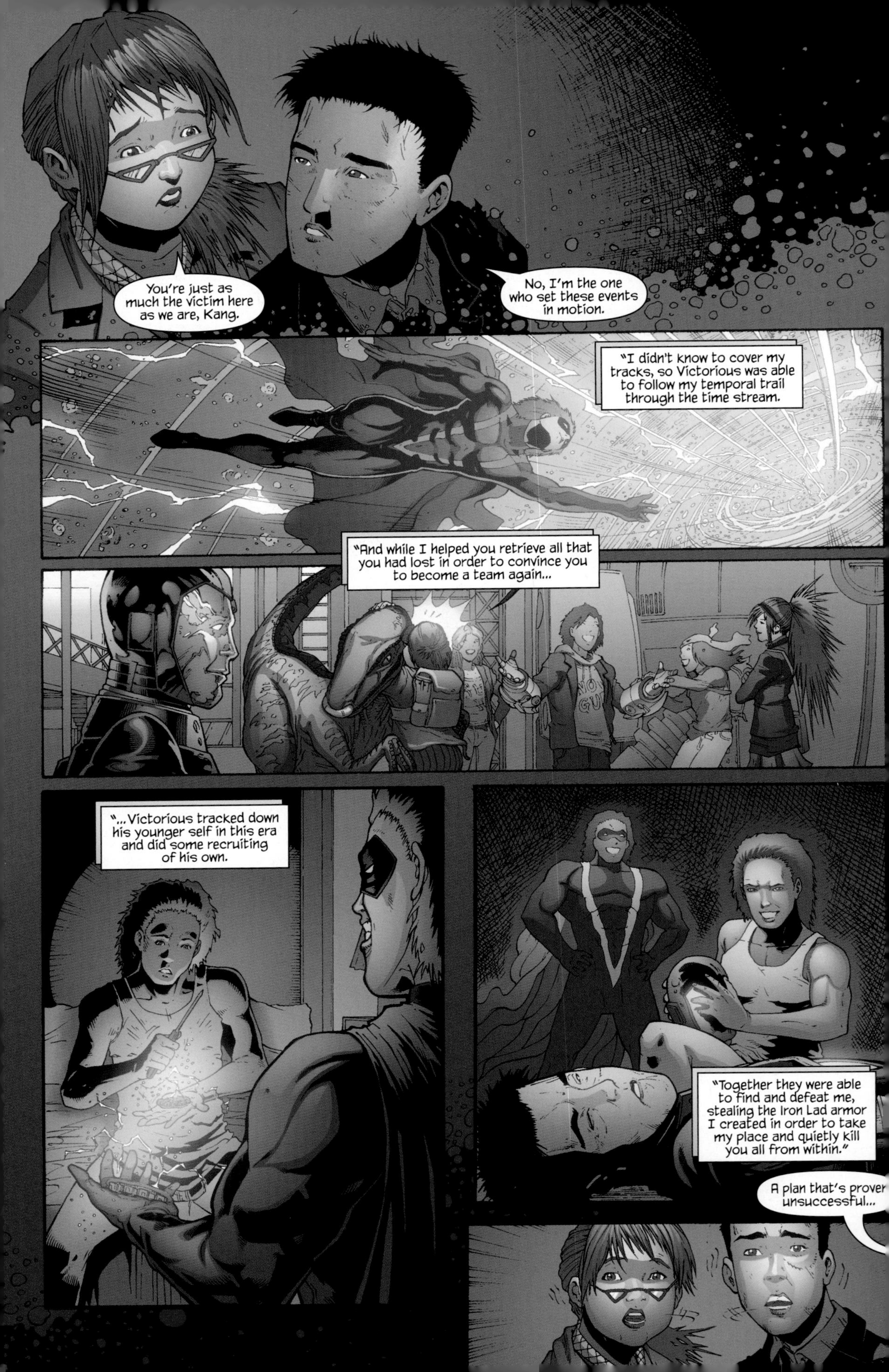
You're just as much the victim here as we are, Kang.
No, I'm the one who set these events in motion.
"I didn't know to cover my tracks, so Victorious was able to follow my temporal trail through the time stream.
"And while I helped you retrieve all that you had lost in order to convince you to become a team again...
"...Victorious tracked down his younger self in this era and did some recruiting of his own.
"Together they were able to find and defeat me, stealing the Iron Lad armor I created in order to take my place and quietly kill you all from within."
A plan that's prove unsuccessful...

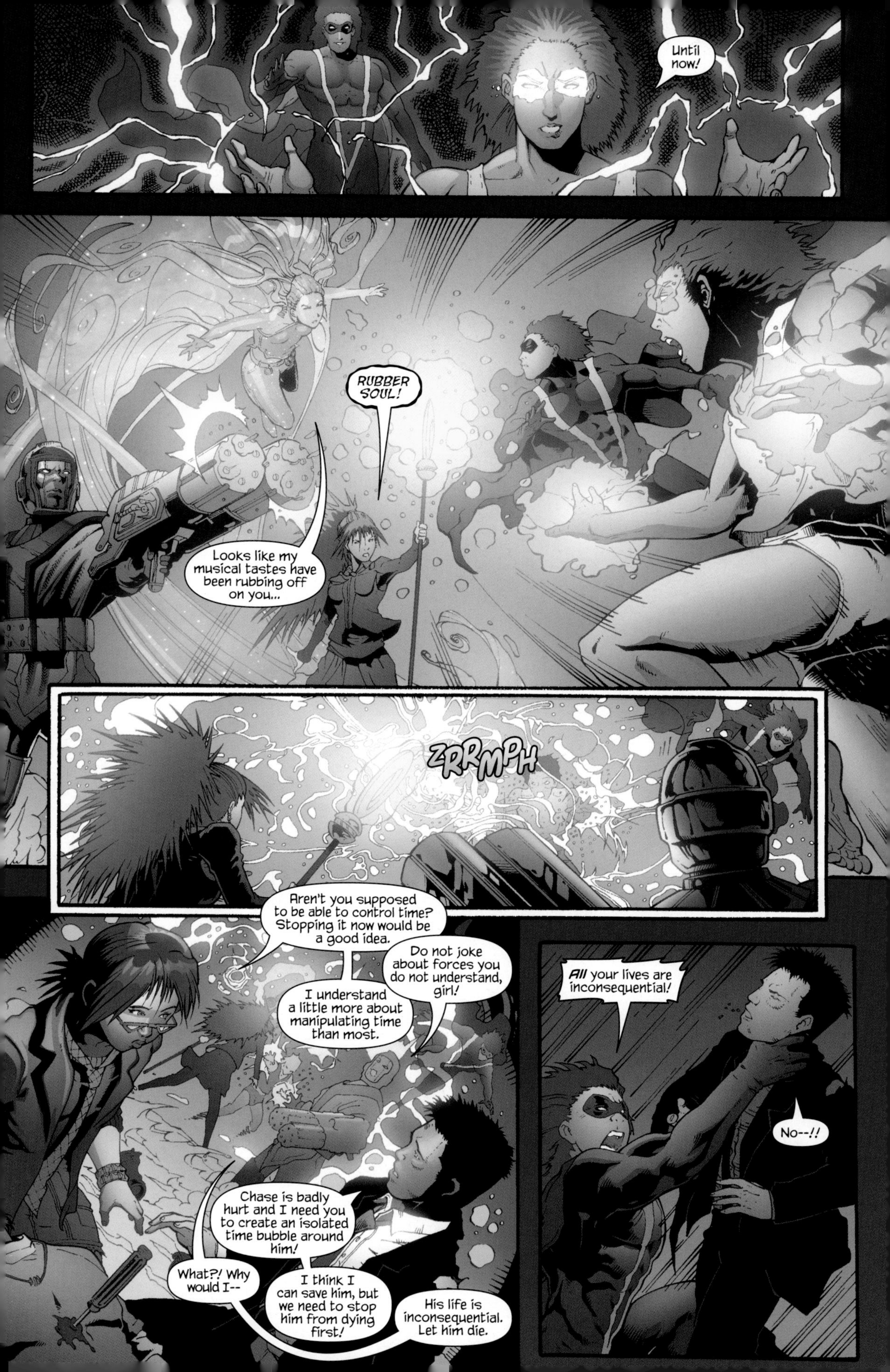

Until now!
RUBBER SOUL!
Looks like my musical tastes have been rubbing off on you...
ZRRMPH
Aren't you supposed to be able to control time? Stopping it now would be a good idea.
Do not joke about forces you do not understand, girl!
I understand a little more about manipulating time than most.
Chase is badly hurt and I need you to create an isolated time bubble around him!
What?! Why would I--
I think I can save him, but we need to stop him from dying first!
His life is inconsequential. Let him die.
All your lives are inconsequential!
No--!!

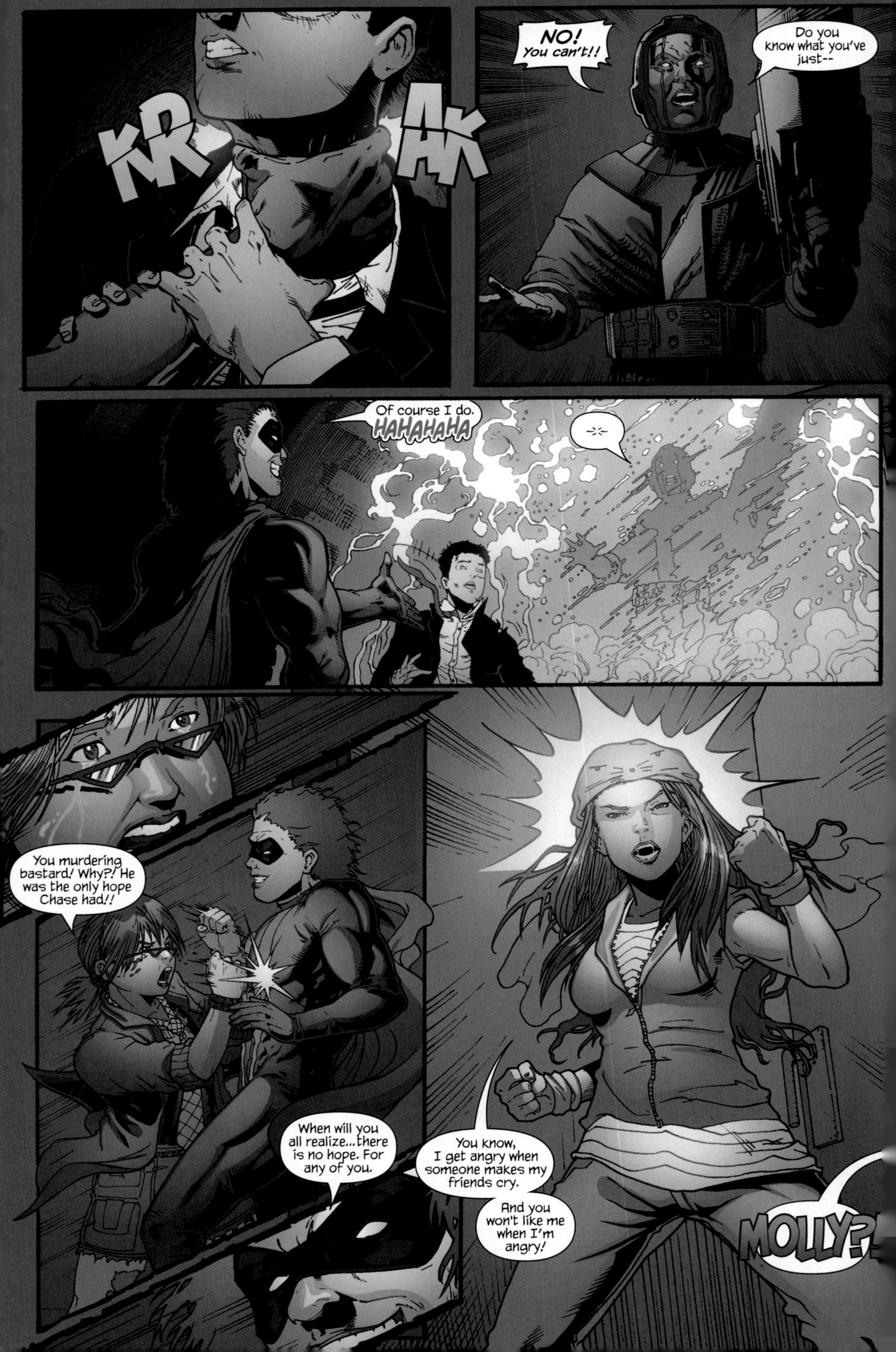

KRAK
NO! You can't!!
Do you know what you've just--
Of course I do.
HAHAHAHA
You murdering bastard! Why?! He was the only hope Chase had!!
When will you all realize...there is no hope. For any of you.
You know, I get angry when someone makes my friends cry.
And you won't like me when I'm angry!
MOLLY?!

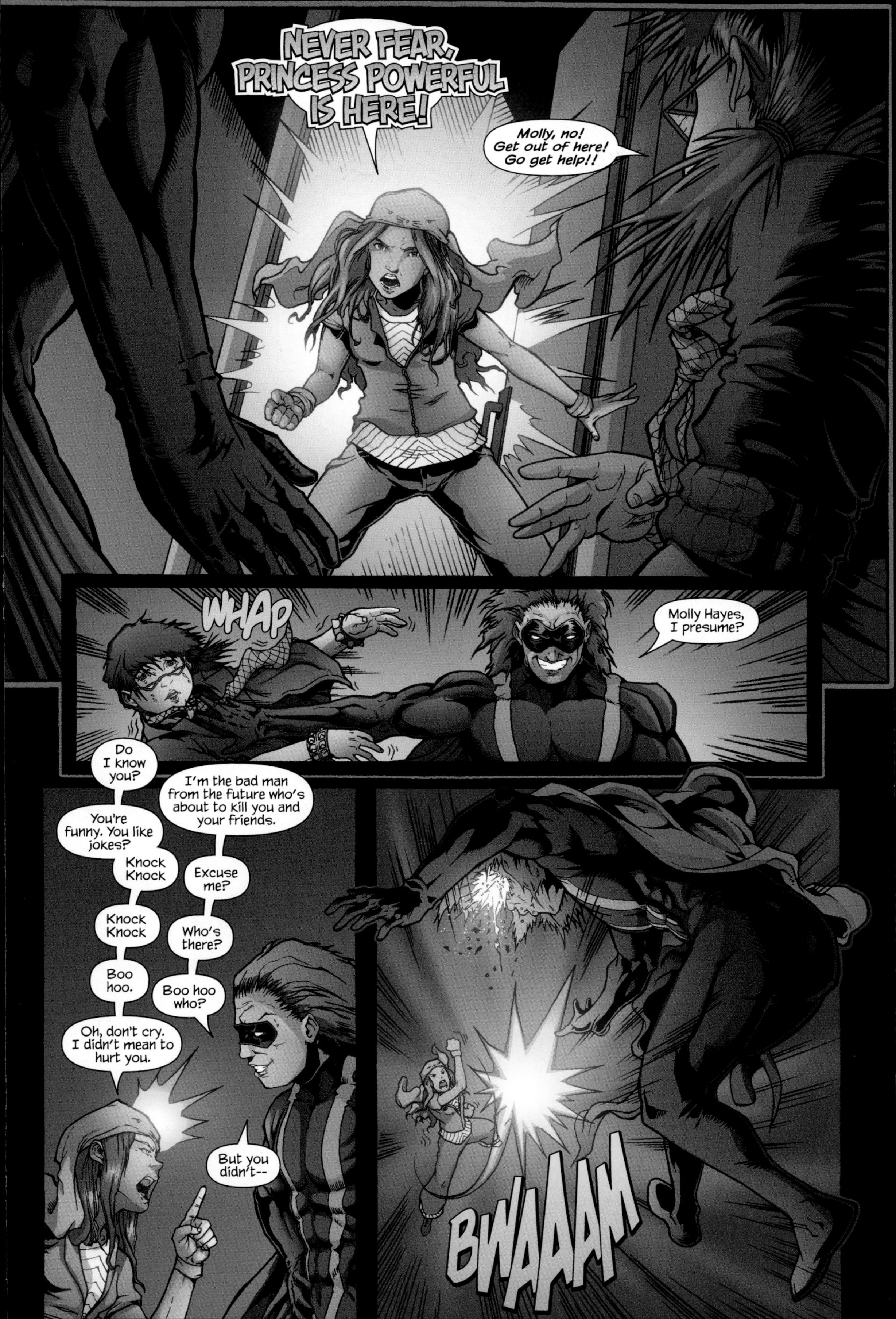
NEVER FEAR, PRINCESS POWERFUL IS HERE!
Molly, no! Get out of here! Go get help!!
WHAP
Molly Hayes, I presume?
Do I know you?
I'm the bad man from the future who's about to kill you and your friends.
You're funny. You like jokes?
Excuse me?
Knock Knock
Who's there?
Knock Knock
Boo hoo.
Boo hoo who?
Oh, don't cry. I didn't mean to hurt you.
But you didn't--
BWAAAM

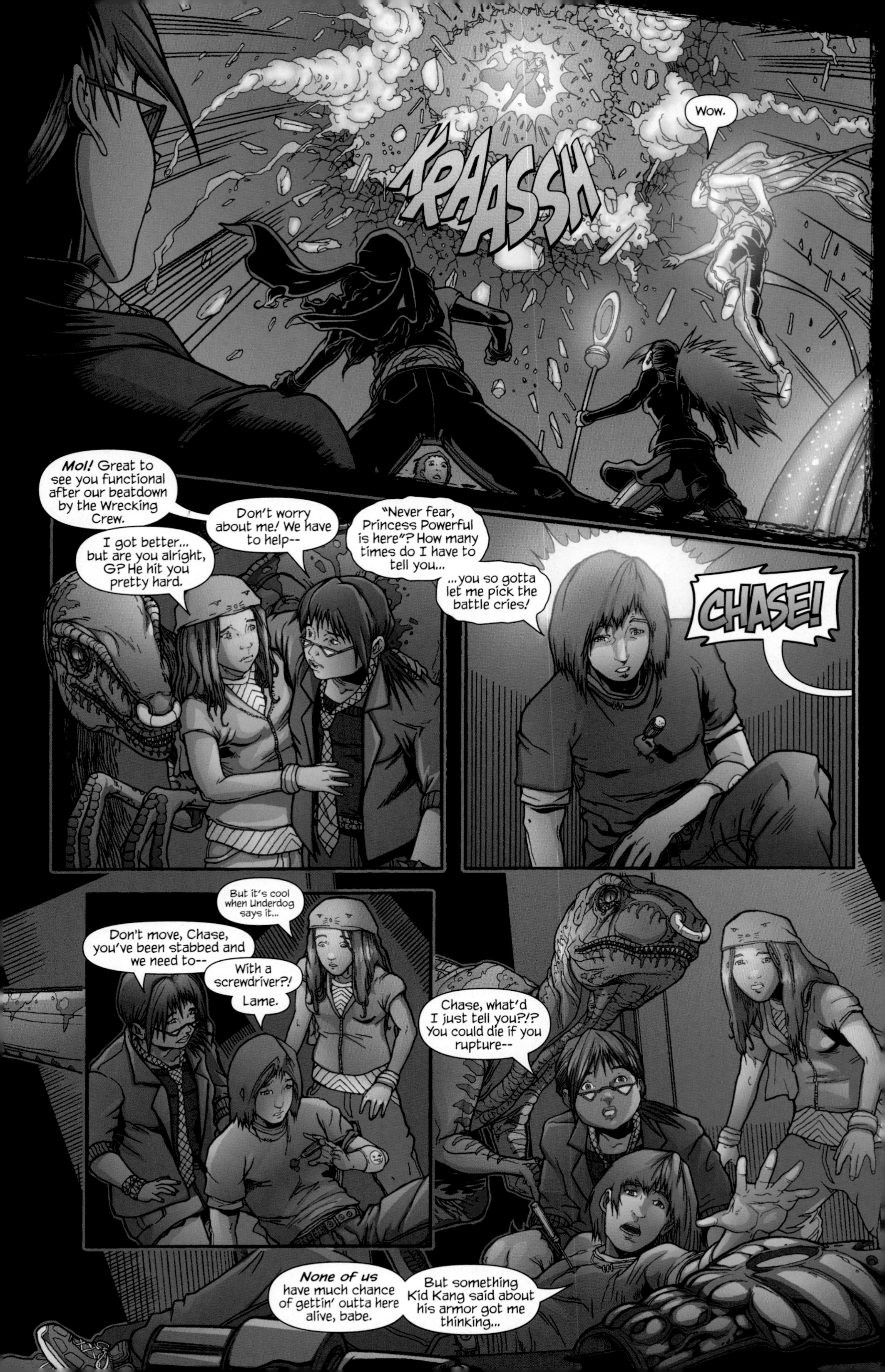
KRAASSH
Wow.
Mol! Great to see you functional after our beatdown by the Wrecking Crew.
I got better... but are you alright, G? He hit you pretty hard.
Don't worry about me! We have to help--
"Never fear, Princess Powerful is here"? How many times do I have to tell you...
...you so gotta let me pick the battle cries!
CHASE!
Don't move, Chase, you've been stabbed and we need to--
But it's cool when Underdog says it...
With a screwdriver?!
Lame.
Chase, what'd I just tell you?!? You could die if you rupture--
None of us have much chance of gettin' outta here alive, babe.
But something Kid Kang said about his armor got me thinking...

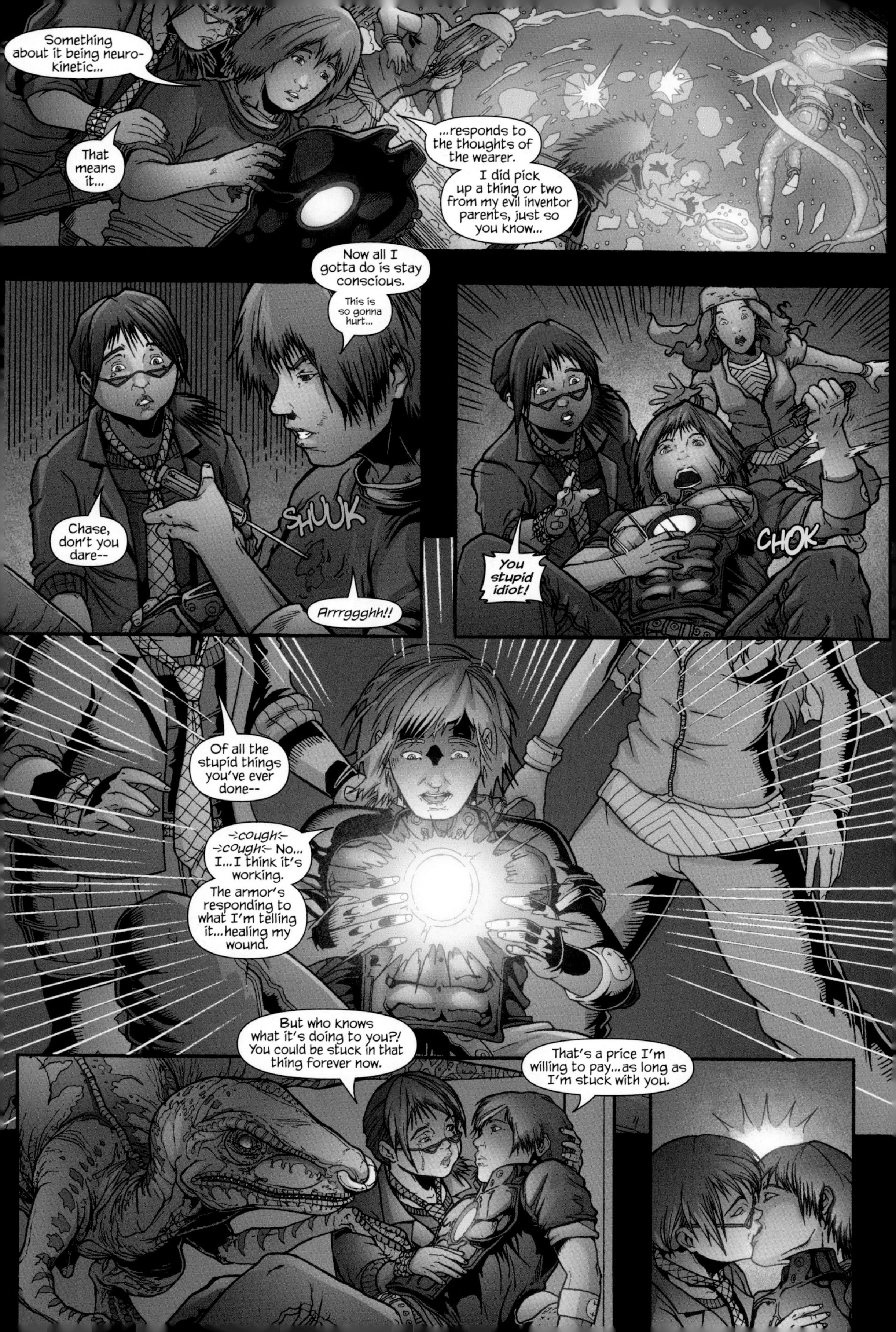
Something about it being neuro-kinetic...
That means it...
...responds to the thoughts of the wearer.
I did pick up a thing or two from my evil inventor parents, just so you know...
Now all I gotta do is stay conscious.
This is so gonna hurt...
Chase, don't you dare--
SHUUK
Arrrggghh!!
You stupid idiot!
CHOK
Of all the stupid things you've ever done--
-cough- -cough- No... I...I think it's working.
The armor's responding to what I'm telling it...healing my wound.
But who knows what it's doing to you?! You could be stuck in that thing forever now.
That's a price I'm willing to pay...as long as I'm stuck with you.

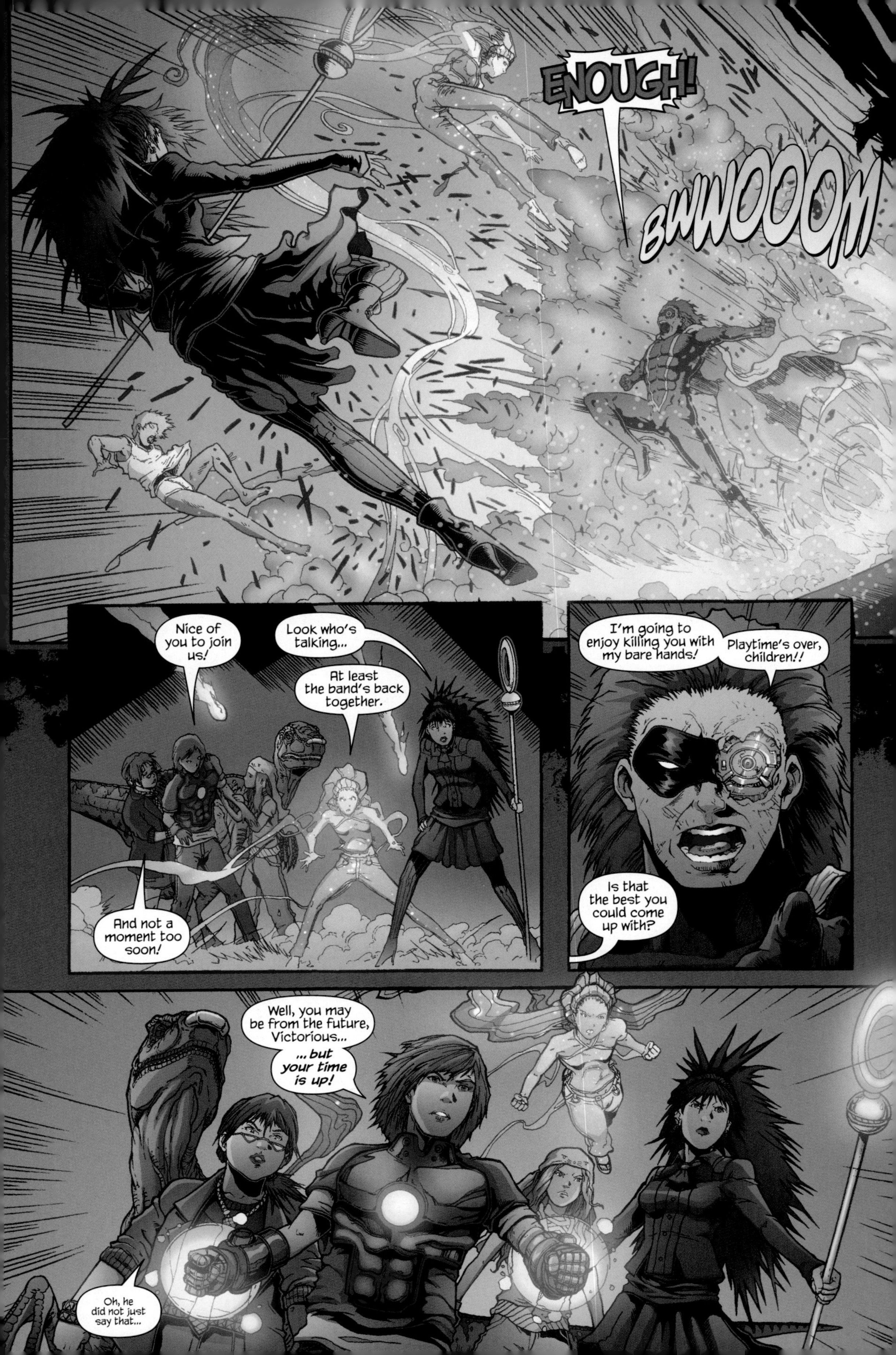
ENOUGH!
BWWOOOM
Nice of you to join us!
Look who's talking...
At least the band's back together.
And not a moment too soon!
I'm going to enjoy killing you with my bare hands!
Playtime's over, children!!
Is that the best you could come up with?
Well, you may be from the future, Victorious...
...but your time is up!
Oh, he did not just say that...

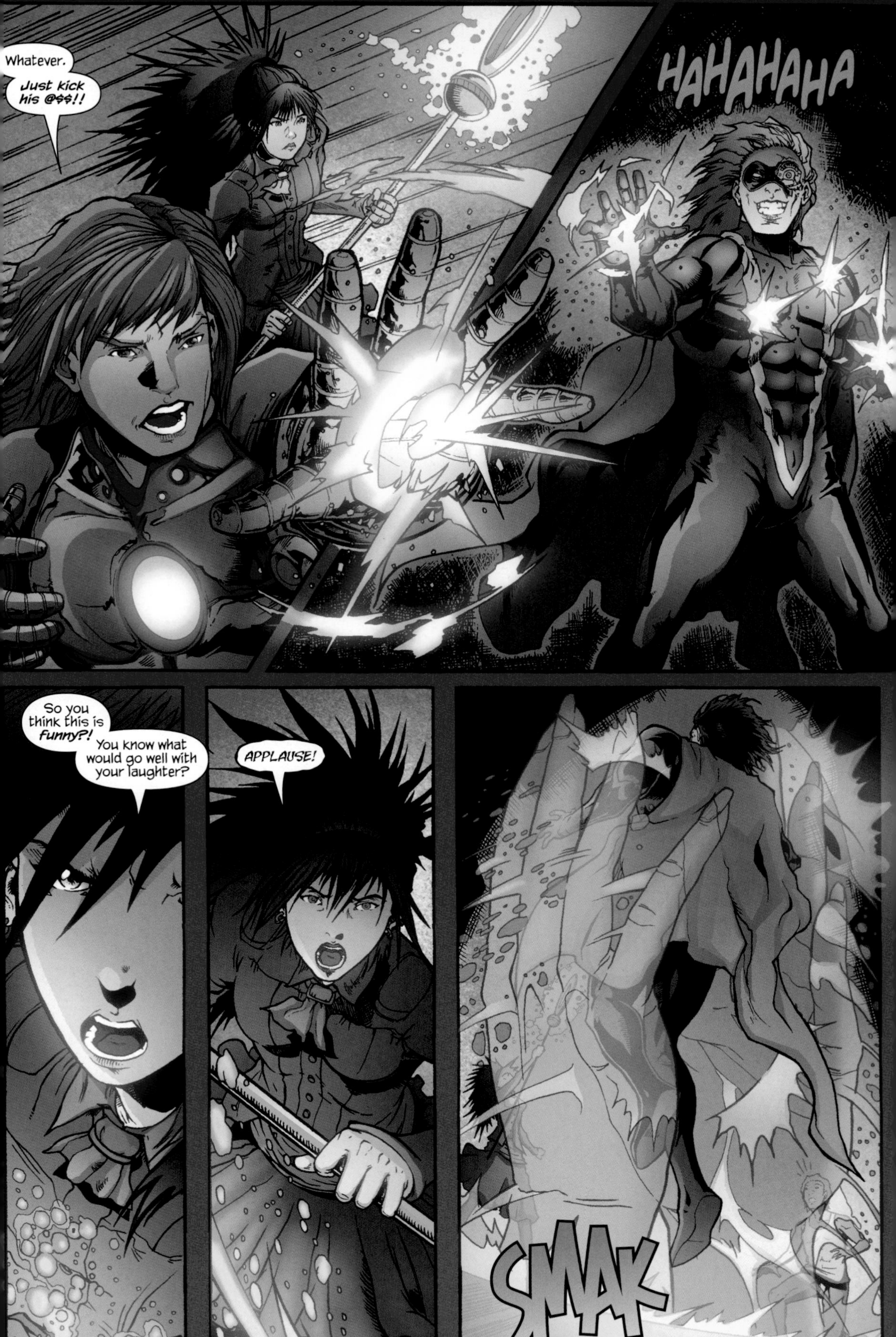
Whatever. Just kick his @$$!!
HAHAHAHA
So you think this is funny?! You know what would go well with your laughter?
APPLAUSE!
SMAK

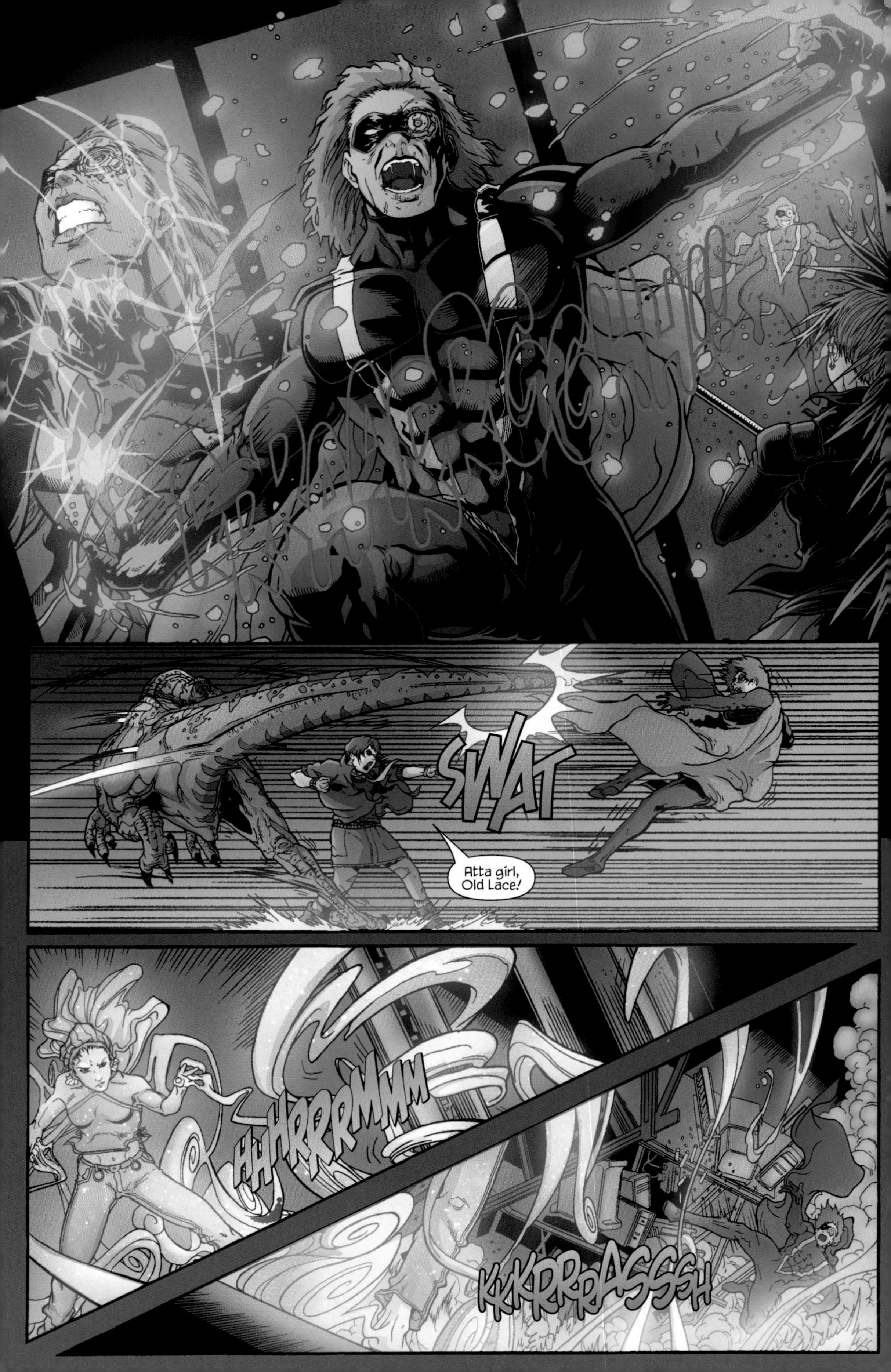
SWAT
Atta girl, Old Lace!
HHHRRRMMMM
KKKRRRASSSH

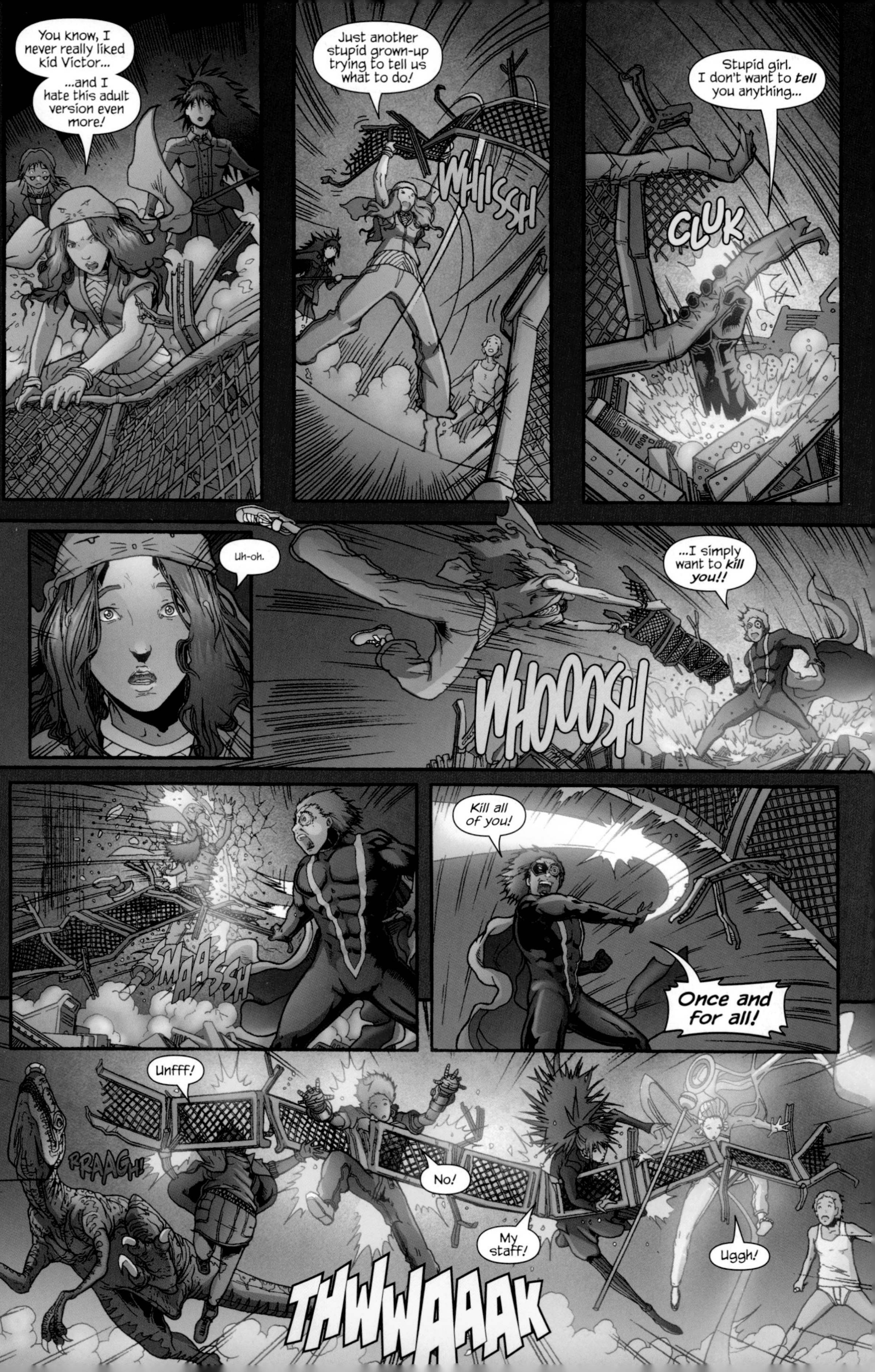
You know, I never really liked kid Victor...
...and I hate this adult version even more!
Just another stupid grown-up trying to tell us what to do!
WHISSH
Stupid girl. I don't want to tell you anything...
CLUK
Uh-oh.
...I simply want to kill you!!
WHOOOSH
SMAASSH
Kill all of you!
Once and for all!
Unfff!
RRAAGH!
No!
My staff!
Uggh!
THWWAAAK

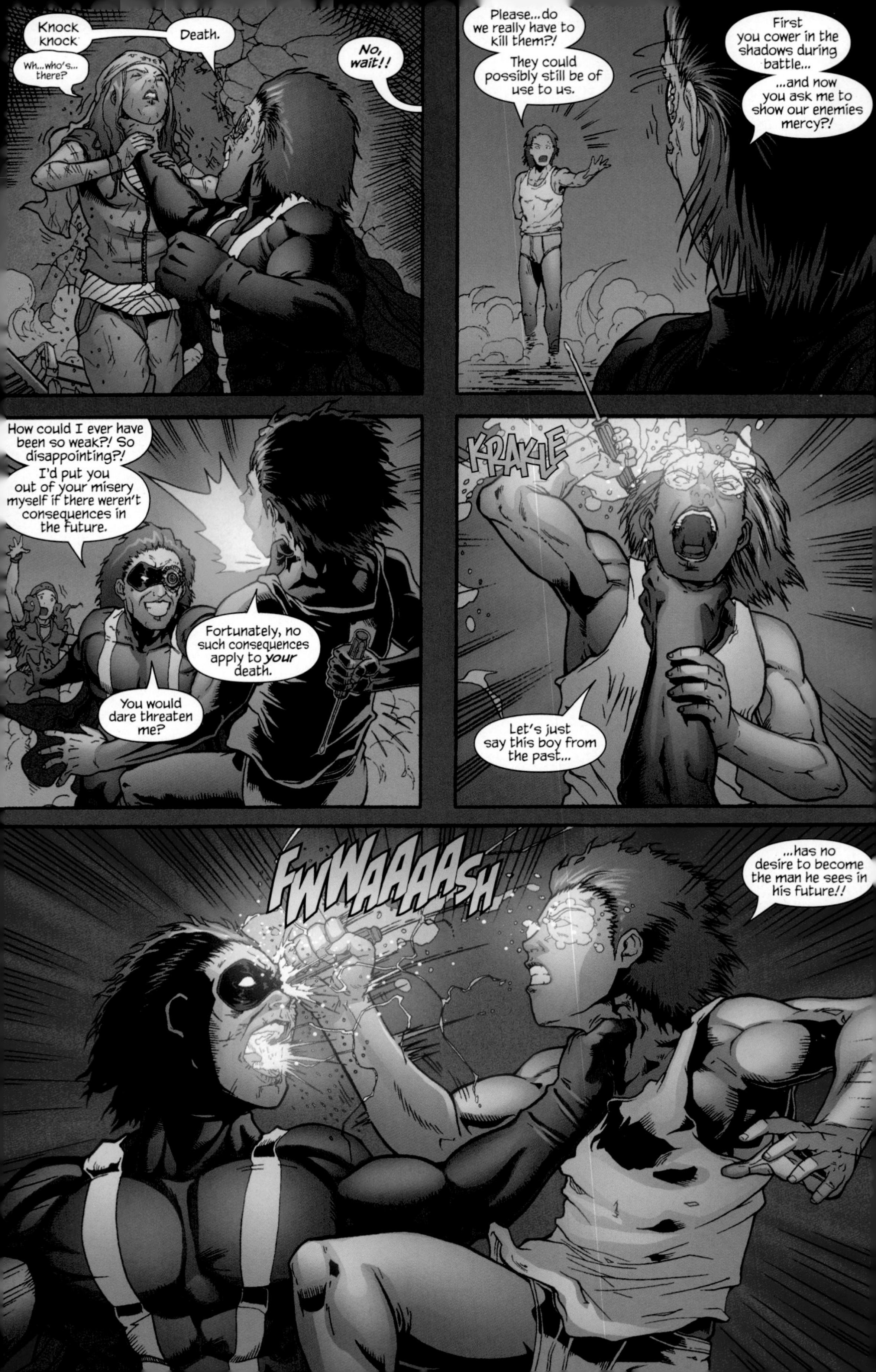
Knock knock.
Wh...who's... there?
Death.
No, wait!!
Please...do we really have to kill them?!
They could possibly still be of use to us.
First you cower in the shadows during battle...
...and now you ask me to show our enemies mercy?!
How could I ever have been so weak?! So disappointing?!
I'd put you out of your misery myself if there weren't consequences in the future.
Fortunately, no such consequences apply to *your* death.
You would dare threaten me?
KRAKLE
Let's just say this boy from the past...
FWAAAASH
...has no desire to become the man he sees in his future!!